Audrey Wood and the Playwrights

Milly S. Barranger

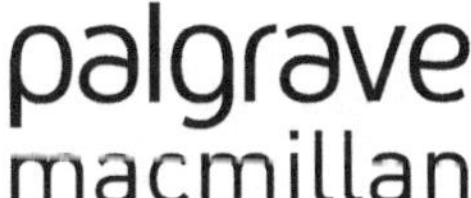

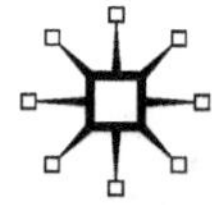

AUDREY WOOD AND THE PLAYWRIGHTS

First published in hardcover in 2013 by PALGRAVE MACMILLAN® in the United States—a division of St. Martin's Press LLC, 175 Fifth Avenue, New York, NY 10010.

Where this book is distributed in the UK, Europe and the rest of the world, this is by Palgrave Macmillan, a division of Macmillan Publishers Limited, registered in England, company number 785998, of Houndmills, Basingstoke, Hampshire RG21 6XS.

Palgrave Macmillan is the global academic imprint of the above companies and has companies and representatives throughout the world.

Palgrave® and Macmillan® are registered trademarks in the United States, the United Kingdom, Europe and other countries.

ISBN: 978–1–137–38547–5

Library of Congress Cataloging-in-Publication Data is available from the Library of Congress.

A catalogue record of the book is available from the British Library.

Design by Newgen Knowledge Works (P) Ltd., Chennai, India.

First PALGRAVE MACMILLAN paperback edition: December 2013

10 9 8 7 6 5 4 3 2 1

Palgrave Studies in Theatre and Performance History is a series devoted to the best of theatre/performance scholarship currently available, accessible, and free of jargon. It strives to include a wide range of topics, from the more traditional to those performance forms that in recent years have helped broaden the understanding of what theatre as a category might include (from variety forms as diverse as the circus and burlesque to street buskers, stage magic, and musical theatre, among many others). Although historical, critical, or analytical studies are of special interest, more theoretical projects, if not the dominant thrust of a study, but utilized as important underpinning or as a historiographical or analytical method of exploration, are also of interest. Textual studies of drama or other types of less traditional performance texts are also germane to the series if placed in their cultural, historical, social, or political and economic context. There is no geographical focus for this series and works of excellence of a diverse and international nature, including comparative studies, are sought.

The editor of the series is Don B. Wilmeth (EMERITUS, Brown University), PhD, University of Illinois, who brings to the series over a dozen years as editor of a book series on American theatre and drama, in addition to his own extensive experience as an editor of books and journals. He is the author of several award-winning books and has received numerous career achievement awards, including one for sustained excellence in editing from the Association for Theatre in Higher Education.

Also in the series:

Undressed for Success by Brenda Foley
Theatre, Performance, and the Historical Avant-garde by Günter Berghaus
Theatre, Politics, and Markets in Fin-de-Siècle Paris by Sally Charnow
Ghosts of Theatre and Cinema in the Brain by Mark Pizzato
Moscow Theatres for Young People: A Cultural History of Ideological Coercion and Artistic Innovation, 1917-2000 by Manon van de Water
Absence and Memory in Colonial American Theatre by Odai Johnson
Vaudeville Wars: How the Keith-Albee and Orpheum Circuits Controlled the Big-Time and Its Performers by Arthur Frank Wertheim
Performance and Femininity in Eighteenth-Century German Women's Writing by Wendy Arons
Operatic China: Staging Chinese Identity across the Pacific by Daphne P. Lei
Transatlantic Stage Stars in Vaudeville and Variety: Celebrity Turns by Leigh Woods
Interrogating America through Theatre and Performance edited by William W. Demastes and Iris Smith Fischer
Plays in American Periodicals, 1890-1918 by Susan Harris Smith
Representation and Identity from Versailles to the Present: The Performing Subject by Alan Sikes
Directors and the New Musical Drama: British and American Musical Theatre in the 1980s and 90s by Miranda Lundskaer-Nielsen
Beyond the Golden Door: Jewish-American Drama and Jewish-American Experience by Julius Novick
American Puppet Modernism: Essays on the Material World in Performance by John Bell
On the Uses of the Fantastic in Modern Theatre: Cocteau, Oedipus, and the Monster by Irene Eynat-Confino

Staging Stigma: A Critical Examination of the American Freak Show by Michael M. Chemers, foreword by Jim Ferris

Performing Magic on the Western Stage: From the Eighteenth-Century to the Present edited by Francesca Coppa, Larry Hass, and James Peck, foreword by Eugene Burger

Memory in Play: From Aeschylus to Sam Shepard by Attilio Favorini

Danjūrō's Girls: Women on the Kabuki Stage by Loren Edelson

Mendel's Theatre: Heredity, Eugenics, and Early Twentieth-Century American Drama by Tamsen Wolff

Theatre and Religion on Krishna's Stage: Performing in Vrindavan by David V. Mason

Rogue Performances: Staging the Underclasses in Early American Theatre Culture by Peter P. Reed

Broadway and Corporate Capitalism: The Rise of the Professional-Managerial Class, 1900–1920 by Michael Schwartz

Lady Macbeth in America: From the Stage to the White House by Gay Smith

Performing Bodies in Pain: Medieval and Post-Modern Martyrs, Mystics, and Artists by Marla Carlson

Early-Twentieth-Century Frontier Dramas on Broadway: Situating the Western Experience in Performing Arts by Richard Wattenberg

Staging the People: Community and Identity in the Federal Theatre Project by Elizabeth A. Osborne

Russian Culture and Theatrical Performance in America, 1891–1933 by Valleri J. Hohman

Baggy Pants Comedy: Burlesque and the Oral Tradition by Andrew Davis

Transposing Broadway: Jews, Assimilation, and the American Musical by Stuart J. Hecht

The Drama of Marriage: Gay Playwrights/Straight Unions from Oscar Wilde to the Present by John M. Clum

Mei Lanfang and the Twentieth-Century International Stage: Chinese Theatre Placed and Displaced by Min Tian

Hijikata Tatsumi and Butoh: Dancing in a Pool of Gray Grits by Bruce Baird

Staging Holocaust Resistance by Gene A. Plunka

Acts of Manhood: The Performance of Masculinity on the American Stage, 1828–1865 by Karl M. Kippola

Loss and Cultural Remains in Performance: The Ghosts of the Franklin Expedition by Heather Davis-Fisch

Uncle Tom's Cabin *on the American Stage and Screen* by John W. Frick

Theatre, Youth, and Culture: A Critical and Historical Exploration by Manon van de Water

Stage Designers in Early Twentieth-Century America: Artists, Activists, Cultural Critics by Christin Essin

Audrey Wood and the Playwrights by Milly S. Barranger

Performing Hybridity in Colonial-Modern China by Siyuan Liu

A Sustainable Theatre: Jasper Deeter at Hedgerow by Barry B. Witham

The Group Theatre: Passion, Politics, and Performance in the Depression Era by Helen Chinoy and edited by Don B. Wilmeth and Milly S. Barranger

Cultivating National Identity through Performance: American Pleasure Gardens and Entertainment by Naomi J. Stubbs

Entertaining Children: The Participation of Youth in the Entertainment Industry edited by Gillian Arrighi and Victor Emeljanow

In Memory of Oscar G. Brockett

Being an author's agent has no precise definition. Broadly put, my work involves locating talented playwrights, wherever and whenever their ability manifests itself, to encourage them to write, either in their earliest stages or as they emerge from the cocoon for the professional theatre. If they accept me as their representative, I will attempt to guide their careers and see to their business affairs. Hopefully, together, we will both enjoy a long and rewarding future.

Audrey Wood

Contents

Photographs

Preface

The small woman lay motionless in the hospice bed surrounded by ever-receding ghosts. Audrey Wood, premier literary agent for over 40 years, collapsed in 1981 when she left a taxi in front of the Royalton Hotel on Forty-fourth Street in Manhattan where she and her husband, William ("Bill") Liebling, had maintained a residence since the late 1930s. Her circle of writers, who depended upon her efforts as adviser, manager, promoter, banker, and reliable friend, included an extraordinary number of recipients of Pulitzer Prizes, Antoinette Perry ("Tony") Awards, Drama Critics' Circle Awards, and Motion Picture Academy ("Oscar") Awards. They were bereft to learn that their redoubtable agent had been felled by a massive stroke that rendered her incapable of speech or movement. She had entered a terrible realm from which there was no return.

This book looks at mid-twentieth century Broadway and Hollywood through the prism of a literary agent whose perspicacity in handling the creative talents of the theater's wordsmiths guided the talents and careers of those who created *A Streetcar Named Desire*, *Tea and Sympathy*, *The Member of the Wedding*, *Bus Stop*, and other notable American plays. Audrey Wood exercised the fierce determination required to set a script on its fearful path to success on stages and in films and to smooth over the troubled relationships that often erupted between writers and their agents.

Before Audrey Wood developed a cadre of playwrights, she married the successful talent agent William Liebling, whereupon they created the Liebling-Wood Agency. In this arrangement, Audrey assumed the care and management of the playwrights, screenwriters, translators, and authors, while her husband represented actors and directors. The two agents were equally famous in their spheres of influence.

This book is about the indomitable Audrey Wood whose firsthand scrutiny of serious playwriting transformed America's commercial theater. Although she signed hundreds of writers during her career, I chose to tell the literary agent's story through her interactions with ten playwrights whose careers she nurtured and shaped for America's stages: Tennessee Williams, Robert Anderson, Bertolt Brecht, William Inge, Carson McCullers, Arthur Kopit, Brian Friel, David Storey, Preston Jones, and Studs Terkel.

Other playwrights, lyricists, and a singular choreographer make brief appearances in this story and further define the literary agent's relationship to the creative world they shared. This group includes Dorothy and DuBose Heyward, E. Y. ("Yip") Harburg, Jay Gorney, John Murray and Allen Boretz, Christopher Isherwood and Don Bachardy, Donald Windham, Louis LaRusso, Maurice Valency, Jane Bowles, Jerome Robbins, Joseph Kesselring, Edward Graczyk, James Costigan, Michael V. Gazzo, Sybille Pearson, Joseph Pintauro, Murray Schisgal, David Berry, and Ruth Wolff.

Audrey Wood's Broadway and the playwrights she represented in mid-twentieth century reinforce the remarkable story of one woman's fortitude, talent, endurance, and guts. Although that theater is no more, it is important to reassess the relationships between agent and playwrights that resulted in many of the greatest plays seen on America's stages in the last century and the reasons for their continuing revival into the millennium.

Acknowledgments

I am indebted to Audrey Wood and Max Wilk for their creation of *Represented by Audrey Wood*, the theatrical memoir that first addressed the story of the famous literary agent and is rivaled in modern letters only by Simon Callow's homage to his London agent Margaret ("Peggy") Ramsey called *Love Is Where It Falls: An Account of a Passionate Friendship*.

Few of Audrey Wood's friends and clients are with us today to contribute to this book. For this reason among others, I have cast her life-story in light of her efforts on behalf of the major playwrights she represented. Their careers, successes, and failures are well-documented in reviews, memoirs, biographies, and theatrical books. Nevertheless, their interactions with the woman behind the scenes who guided them, negotiated their successes, and comforted them in their failures, have not been explored as an essential part of American stage history. The work of the literary agent is, necessarily, upstaged by the playwrights, their plays, the directors, the choreographers, and the performers who receive the applause. However, it is my purpose here to highlight the personality and tireless work of the backseat driver who encouraged and guided the writing talents that produced *A Streetcar Named Desire, Tea and Sympathy, The Member of the Wedding, Bus Stop, The Faith Healer, Oh Dad, Poor Dad Mama's Hung You in the Closet and I'm Feelin' So Sad, and The Texas Trilogy* and in a time before Broadway was overtaken by mega-musicals, revivals of tested plays and proven musicals, and staging of new works by established playwrights.

I am grateful to those who shared their stories and experiences of Audrey Wood. They are Daphne Athas, Don Bachardy, Melvin Bernhardt, David A. Berry, Andreas Brown, Martha Coigney, Richard G. Fallon, Brian Friel, Sondra K. Gorney, Adrian Hall, Isobel Robins Konecky, Gilbert Parker, Richard Seff, David Storey, Dolores Sutton, Max Wilk, Walter Willison, George C. White, Ruth Wolff, and Liz Woodman. Others who provided sources for this book were Carole Brandt, Jack Clay, Lenore DeKoven, Allan Deptula, Robyn Baker Flatt, Pat Galloway, Alexis Greene, Greta A. Hays, W. Kenneth Holditch, Julie Jensen, Kevin Kerrane, Martin Kettling,

Margery Klain, Cheryl Raymond, Lynne Rogers, David Samples, Bonnie Nelson Schwartz, Marion Simon, Helen Sneed, Tazewell Thompson, Robert Vaughn, Preston Whiteway, and Don B. Wilmeth.

Moreover, I have benefited from personal histories, biographies, interviews, articles, and firsthand accounts by Thomas P. Adler, David Bogle, Andreas Brown, Virginia Spencer Carr, Tony Coult, Cheryl Crawford, Hume Cronyn, Samuel G. Freedman, Brian Friel, Lewis B. Funke, Sondra K. Gorney, Brenda Gross, Wilborn Hampton, Theresa Helburn, Deborah Jowitt, Elia Kazan, Lawrence Langner, Lyle Leverich, Joshua Logan, James K. Lyon, Fred Nelson, T. W. Sanford, Josyane Savigneau, Robert A. Schanke, Richard Schickel, Alan Schneider, Richard Seff, Irene Mayer Selznick, Wilfred Sheed, Helen Sheehy, Robert Sherwood, Don Shewey, Donald Spoto, Dan. P. Terkell, Kenneth Turan with Joseph Papp, Ralph F. Voss, Eli Wallach, Margaret Webster, John F. Wharton, David Wilk, Max Wilk, Tennessee Williams, Ruth Wolff, and Audrey Wood.

The collections of letters containing correspondence between Tennessee Williams and Audrey Wood, edited by Albert J. Devlin and Nancy M. Tischler, and the notebooks of Tennessee Williams, edited by Margaret Bradham Thornton, are invaluable sources of firsthand material on interactions between Audrey Wood and her famous client during key stages of the playwright's career.

On a personal note, I wish to express my gratitude to George C. White, founder of the Eugene O'Neill Memorial Foundation and Theater Center, for sharing his thoughts on Audrey Wood's early collaboration with the O'Neill Center.

Moreover, it is important to acknowledge that without the support and generosity of Alan Q. Schwartz, Executor of the Audrey Wood Estate, and David Wilk, son of writer Max Wilk who assisted the literary agent in the final preparation of her memoir for publication, it would not be possible to hear the "voice" of Audrey Wood in moments of frustration, disappointment, and success as she responded to clients and industry pressures.

I am also indebted to the generosity of the Harry Ransom Humanities Research Center at the University of Texas, Austin, for awarding a travel fellowship from the Fleur Cowles Endowment in support of my research into the considerable Audrey Wood Papers housed within the Center. I am also appreciative of the assistance and many courtesies of Richard Workman and the staff in the Center's Manuscript Room.

Milly S. Barranger
New York City

Introduction

The theater is a venture [one hesitates to call it a business] built of equal parts of faith, energy and hard work—all tied together with massive injections of nerve.[1]

Among the theatergoing public, very few of us know what an "author's agent" does, and most likely, as ticket-buyers we have never met one. For a time, Audrey Wood, who first put "represented by Audrey Wood" in a Broadway playbill, was the American theater's most famous play agent. Working behind the scenes, the diminutive New Yorker (scarcely five feet tall without her signature hat) encouraged talented writers and guided their careers through business deals with producers, theater managements, film companies, and publishers. She wrote her autobiography, *Represented by Audrey Wood*, with author and screenwriter Max Wilk, but succumbed to a cerebral hemorrhage on the streets of New York City shortly before its publication. Since then, few in the profession remember Audrey Wood with the exception of scholars and critics researching the lives and careers of America's playwrights in the last century.

Unlike actors whose accomplishments are defined by their roles (Laurette Taylor as Amanda Wingfield and Marlon Brando as Stanley Kowalski), the theater's literary agents are permanently associated with playwrights and their greatest hits. The first encounter between Tennessee Williams and his future agent is the stuff of theatrical legend. Audrey Wood walked into the outer office of the new Liebling-Wood Agency on the twelfth floor at 551 Fifth Avenue, and came face to face with a slender young man of medium height with slightly curly hair, a sandy moustache, and pale blue eyes who had come to see her without an appointment. She walked over to him and said, "Did you want to see me about something?" "If your name is Audrey Wood, I do," he replied in a Southern drawl, and introduced himself, "My name is Tennessee Williams."[2] The meeting set in motion a collaboration that lasted over 32 years—several lifetimes in the commercial theater.

I have been circling the story of Audrey Wood for ten years or more. I wrote books on Anglo-American director Margaret Webster, who staged the ill-fated Boston premiere of Tennessee Williams's early full-length play, *Battle of Angels*, and on Broadway producer Cheryl Crawford, who produced four of his major plays. In both books, Audrey Wood appeared as an enabling presence to the playwright, directors, and producers.

Born into her father's world of vaudeville entertainers, stock companies, and Broadway's Palace Theatre where William H. Wood excelled as a theater manager, his daughter at the age of 22 found a niche as a theatrical agent and began her future career. Audrey put her name on the door of her first agency in 1937, the same year the Hindenburg burst into flames over New Jersey, Lillian Hellman and Dorothy Parker reported on the civil war in Spain, and Adolf Hitler positioned German tanks on the borders of Czechoslovakia and Poland. The year was ripe for Broadway to respond to a changing political, social, and cultural landscape in America and welcome a woman into the ranks of Broadway's "author's agents."

For the next 40 years, Audrey Wood remained focused on her clients whose contributions shaped the American theater during the middle of the last century and whose present-day revivals continue to enrich stages across the United States, England, and Europe. Moreover, their screenplays, many based on their plays written for the stage, are admired and studied for their craft and notable performances.

Audrey Wood's circle of playwrights eventually included Dorothy and Dubose Heyward, Tennessee Williams, Robert Anderson, William Inge, Carson McCullers, Maurice Valency, Arthur Kopit, Preston Jones, Brian Friel, David Storey, and Studs Terkel, along with more than a hundred other writers. Their ever-expanding numbers accounted for new plays that made the journey from Miss Wood's desk to the stages of America's theaters—and beyond.

Since 1927, when she began as a play-reader for the Century Play Company in Manhattan, Audrey Wood labored for her clients as a largely invisible player. The play-agent's business is reading scripts, signing authors, negotiating with producers, writing contracts, arranging writer's fees, holding hands through casting and rewrites in the pressure cooker of the commercial theater with its stream of lawyers, accountants, investors, and creative temperaments. And, finally, during the wait for the late-night reviews in some nearby watering hole, she knows that regardless of the verdict, the next morning she will be back in her office preparing to begin the cycle again with the next one.

The attendant arguments, crises, and daily eruptions experienced in the crucible of the commercial theater bind the agent and the writer, often in a love-hate relationship. Nevertheless, for the time they are conjoined in an enterprise, the agent remains a polestar guiding their lives and careers, hopefully, to safe harbor in the columns of the *New York Times* and in lines of ticket buyers at box-office windows.

Audrey Wood remarked on her chosen niche in a tough profession: "It is a peculiar line of work, precarious, filled with a certain amount of success, many disappointments and often disaster."[3]

Audrey Wood's name is permanently linked today with a number of gifted writers. Considered in tandem, the story of the 40 years of her labors begins and ends in the theater with the curtain rising on the well-crafted play that began its commercial life in a stack of manuscripts on her desk, followed by a telephone call inviting the writer to come to her office to discuss his or her submission. Her intuition, the mysterious inner instinct that manifest itself within the first 10 to 15 pages of a script, cried out from time to time that this one might be the next Eugene O'Neill. She then telephoned the playwright and said in a calm, cultivated voice, "This is Audrey Wood. I would like to represent you."

Part I Genesis of an Agent 1905–1940

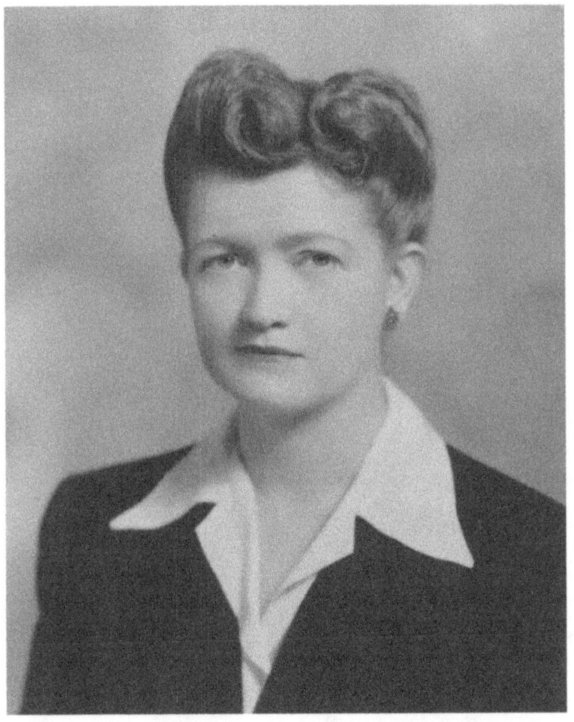

Audrey Wood, c. 1937. Billy Rose Theatre Division, The New York Public Library for the Performing Arts, Astor, Lenox, and Tilden Foundations.

1. Stagestruck

To lose a troupe of full-grown elephants is not an easy feat.[1]

The Century Play Company at 1440 Broadway was the place of Audrey Wood's seven-year apprenticeship that followed a childhood of weekend matinees of vaudeville shows and touring productions in New York theaters managed by her father. She was stagestruck at an early age by Weber and Fields' Dutch act in mock-Germanic accents, by the reenactment of the English derby in *The Sporting Life*, and by the tribute to the Divine Sarah, seated in a high-back chair while assembled stars paid homage by crowning her with a golden wreath on the stage of Broadway's Palace Theatre.

Nevertheless, nothing rivaled the breathless anticipation of the eight-year-old in the manager's box at the Palace for the opening act with a family of elephants. The elephants, guided by their trainer, lumbered up Broadway in single file from the Forty-second Street ferry to the entertainment of passersby, and, just as the Palace orchestra began the overture, the pachyderms arrived at the stage door on Forty-seventh Street to make their entrance.

Born on a dining-room table in a New York apartment on West Fifty-first Street on February 28, 1905, Audrey Violet Wood called herself a "cut-rate baby."[2] The physician, who delivered her, was also the "house doctor" on 24-hour call at the Broadway Theatre on Fortieth Street where her father was then employed as business manager. Her parents, William H. Wood and Ida Gaubatz Wood, named their daughter for a character in a dramatized novel by Mary Johnston produced on Broadway before Audrey was born. They added Violet as a middle name, but Audrey became less than thrilled with "Violet" and managed to rid herself of her middle name without serious complaint from her parents.[3]

The Wood family had immigrated to Milwaukee from a "genteel suburb" in London when William was seven years old. The Gaubatz family had come to America from Germany in the 1860s, and eventually migrated to Milwaukee where Ida May Gaubatz was born. After completing eighth grade, Audrey's future parents decided to get on with the serious business of their adult lives. Her mother became a bookkeeper at a local bookshop, and her father, after several adventures as a legal clerk and a book salesman, so impressed impresario Jacob Litt of Milwaukee's Bijou Theatre, who owned and managed other theaters in the Midwest, that he gave the young man his choice of managing theaters in Chicago or New York. William Wood chose the theater capital of the United States.

Once established as Jacob Litt's up-and-coming manager of his various touring shows, Wood was promoted to the staff of the Broadway Theatre at Fortieth Street. At this point, Wood sent for Ida and they were married. Their daughter was born in Manhattan and grew up six blocks from where she would eventually reign over the Leibling-Wood Agency at 551 Fifth Avenue.

Playing in the aisles of the Broadway Theatre while her father reviewed box-office statements on weekends, Audrey was infected by the show business bug. Seeing shows at matinee performances, "usually from a good seat," the manager's daughter vividly recalled the great spectacles of *The Sporting Life*, *Shenandoah*, and *Ben Hur*. Nevertheless, around the family dinner table, Audrey came to understand that behind the scenes the theater business was not so glamorous. Oftentimes it was a treadmill of constant hard work with low pay, harsh living and travel conditions, and frequent exploitation of the hapless performers by small-time managers.[4]

When the popularity and cheap prices of motion pictures forced the Broadway Theatre to close as a home for legitimate theater, William Wood, disdaining the "five-and-ten-cent entertainment," accepted producer B. F. Keith's invitation to work with him and with vaudeville impresario Martin Beck at a new theater they were building at Forty-seventh Street and Broadway. The Palace opened in the spring of 1913, and the eight-year-old Audrey marveled at the progression of vaudeville turns by actors and actresses in one-acts, along with magicians, acrobats, jugglers, and animal acts. At the Palace, Audrey saw the reigning queen of the French theater, Sarah Bernhardt, with members of her company, perform scenes from *The Lady of the Camellias* and other plays on the same bill.

From her matinee house seat (granted as a weekly treat from her parents), Audrey saw the Palace headliners and discovered Ethel Barrymore, Alla Nazimova, W. C. Fields, Sophie Tucker, and Bert Williams. When she was not at the Palace, she attended Public School No. 84 on West Fiftieth Street, and on Sundays sporadically attended Lutheran Sunday

School at Sixty-fifth Street and Central Park West. Her parents were indifferent to her churchgoing but her neighborhood girlfriends insisted that she accompany them on Sundays to learn something more than the names of headliners at the Palace.

Her father was a shrewd manager and was selected by B. F. Keith's executive office to manage the Hudson Theatre, part of the Keith-Albee circuit in Union Hill (later Union City) across the Hudson River in New Jersey. Audrey and her mother now acquired a new routine on weekends. Every Friday evening, they took the ferry from Forty-second Street across the river, and then a streetcar or bus ride to the theater, where they were ushered into the manager's box. They would see a show and return to their Manhattan apartment long after normal bedtime hours for a preadolescent. The same schedule was repeated for Sunday matinees. At no time did her parents censor the plays that she saw.

Audrey recalled a smorgasbord of entertainment at the Hudson: the melodrama *The Traffic* (billed as "An Astounding White Slave Play"), *Graustark* (later known to moviegoers as *The Prisoner of Zenda*), *Rip Van Winkle* (who awakened from a long sleep a changed man), *Uncle Tom's Cabin* (with Eliza crossing the ice, clutching her infant in her arms), along with the many personalities appearing at the Sunday vaudeville matinees. On one such occasion, the "Sultan of Swat," Babe Ruth, made a personal appearance to the audience's delight.

In a moment of fatherly pride when his daughter was 11, William Wood sent her a press photograph of himself inscribed,

> To little auburn Audrey:
> If you grow up to be as good a woman as your mother, and
> as smart as your father—Gee, what a success you'll be.
> W. H. Wood, alias "Father," March 18, 1916.[5]

Audrey Wood's not-so-formal education took place in the theater, where she was exposed to classic and not-so-classic plays.[6] During weekdays at Public School No. 84 and then at Washington Irving High School, 40 Irving Place, Audrey, by her own account, was "never a really good student." She was proficient in English classes and was encouraged to write for the school magazine, *The Sketch Book*. She took pride in knowing as much about the theater as Alexander Woollcott of the *Times* and Heywood Broun of the *Morning World* whose columns she read every morning in the subway on the way to Irving Place. When she became editor of the school magazine, she started a drama review department and cleverly gave all of the assignments to herself. Mesmerized by Eleonora Duse's performance as Mrs. Alving in Henrik Ibsen's *Ghosts* at the Century Theatre, the novice reviewer gave Duse a "rave," as did her better-known compatriots Woollcott and Broun.

In the hope that she would become an actress, her father gave his daughter a small part in Booth Tarkington's *Seventeen* at the Hudson. At 16, she played the bit part "as though I had been playing on Broadway for years!" She marveled that she experienced no stage fright and reasoned, "I had such belief in myself I was unafraid."[7]

After high school, she enrolled in Hunter College of the City University of New York, but by the end of the third month her father suffered a stroke (he died shortly thereafter) and Audrey withdrew from college. She felt an obligation to support her mother and turned to theatrical agent Max Hart, a friend of her father's, to secure an acting job. She auditioned for Richard Herndon, and the ingénue was offered a job in his Chicago company, but in the face of the cold reality of supporting two households on $75 a week, she turned down the offer. In later years, she mused, "My loss was the audience's gain."[8]

She was very much aware that the theater business was a male fiefdom with limited opportunities for a young woman who was not an actress. Nevertheless, as the daughter of a successful manager with many contacts in front offices, she was determined to break down doors. In 1923, she knocked on Tom Kane's door at the Century Play Company, and found her way into the business for the next 50 years.

2. Starting Out

Many, many scripts call, but few are chosen.[1]

Aware that the seat of theatrical power in the front offices of managers, booking agents, and producers was male turf, the 22-year-old Audrey Wood was too busy looking for a job to be concerned about what was later called the glass ceiling. She knew that most women in theatrical offices labored as telephone operators, receptionists, and typists in undistinguished and badly paid jobs. Even in the mid-1920s, when Rachel Crothers, Zoë Akins, Rose Franken, and Anne Nichols were making names as playwrights, there were few opportunities for women to be hired at the managerial level. As she walked down Broadway toward the offices of the Century Play Company, she did not consider herself a modern-day heroine breaking down doors to invade male territory. She wanted a job—any job.

For the second time, Audrey found that her father's connections opened doors for her. Owned by Tom Kane and James Thatcher, the Century Play Company at 1440 Broadway acted as agents for playwrights. Kane had been a friend of William Wood, and when approached by his daughter, he offered the young woman the lowest-rung position on Century's corporate ladder. He hired her as a playreader for $3 a report. The Century's mail room was filled with an endless stream of manuscripts submitted by aspiring writers. It was Audrey's job to take home a stack of scripts, read them, and write reports on their potential for the commercial stage.

In 1927, Century was hugely successful. Tom Kane advanced playwrights large sums of money for their plays produced on Broadway to secure the "stock rights" for the firm. He proceeded to secure touring productions for his clients' work chiefly with road impresarios Poli in New England and Henry Duffy in key cities in California and the Northwest. Touring companies changed bills of fare weekly, thereby generating enormous incomes for Century and its playwrights along with a large volume of paperwork and bookkeeping.

Audrey's future in the business increased a rung on Century's corporate ladder when she arrived at the office one morning to deliver her reports and found Gus Diehl, manager of Century's stock department (also a friend of her father's), waist-deep in problems with licensing and touring schedules.

In those days, the stock business was Century's "cash cow." There were literally hundreds of local stock companies in cities and towns and each license had to be negotiated 50-odd times a year. In this thriving market, a playwright, managed by Century, could sell a play to Henry Duffy for his theaters in Los Angeles, then San Francisco, and then northward in the circuit to Portland and Seattle. This business, in which the stock company's entertainment or bill changed weekly in myriad towns and cities, generated an enormous income for Century and its playwrights. Harry Delf's family comedy, *The Family Upstairs*, with little impact on Broadway, could still make the writer a fortune in royalties for years to come. In the absence of computers, the company's bookkeeping and contracts were handled by hand, and the manager of Century's stock department lived in a state of disarray in his effort to keep up with the coast-to-coast business.

Face to face one morning with the highly agitated Gus Diehl, Audrey spoke up with little forethought: "You know, Mr. Diehl, it seems to me you need somebody to help you and I think I'm the one to do this job."[2] Diehl looked at the small woman with the quiet, cultivated voice and nodded in agreement. The next morning, Audrey Wood went to work as a full-time employee for the Century Play Company and forever after remained a *play agent*.

Not only was Audrey Wood a skillful taskmaster, but she had acquired in her younger play-going days a vast knowledge of the dramas and comedies of the recent past. Whenever there was a question about a dramatic property, Audrey could usually remember what the play was about and who had been in the cast. With her encyclopedic memory, she became indispensable to Century.

In a serendipitous moment, the woman running Century's new play department went on holiday with no plans to return but withheld this information from Tom Kane who asked Audrey to fill-in during her absence. When the absence became permanent, Kane tapped Audrey to head the new play department. Audrey Wood was now poised to leave behind Alexandre Dumas, Lew Wallace, and George L. Aiken for the living presence of Lawrence Hazard, Joseph Kesselring, and Doris Frankel.

In her new capacity, and in an inspired act of personal initiative, Audrey took the train to New Haven to begin her search for new playwrights who would someday need an agent to represent their work. She had written to George Pierce Baker, then Dean of Yale University's School of Drama and legendary creator of the 47 Workshop at Harvard, where he taught the principles of playwriting that influenced Eugene O'Neill, Sidney Howard, Edward Sheldon, and Philip Barry. Lured to Yale in 1925, his workshop for the writing and production of plays became the keystone of the new drama school.

In her letter to Professor Baker, Audrey asked if she could meet with him to discuss young playwrights and the problems that confronted them. Baker replied and offered her an appointment the following week at 8:30 a.m. on a weekday morning. To keep the appointment she took the train to New Haven and spent the night in the Taft Hotel which adjoined the Shubert Theatre, a well-used tryout house in downtown New Haven. In years to come, Audrey would spend many hours in the Shubert and many nights in the Taft while attending the out-of-town tryouts of plays whose authors she represented.

The ever punctual Audrey Wood arrived at Baker's office at 8:30 a.m. George Pierce Baker had never heard of Audrey Wood or the Century Play Company but listened to her offer to represent his "tyro" writers. Rather than dismissing the youthful agent on the spot, Baker offered to put her name on the Drama School's mailing list so she might know when a new play, whose author had no agent, was being produced. Audrey returned triumphantly to New York as an agent for "new" playwrights.

Shortly thereafter, Baker referred David Hertz, an up-and-coming writer, to her. Audrey signed Hertz, who had written a play called *Miles of Heaven*, and went in search of a producer. In time, she found one in California where the play was eventually staged but without success. Nevertheless, *Miles of Heaven* attracted Hollywood film people and David Hertz became a well-paid screenwriter. The playwright's agent now added a new component to her business—the screenwriter.

THE NEW AGENCY

Audrey remained at the Century Play Company for seven years during which she was paid a weekly salary and gave scant attention to the troubled national economy and the burgeoning "talkies." She was intent on meeting the increasing demand of the Hollywood studios for "word" men, that is, playwrights who could supply actors and actresses with dialogue. As vaudeville disappeared from Broadway and the road bookings vanished beneath the impact of Al Jolson's acting and singing on the silver screen in *The Jazz Singer* at popular prices, the weekly paychecks from Hollywood were hard for writers (and their agents) to refuse.

Audrey worked relentlessly to meet aspiring authors. During the turbulent years of the Depression, she met DuBose and Dorothy Heyward, who would later become the first clients of the new Audrey Wood Agency. She also represented a young playwright from Yale, named Arnold Sundgaard, whose play *Everywhere I Roam* was produced in New York and received respectable notices. Marc Connolly, known for his collaborations with George S. Kaufman on *Dulcy* and *Beggar on Horseback*, was the director and coproducer, but Connolly did not offer his Pulitzer-Prize winning *Green Pastures* to the disappointed agent.

Several of the early collaborations paid off, however. The young Yale authors remained loyal clients during the Depression years and thereafter. Oftentimes, they did not have a quarter to buy a meal at Child's Restaurant, located across the street from the Century offices at Fortieth Street and Broadway, where the Century staff ate lunch. Audrey carried a pocket full of quarters when she went to Child's, knowing that her "friends" often did not have the price of a meal—yet.

Lawrence Hazard was one of these "friends." Audrey sold his play to a film company and he returned to New York to give her $500 for her hard work that had resulted in a lucrative film contract, a house, and swimming pool. Tom Kane objected to Hazard's gift and a "terrible row" ensued between the two men, with Hazard prevailing. Audrey was permitted to take the $500, "a staggering sum in those days," which she took home to her mother who frequently subsidized her daughter's 5 cent bus fare and the 25 cent lunches at Child's.[3]

One day in the darkest Depression year, Tom Kane announced that he was closing the new play department and gave Audrey a year's notice. She had given little attention to the devastating affects on Century's business caused by the burgeoning talkies and the shrinking legitimate theater. Audrey recalled the year's notice as "a very decent gesture" in those dreadful times of bread lines, apple sellers on every corner, and darkened, empty playhouses.[4]

Undaunted, Audrey sallied forth to look for a new affiliation. She was helped by another agent, Kay Brown, who was working in the New York offices of the legendary agent Leland Hayward, whose agency was known as "the Tiffany of agencies" and represented such celebrity talents as Katharine Hepburn, Fred Astaire, Ingrid Bergman, Henry Fonda, and James Stewart, along with such successful authors as Edna Ferber, Paul Osborne, Ben Hecht, and Charles MacArthur.

Kay Brown, who later served as story editor for David O. Selznick and was instrumental in his purchase of the screen rights to *Gone with the Wind*, promoted Audrey to the powers-that-be within the Hayward office. She arranged an invitation for Audrey to lunch at Sardi's with Hayward's New York drama agent, Paul Streger. Audrey entered the famous restaurant in the full knowledge that to sign with the powerful national agency would constitute a giant step forward. Nevertheless, when Streger offered her a job in his department, she asked, "If I work with you and if a play comes along and I like it but you don't, what happens?" His reply was swift: "We do not handle the play."[5]

Faced with a difficult choice, Audrey reflected for several days and finally listened to an inner voice that told her she needed to make her own decisions about a writer's talent. She trusted her instincts and knew that in the Hayward office she would be cut off from her intuitive assessment of a writer's abilities honed over seven years at Century. Once her decision was made, she sent Leland Hayward a wire regretfully declining the offer to work with his prestigious firm.

Unaccustomed to being turned down by novice agents, Hayward called up Kay Brown to complain about the cheeky young woman. "Who the hell does Audrey Wood think she is?" Years later, Audrey learned Kay's answer ("She's good and she knows it.").[6] By then, Hayward was a successful Broadway producer of *Mr. Roberts*, *South Pacific*, and *The Sound of Music*, and regularly telephoned the established Audrey Wood of the Liebling-Wood Agency to ask her to find him a producible script.

Audrey continued to interview with other theatrical agencies but nothing came of her efforts. Then, her client Doris Frankel—who was working on a play later produced on Broadway and who also taught at the Yale Drama School and was married to Philip Barber—the New York director of the Federal Theatre Project, came to her with a suggestion. Frankel's father had a vacant office space in the Heckscher Building and she proposed that they form a business partnership and open their own office.

Knowing that success as an independent agent was a long shot, especially for a woman in the early 1930s, Audrey, nevertheless, teased the pros and cons of the empty office waiting on Fifty-seventh Street and Fifth Avenue. The office would be rent-free, but she would draw no weekly salary. Furthermore, the women could not afford a secretary, not even an office boy for errands.

At home later that evening, she discussed the opportunity with her mother. Ida Wood, who had been around the theater long enough to know the risks and the rewards, encouraged her daughter to make the leap. "Go ahead," she said, "I'll give you a year."[7]

In the months to come, she continued to dole out bus fare to her daughter who also did a great deal of walking to save a nickel.

Once the Audrey Wood Agency opened, the women sent out invitations to their launch party. As Audrey opened the door to their first guest, she was astonished to see Broadway producer Harry Moses, responsible for the hit *Grand Hotel*. Unable to conceal her astonishment that someone so important would come to their celebration, she concluded that the appearance of Harry Moses meant that they were truly launched in the business.

FIRST CLIENTS

The playwrights that Audrey Wood eventually represented began their journeys in a variety of locales and backgrounds, not the least was Charleston, South Carolina. Dubose and Dorothy Heyward followed her to the new agency. The same year that Audrey became a script-reader at Century, the couple adapted *Porgy* from DuBose Heyward's novel about black residents of Catfish Row in South Carolina, and the Theatre Guild produced it with great success. By the time composer George Gershwin proposed creating an opera from *Porgy*, Audrey Wood represented the South Carolinians. The Guild wanted a musical as a starring vehicle for Al Jolson, but Audrey favored Gershwin's proposed operatic version. She later recalled the dilemma in an interview: "What to do? Jolson had the dough, Gershwin the dream. We settled for the dream, and you know the rest."[8]

Audrey spoke candidly to the Heywards and they agreed to wait for Gershwin's availability. As they waited, Jolson went to Hollywood to film *The Jazz Singer*. When Gershwin was free of other commitments, Audrey drew up contracts for the collaboration and took the papers to the composer's apartment in the West seventies, and then across the street to Ira Gershwin who was collaborating on the lyrics with Dubose Heyward. With trips to South Carolina to immerse himself in the life rhythms and speech patterns of the Gullahs, George Gershwin took 11 months to write the score for *Porgy* (with *Bess* added to the title). The score comprised seven hundred pages of music, which Audrey calculated would take four and a half hours to perform. It was Gershwin's masterpiece, but by the time the Theatre Guild produced *Porgy and Bess* at the Alvin Theatre in 1935, it was described by the press as "a Broadway musical slowed down by gobbits of opera."[9]

Porgy and Bess had a respectable (Broadway lingo for a modest success) run of 124 performances. Only with the folk opera's revival under the producing hand of Cheryl Crawford, who worked with the Gershwin estate and with conductor Alexander Smallen to reduce the recitatives, did the opera become a commercial success—and an American classic.

By 1939, the Heywards sent *Mamba's Daughters*, based on DuBose Heyward's novel about the struggles of a black matriarch to raise her family in segregated Charleston, to Audrey at the newly-opened Leibling-Wood Agency. In her search for a producer, Audrey found Guthrie McClintic, married to Katharine Cornell, who optioned the drama and proceeded to cast Ethel Waters, a popular nightclub singer and musical revue headliner, to play the matriarch's oldest daughter. Audrey was subsequently thrown into the country's troubled race relations that spilled onto Broadway's stages.

It was a bold idea to cast the singer, even though she had been given equal billing with her white costars in Irving Berlin's 1933 revue *As Thousands Cheer*. Nevertheless, Audrey worked for months to find a producer for a serious play helmed by a black entertainer. She was aware that Broadway audiences would accept Ethel Waters as an entertainer, but in the 1930s, black actors were not offered dramatic, non-singing roles in the Broadway theater. Also, it was not unusual for black actors routinely to be directed to the service elevator when staying in hotels during tours, and even upon occasion in New York hotels.

Mamba's Daughters opened with the first African American performer ever to star on the stage of the Empire Theatre, but the reviewer for the *New York Times* was unenthusiastic. Incensed by Brooks Atkinson's review, friends of the actress and other theatrical people raised money to buy an ad in the *Times* to rave about Ethel Waters' performance and to plead with New York audiences to support the actress and the play.

The following Sunday, Atkinson wrote a reappraisal (titled "Mamba's Waters") in which he praised the actress and apologized to readers for slighting the performance in his earlier review.[10] Nevertheless, business did not improve and *Mamba's Daughter's* closed as a financial failure after 162 performances but a great personal success for Ethel Waters and for minority actors in the New York theater.

Two years later, Waters played the lead in the musical fantasy, *Cabin in the Sky*, the first successful musical represented by the new Liebling-Wood agency. With the musical book by Audrey's clients Lynn Root and John La

Touche, and directed by George Balanchine, the fantastical show pitted the forces of good and evil in battle for the soul of Little Joe, a gambling man, played by Dooley Wilson (later immortalized in film as Sam, the piano player who sings "As Time Goes By" in *Casablanca*). Ethel Waters was cast as Joe's faithful wife who joyously battles the Devil to save her husband's soul. Night after night, Waters stepped in front of the curtain and stopped the show with composer Vernon Duke's melody, "Taking a Chance on Love," with John La Touche and Ted Fetter's memorable lyrics.

Waters' film career was launched in 1943 with the film version of *Cabin in the Sky*, wherein she costarred with Eddie "Rochester" Anderson, Lena Horne, and Louis Armstrong. Within seven years, Ethel Waters returned to New York to appear as the housekeeper, Bernice Sadie Brown, in a play by Audrey's new client, the novelist Carson McCullers.

During Audrey's post–Century Play Company representation of writers, Arnold Sundgaard became a highly paid screenwriter, Joseph Kesselring wrote his hit comedy, *Arsenic and Old Lace,* and Harry Segall wrote the comedy *Heaven Can Wait*, twice made into a classic film. Lawrence Hazard and Richard Flournoy started out writing plays and also ended as highly paid screenwriters. Audrey always regretted when one of her writers turned entirely away from the legitimate theater. Nonetheless, she appreciated the lucrative call of Hollywood and took satisfaction in those clients who continued writing both plays and filmscripts.

ENTER LIEBLING

After *Mamba's Daughters*, Audrey struggled to eek out enough income to sustain the office. One day, the telephone rang and Broadway's leading casting agent asked to speak with Miss Wood. She had never met William H. Liebling (known as "the King of Forty-fifth Street), but she knew his reputation as the casting agent of choice for major theatrical producers. He handled the shows of George M. Cohan, Sam H. Harris, and Max Gordon. He read their plays, suggested appropriate actors, and brought those actors to auditions for such hits as *You Can't Take It With You* and *Abe Lincoln in Illinois*.

Audrey recalled her first conversation with Liebling (the name means "darling"). "They tell me you are a bright young agent," he said, "who has interesting plays to sell. I would like to read some of them."[11] Since the Audrey Wood agency could not afford an "office boy," as they were called in those days, to make deliveries, she promptly carried the scripts herself to 551 Fifth Avenue.

Liebling—described as a small, dapper man with a receding hairline and ubiquitous black suit, stiff white collar, and dark tie—had arranged his outer office with a receptionist cubicle and a convenient bench to seat the stream of actors looking for jobs. It was dubbed "Mr. Liebling's bench" by grateful actors who often sat in his outer office simply to rest after making the rounds of offices seeking work. He was always courteous to the waiting aspirants and invited them to remain seated as long as they liked.

Audrey entered with manuscripts in hand and found a place on the bench beside several actors. She observed the small man with dark receding hair, who was to become her future business partner and husband, as immaculately dressed with a high collar and elegant tie and unfailingly polite to the actors in the outer office, treating them as creative human beings rather than as pawns in the casting game.[12]

Bill Liebling was known throughout Times Square as a soft-spoken, self-effacing gentle man who was the antithesis of the popular conception of the brusque, cigar-smoking casting agent. He had a reputation for kindness and courtesy to his many clients.[13]

On the day Audrey arrived bearing scripts, he gently dismissed the actors and ushered her into his office. As she handed over the scripts, he startled her by asking if she had plans for dinner. Since she had never met William Liebling, she found his invitation arrogant and even suspicious. She made a quick exit declaring, somewhat haughtily, that she had other plans for the evening.

When she returned to collect the manuscripts, Liebling ushered her into his office once again. Audrey recalled their conversation: "I want to talk to you, Miss Wood. I have been thinking about you and have decided I want to open a play department and I'd like you to run it."[14]

Startled by his abruptness, she declined the invitation, citing her responsibilities to her own agency and business partner. With the confidence of a man who always gets his way whether casting the ideal actress or a business partner, Liebling announced that he would postpone his decision for a time.

Following on the heels of Audrey's second encounter with William Liebling, Doris Frankel announced that she was pregnant and had decided that she could not continue as partner in the agency. Coincidences, which Audrey regarded as a tired device that skilled playwrights avoided, began to accumulate. That same day, Liebling called to invite her to dinner. This time, she accepted. As soon as they were seated in Sardi's, Audrey, without preamble, told him of Doris Frankel's imminent departure. Liebling nodded to confirm his earlier decision: "I've been waiting for months, now. Come."[15]

The genesis of the famous Liebling-Wood Agency occurred at Sardi's one evening in 1937, and the partnership lasted until William Liebling's retirement 20 years later.

3. A Room of Their Own

. . . ours is a business that has hope for its cornerstone.[1]

John Murray and Allen Boretz, resembling nothing so much as a New York version of the Bobbsy twins, walked into the suite on the twelfth floor at 551 Fifth Avenue with a revised script of *Room Service*, and handed the newly merged team of Liebling-Wood their first Broadway success. *Room Service* opened on May 19, 1937, and registered a smash hit for the new agency.

Liebling brought an earlier version of the Murray-Boretz script to the new partnership when it was formed on Shakespeare's birthday in April of 1937. Until he represented the writing team, he had been solely an actor's agent with a reputation for being a shrewd judge of talent and a tenacious advocate. Earlier that season, *Room Service* had tried out in Philadelphia under the auspices of producer Sam Harris—and closed there. Convinced that the play would work if rewritten, Liebling installed the authors in his hotel room at the Piccadilly on West Forty-fifth Street and set them to revising their material. Audrey described the playwrights as "earnest, eager, willing, and hungry," and extravagantly prone to ordering room service.[2] With the steady trundling of carts from the kitchen to Liebling's suite, life and art came face to face at the Picadilly Hotel.

Room Service plots the machinations of a penniless producer who installs himself in his brother's suite at the White Way Hotel along with his equally penurious playwright, director, and cast. As the bills mount up, desperate ploys are tried to forestall eviction until the exasperated hotel owner agrees to finance the play, which then becomes a hit.

FAST, FRENZIED, FUNNY

Audrey's account of Bill Liebling's maneuvers on behalf of *Room Service* took up the story with the search for the right director, namely George

Abbott. At the time, Abbott was Broadway's premier producer-director of farcical comedy with a record of hits that included *Three Men on a Horse, Boy Meets Girl*, and *On Your Toes*. Determined to secure Abbott for his clients, Liebling had to circumvent Sam Harris who, as producer of the failed Philadelphia tryout, still had first refusal of the revised script. Liebling's dilemma was compounded by the fact that both Harris and Abbott, theatrical royalty, were not inclined to be the first to pick up the telephone to discuss the property.

A cagey Bill Liebling called Abbott's New York residence and left a message: "Sam Harris had phoned and wished to discuss *Room Service* with George Abbott."[3] Abbott then called Harris and learned that he was not interested in producing the play a second time. With Sam Harris out of the picture, Abbott was determined to produce and direct the comedy himself. It was Audrey's turn to draw up production contracts for Murray and Boretz—the first of many authors' contracts generated by Liebling-Wood.

In mid-May, a few weeks after Liebling-Wood had opened for business, *Room Service* with a cast of farceurs that included Sam Levene, Philip Loeb, Eddie Albert, and Betty Field opened to roars of laughter, waves of applause, and critical raves that declared it the "funniest play New York has seen in years and years."[4]

Nevertheless, the agents' work had only begun. As Abbott began casting actors for touring companies and a London production, bidding began for the sale of rights for a motion-picture version. While Audrey generated multiple production contracts for the authors, Liebling was determined to secure a lucrative film contract for his clients. Warner Brothers had a prior relationship with George Abbott and presumed that they had preference in any film deal, but in an effort to get the best price for his clients, Liebling took the matter to the Dramatists Guild—established to protect the rights of playwrights for US productions of plays and musicals—and argued that any negotiations for screen rights must be handled at an open auction. In the end, RKO Pictures paid $250,000, agreed to hire Murray and Boretz to write the screenplay, and subsequently made the film with the Marx Brothers, Lucille Ball, and Ann Miller.

DIVISION OF LABOR

The Liebling-Wood Agency was a small suite of offices configured so that each of the three offices had a single window. The outer reception area was furnished with Liebling's bench, a standing ashtray, and several small chairs. A glass partition separated the receptionist and a "Lily Tomlin switchboard," made popular in actress Lily Tomlin's skit on television's *Laugh-In*, from the waiting clients. Sometime in the late 1940s, an agent, representing television interests, occupied the third office. Space was so limited that a large closet was used as the agency's "file room."[5]

Audrey's office, which she shared with her secretary, was located on the western side of the three offices and Liebling occupied the middle office that placed him closer to the traffic of hopeful actors.

Room Service was Liebling-Wood's first commercial hit. In the theater district, Bill Leibling had a reputation as a shrewd judge of talent as a casting agent, and, in time, represented both actors and directors. Well-known around Times Square in the 1930s, he was constantly involved in casting plays by legendary producers. Audrey described his casting technique as simple and direct, but largely intuitive. He studied a play, made up a list of actors he felt were right for individual parts, and, after he made his selection, seldom considered alternatives. By Audrey's account, he refused to waste time—his own, the producer's, the director's, and, most importantly, the actor's.[6] In this way, he cast *Dinner at Eight*, *Inherit the Wind*, *The King and I*, *You Can't Take It With You*, and *Abe Lincoln in Illinois*.

In those days, a casting agent (called a casting director today) could represent an actor for a part in a play, provided he or she reached the actor with the *first* offer. Audrey was representing Tennessee Williams when preparations began for *A Streetcar Named Desire*. The producer, Irene Mayer Selznick, had engaged Elia Kazan to direct. Casting the various roles of Blanche, Stella, and Mitch took several months but the major role of Stanley Kowalski presented problems. All had agreed that John Garfield was ideal for the part but his agent insisted on a "get-out" clause that would permit the actor to leave the play should he receive a bona fide offer for a motion picture. This was a deal breaker for the *Streetcar* people. Liebling stepped forward to suggest Marlon Brando. Although he was not a star, Brando had appeared on Broadway in 1944 in *I Remember Mama* with Mady Christians, and then in *Truckline Café* with Paul Muni, and as the young Marchbanks in Katharine Cornell's revival of *Candida*. Although unenthusiastic at first, Kazan agreed to see the actor and listen to him read the part.

Liebling now faced the problem that no one knew where to find Brando, who was prone to sudden disappearances. The agent sent word through friends and acquaintances for the actor to get in touch with him. Days passed with no sign of Brando. Then, without warning, the receptionist announced that there was a young man in the outer office looking for Mr. Liebling.

Liebling hastily escorted Marlon Brando to Henry Miller's Theatre on West Forty-third Street and into the presence of Irene Selznick and Elia Kazan. As they walked to the theater, Liebling explained the purpose of the meeting, described the part of Stanley Kowalski, and warned the actor that he was about to audition for Elia Kazan. Brando, in turn, asked "Willie the Bass" if he could sing, and they proceeded to the theater harmonizing "Dear Old Girl."

The producer and director were so impressed with Brando that they immediately wanted the playwright to hear him read. Kazan wired the playwright, then staying on Cape Cod, that he was sending an extremely gifted actor to the Cape for an audition and Williams's approval. Liebling, now Brando's agent-in-place, advanced the actor bus fare to the Cape, whereupon he vanished for three days.[7] When Brando finally arrived at Williams's rented beachfront cottage, accompanied by a female companion, he found the playwright and the cottage in a state of crisis. The electricity had gone out and the plumbing had failed.

With a penny placed in the fuse box, Brando restored the electricity and proceeded to fix the plumbing. Only then did he pick up a copy of *Streetcar*, and with the playwright cueing him, proceeded to read *Streetcar* for an audience of two—Tennessee Williams and his good friend Margo Jones, the Texas producer-director who founded the arena-style Theatre 47 in Dallas. When they arrived at the card-player's last line ("The game is seven-card stud."), Jones shouted that it was the greatest reading she had even heard "in or outside of Texas."[8]

Ecstatic telephone calls were made from the Cape to Kazan and Selznick. In New York, Liebling proceeded to negotiate a contract for his new client. Nevertheless, the actor had vanished once again. Liebling sent word on the Broadway grapevine for Brando to contact his agent. Several days later, Brando reappeared disheveled and unshaven, whereupon Liebling pressed a contract in his hand for signature. Liebling had negotiated an excellent salary for his client; $550 per week was a fat fee in those preinflation days.

Because of Liebling's reputation as a successful casting agent, the outer office at Liebling-Wood was always crowded with actors making daily rounds to casting offices. In a shrinking theater season, Liebling would appear and regretfully announce, "Sorry, kid, nothing today, but you're welcome to sit for a while."[9] Over time, future stars such as Tony Randall, Julie Harris, Paul Newman, Karl Malden, Lee Grant, Yul Brynner, Montgomery Clift, and Cloris Leachman sat in the outer office waiting their turn to see "Mr. Liebling."

In the division of their labors, the writers were Audrey's bailiwick. Based upon Audrey's experience at the Century Play Company's new play department representing authors, she and Liebling divided their representation. Audrey (Bill Liebling always addressed her as "Miss Wood") was the play broker and author's representative. This involved not only the writers' plays and adaptations of nondramatic works, but also their screenplays, television scripts, short stories, and novels. Her efforts consisted of reading manuscripts, negotiating terms for the writers, and often finding a producer and financial backing for the production, and being party to endless decisions in the pressure cooker of Broadway. In her spare time, she held conferences with writers to address the early stages of their work, went to lunch at the Dorset Café or Sardi's with producers to discuss options, attended staged readings of her clients' plays, and saw new plays by playwrights in need of agents.

Despite years of theatergoing, Audrey operated largely on instinct and intuition—"a green light flashing in her head"—as she called her moments of inspiration when deciding to take on a playwright's script. She frequently explained to interviewers that she could pick up a new script by an author whose work was unfamiliar, and within the first ten pages or so, she usually knew whether or not she was reading the work of someone with talent. She insisted that it was rare to turn up, from beneath the haystack of typed pages, that "shining needle."[10]

Once she went to work for the author's play, however, she was indefatigable. She exhausted every possible chance to get it produced and to see the playwright through the tribulations of rewrites under pressure and the critical battering that often accompanied opening nights.

In 1937, when the Liebling-Wood agency was formed, Audrey Wood, as was expected of a "proper unmarried female," was living with her mother on West Fifty-first Street and dutifully brought her paycheck home each week.[11] At first, she viewed her relationship with the Jewish Liebling, who was eleven years older, as strictly a business partnership except for the fact that she saw a great deal of the unmarried gentleman. Not only did they share a suite of offices, they dined together, and went to the theater together in the evening after which Audrey went home to the apartment she shared with Ida Wood.

One morning, Liebling walked into her office, pounded his fist on the desk, and shouted, "Audrey, are you, or are you not, going to marry me?"

Speechless at receiving a fist-pounding proposal of marriage, she failed to reply. The routine continued each morning until Audrey realized that she was not opposed to the suggestion. The two agents closed their negotiations for a second partnership on Liebling's terms: "If you'll marry me, you don't have to live with me until you work out all of your problems with your mother and your home life."[12] In effect, the bedrock of Liebling's marriage proposal was the creation of an inclusive theatrical agency.

Their marriage presented the complications of mixed religious traditions. William Liebling had been born in a small Polish village on the outskirts of the city of Lodz. Like many East European Jews fleeing oppression at the turn of the twentieth century, the Liebling family was determined to secure passage to America, the land of opportunity.

In 1902, Liebling's mother and her two sons began the journey from Poland to London and then to the United States with money sent by Morris Liebling, who had made the trip earlier to earn enough money to pay for the family's journey. Young Bill Liebling developed an eye infection on the journey and remained behind in London to avoid the possibility that US medical authorities would refuse him entry. Months later, he made the trip in steerage aboard another ship, passed through Ellis Island, and joined the family in their tenement flat on Essex Street on the lower Eastside of Manhattan. In time, the family moved uptown into the Harlem district.

Liebling earned the nickname "Willie the Bass" for his bass baritone voice and sometime after the eighth grade, entered show business with his own act and a steady salary touring in vaudeville. The First World War interrupted his singing career, but as an army corporal, he was a member of the Argonne Players who performed for soldiers in a theater liberated from the Germans. At war's end, he returned to New York and faced the realities of show business casting. He was too short of stature for leading roles in vaudeville or on Broadway. Nevertheless, his fellow performers sought his advice and counsel. Convinced he could get paid for his advice, Liebling became a casting agent and eventually "King of Forty-fifth Street."

The obstacles to the interfaith marriage were, namely, Liebling's Jewish heritage and Ida Wood's devotion to the Lutheran Church. The couple was determined to marry first and deal with their parents later. On February 12, 1938, they stood before a justice of the peace in Armonk, New York, and once back in Manhattan, continued to live apart. Liebling sequestered Audrey's ring and the marriage license in his hotel room.

After three weeks of this arrangement, Audrey was determined to change the situation. She knew that Ida Wood would expect a church wedding for her daughter and set about identifying a church that would marry an interfaith couple. She was turned down by her own pastor who had no objection to an interfaith marriage but in Lutheran doctrine there was a rule that forbade a religious ceremony after a civil one had taken place. Finally, as a special concession, Dr. Randolph Ray, who presided at the Little Church Around the Corner on Twenty-ninth Street near lower Park Avenue, agreed to marry the couple with certain stipulations.

Weeks earlier, Liebling made a proper request of Ida Wood for her daughter's hand in marriage, but received no answer from his future mother-in-law. With a church service planned for March 24, 1938, at five o'clock in the afternoon, Audrey had to tell her mother that she and Liebling were going to be married, but not in the Lutheran Church on Central Park West and not before a church altar but in a parsonage, and not at midday but in the late afternoon.

Reconciled to an abbreviated ceremony, Ida Wood attended her daughter's wedding, but her son's marriage was never revealed to Mrs. Morris Liebling. Audrey invented four lines of dialogue to caricature Liebling's efforts to bring up the subject of an interfaith marriage with his orthodox mother:

Liebling: Mom, what would you say, if I married a *shiksa*?
Mrs. Liebling: You're a good son, you've always taken care of me. If that is what you want to do, you must do it. As for me, I'll just kill myself.[13]

On the rare occasions that Audrey attended family dinners in her mother-in-law's home, she was introduced as a "secretary," never as her daughter-in-law. At the time, no one remarked that the Liebling-Wood marriage had elements of a nineteenth-century mother-in-law farce written by Victorien Sardou.

Determined not to create a rift between her husband and his orthodox mother or to interfere with Liebling's faith, Audrey played along with the charade. Bill Liebling was a pious Jew, who attended services at his synagogue and kept the rituals of his faith. In contrast, Ida Wood embraced her son-in-law, and upon her death, he acknowledged his own affection by placing an obituary notice in the *New York Times* for the "loving mother-in-law of William Liebling."[14]

The twice-married Lieblings took up permanent residence in the Royalton Hotel on West Forty-fourth Street—lived there for the thirty-two years of their marriage—and Audrey continued to reside there after Liebling's death. The couple agreed that the agency would be better served if their mutual existence did not include house-cleaning, laundry, and cooking. Moreover, many literary and theater people were residents of the Royalton, including George Jean Nathan, Robert Benchley, Julie Haydon, and Jed Harris.

PARADOX OF BROADWAY

By the early forties, Audrey Wood had gained her footing as the premier literary agent for playwrights and screenwriters. Always ladylike in demeanor, Audrey was nonthreatening to insecure and often paranoiac writers; her soft, cultivated voice (brisk at times) lent reassurance; her determination and frankness were masked by velvet gloves; and her girlish smile hinted at flirtation even as she brusquely handed over contract and pen for the writer's signature. Once she decided that the writer possessed an original (and commercial) talent, she went the extra mile as friend and business partner to aid and abet the writer's career. In turn, they called her "Audrey," signifying the warmth, affection, and trust that passed between them.

One of her coworkers described her as "beautiful with auburn hair, cornsilk blue eyes, a button nose, and a charming, dulcet voice."[15] Writer Max Wilk added that she had "the grace and inner delicacy of the most womanly woman . . . with the combative instincts and vigor of a man and his greater taste for frankness. Her small hands can be firm and strong as iron inside their velvety gloves, and, when a situation calls for it, she is not reluctant to take the gloves off."[16]

When Audrey was contacted by Molly Day Thacher, head of the Group Theatre's play department and married to Elia Kazan, with the message that an unknown playwright, who had just received a special award from the Group, was her kind of writer, Audrey Wood responded almost immediately:

> Dear Mr. Williams:
>
> I have heard of your successfully winning one of the Group Theatre prizes recently distributed. It seems to me, from what I have heard about you, that you may be exactly the kind of author whom I might help. I have a reputation for showing interest in the talented unknown playwright, which was proven rather forcefully a few weeks ago when four of the six Rockefeller Fellowships awarded were given to clients of mine. I can refer you to the Dramatists' Guild for further information regarding my status as a playbroker. I should like very much to be aware of your work if you are not at this time tied up with any other agent.[17]

The early correspondence between Audrey Wood and, arguably, her most famous client-to-be revealed a great deal about Audrey's business acumen, frank dedication to her clients, and her unshakable rule that the playwright had to demonstrate talent for the commercial theater. Williams's biographer Lyle Leverich was convinced that Audrey would never have continued in her representation of Tennessee Williams in those early years if she had not been convinced by his unshakeable tenacity to succeed in the commercial theater.[18]

In a forthright manner, Audrey assured her reluctant playwright that she had been in touch with the Group Theatre and they were sending her copies of his materials that they had on hand. "I'll let you know whether I think I can help you after I see your work," she wrote. Responding to his earlier hint that he was "high and dry on the beach," she urged him to apply for a Rockefeller Fellowship awarded solely on the basis of "need and merit" through the Dramatists Guild.[19]

Despite Williams's fog of indecision and the persistence of another agent, he reported that he was sending Audrey several plays and hoped that she would read them and let him know, as soon as possible, if she would act as his agent. When the parcel arrived, among the manuscripts of one-acts and a full-length draft of *The Fugitive Kind*, Audrey found a short story, "The Field of Blue Children," that excited her interest and resulted in a commitment to the writer that lasted 31 years.

In the early years of their collaboration, the vicissitudes of life, shortness of money, and plagues of self-doubt and self-loathing afflicted the writer during his climb to eventual success. In 1939, agent and playwright reached an agreement. Audrey proceeded to file an application on Williams's behalf for a Rockefeller fellowship, submitted the one-acts and short stories to *Story* magazine run by Whit Burnett and Martha Foley, and sent *American Blues* to the Actors' Repertory Theatre, a group that had originally produced Irwin Shaw's *Bury the Dead* and E. P. Conkle's *Two Hundred Were Chosen*. Although Audrey was impressed by the one-acts, she had reservations about the limited market for short plays. "It is a very special medium and one that is not too commonly used," she advised the playwright.[20]

When she shared her thoughts on the weaknesses of *The Fugitive Kind*, she sought to lessen the blow. "One of my virtues, unfortunately, is extreme honesty," she told him in late April. "I cannot at this point promise you any kind of a quick sale on anything. As a matter of fact, the theatre isn't an easy market and one has to, very often, play a waiting game before the breaks come. Also, on the basis of what I have read, you are not a finished dramatist, although I do say I think you are highly promising."[21]

Convinced of Audrey's integrity, Williams assured her that he had chosen her to be his agent, adding, "As for future efforts, I have two long plays in progress and another probably the best, only in mind."[22]

Six months after their correspondence began, Williams appeared in the offices of Liebling-Wood. Unshaven, broke, and disheveled, he sat quietly on Liebling's bench to watch the soft-spoken casting agent interview a roomful of chorus girls for a musical. When Liebling finally noticed the young man, he assumed he was an actor, and said, "Sorry, nothing for you today."

Williams replied to the reputed King of Forty-fifth Street, saying, that he didn't want anything today, except to meet Miss Wood. Whereupon she entered the outer office and asked, "Did you want to see me about something?" He nodded, "If your name is Audrey Wood, I do. My name is Tennessee Williams." Williams recalled that she responded, "Well, well, you've finally made it," to which he replied quite literally, "Not yet."[23]

Audrey remembered the young Tennessee as speaking with a soft Southern accent and having a slight build, looking like a teenage country boy in contrast to his rather athletic appearance in the photograph that he sent from Laguna Beach. His physical appearance defied her expectations because she was anticipating someone "more in the Southern mold of Thomas Wolfe."[24] In turn, Williams was surprised to find his agent "a very small and dainty woman with red hair, a porcelain complexion and a look of cool perspicacity in her eyes."[25]

The shrewd, all-business Audrey Wood began a series of introductions and conferences for her new client. She took him to the Group Theatre where he met Molly Day Thacher and to the Eastern offices of Metro-Goldwyn-Mayer for a possible writing job with the film studio. Williams was determined to attend Broadway plays and to learn badly needed craftsmanship. Audrey and Molly Thacher facilitated his introduction to Broadway by providing tickets to Lillian Hellman's *The Little Foxes* with Tallulah Bankhead and to S. N. Behrman's *No Time for Comedy* with Katharine Cornell.

In 1939, there were no Off or Off Off Broadway theaters to nurture the work of new playwrights, nor was Audrey Wood an agent to represent non-commercial writers. She was fond of Williams personally, and dedicated to him professionally, but it was his unshakable tenacity that convinced her of his future success.

While Audrey was representing the composer and lyricist for *Cabin in the Sky* opening on Broadway in October of 1940, Williams settled down in a nearby hotel to write "furiously with seven wild-cats under my skin" on a new play, labeled "Opus V Written on Subways."[26] He sent a rough synopsis of "Opus V" to Audrey with a cautionary note warning: "You won't like the pathological characters or violent theme but I'm hoping my final treatment of it will please you somewhat better."[27]

Always mindful of taking telephone calls and answering letters from imploring writers, Audrey wasted no time in replying. Having read the synopsis of his new play, titled *Shadow of My Passion* (later *Battle of Angels*), she replied, "Don't ever think I don't like violent themes. Also don't think I go for plays about hearts and flowers. If you can write a play with a violent theme well enough to make me think it is commercial, I will go screaming down the street like a mad woman and deliver you a sale as soon as I can get someone to go mad with me." She added, "Contrary to your opinion, I am very interested in the material in the synopsis, *Shadow of My Passion*. If you could write this in dramatic form (which is unfortunately usually the three-act form), making the play come alive, I think it may well be exciting theatre."[28]

Three weeks later, Williams sent his agent a draft of *Battle of Angels*.[29] The Lieblings had left for Los Angeles earlier that month to open a West Coast office, but Audrey's assistant, most likely Bertha Case, acknowledged receipt of the manuscript. On December 21, Audrey wired the playwright, who had taken refuge for the holidays with his family in St. Louis, that he had won the Rockefeller fellowship:

> SO PROUD THAT YOU WON ROCKEFELLER FELLOWSHIP. LIEBLING AND I DELIGHTED. HAVE READ NEW PLAY AND LIKE A GREAT DEAL OF IT. WILL WRITE TO YOU.[30]

When Audrey Wood referred to the theater as "a venture (one hesitates to call it a business) built of equal parts of faith, energy and hard work—all tied together with massive injections of nerve," she did not know that the Theatre Guild would call out of the blue with a decision to produce the first full-length play by Tennessee Williams, called, prophetically, *Battle of Angels*.[31] She also had not received the telephone call from actor Charles Laughton that thrust her into the political arena of the McCarthy era. Both ventures would require massive injections of nerve on the part of the diminutive agent.

Part II The Fearful Path 1941–1970

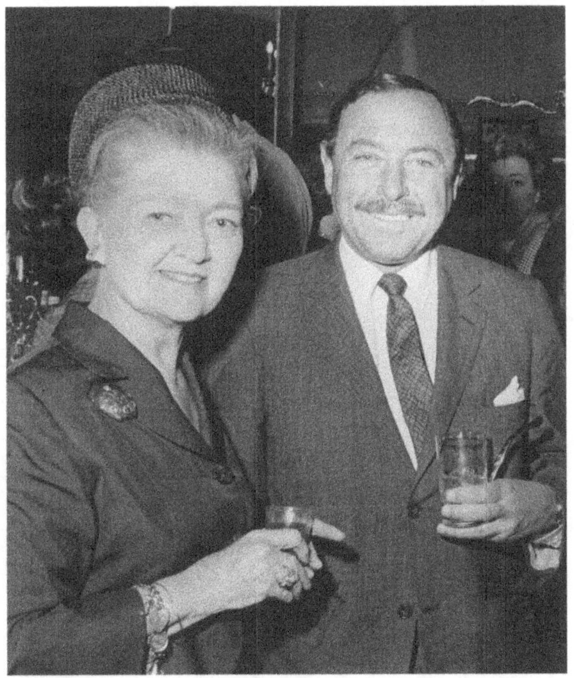

Audrey Wood and Tennessee Williams. The New Dramatists honored the literary agent and the playwright at a luncheon. (Photograph by Friedman-Abeles.) Billy Rose Theatre Division, The New York Public Library for the Performing Arts, Astor, Lenox, and Tilden Foundations.

4. The Bitch Goddess

How wonderful to be an author. How wonderful to be a producer. How confining to be an author's representative.[1]

Audrey Wood's world was dominated by Tennessee Williams for over three decades. At the outset, she was thrust into the playwright's need for survival. Then, when the successes kicked-in with *The Glass Menagerie* and *A Streetcar Named Desire*, she was bombarded by producers wanting his next project. Accompanying the successes were her client's demands for attention, very much like William James's homesick child who wanted "absolute protection and utter effortlessness" as he embraced the Bitch Goddess.[2] In time, the playwright's dependencies took on an ominous need for alcohol and drugs that acerbated his paranoiac moods, which, in their ferocity, shattered Audrey's exterior calm and unraveled their relationship of 32 years.

NOTHING SUCCEEDS LIKE SUCCESS

In the early forties with *Cabin in the Sky*, *By Jupiter!*, and *Bloomer Girl*, the Liebling-Wood agency quickly earned a reputation for representing the creators of winning musical comedies. With a nose for interesting material and musical talent, Willie the Bass exercised his musical know-how in search of performers who required representation. Audrey looked to the book-writers and lyricists.

While Audrey developed the financial and legal documents for their growing number of clients, Liebling scouted for new talent. One evening in 1941, he went to the New School for Social Research in lower Manhattan to observe the performance of an actor in the revival of a comedy by Julian F. Thompson, called *The Warrior's Husband*. Loosely based on Aristophanes' *Lysistrata*, depicting the revolt of the Trojan women against their warrior men, *The Warrior's Husband* originally starred Katharine Hepburn in her Broadway debut. As he sat in the audience, Liebling decided the Thompson play would make a successful musical comedy. The next day, Liebling-Wood optioned the musical rights. Looking around for the best talent to adapt the comedy, Liebling turned to the team of composer Richard Rodgers and lyricist Lorenz Hart.

Liebling arranged a meeting and brought along a copy of *The Warrior's Husband.* His enthusiasm for the farce sparked their interest and Audrey drew up contracts for *By Jupiter!* Beginning in June of 1942, the "melodious laugh-rouser," starring Ray Bolger and Constance Moore, played for 427 performances. Unknown to them at the time, the Liebling-Wood agency represented the final collaboration of Rodgers and Hart as a creative team.

While Liebling exercised his instincts for casting actors and musicians, Audrey reached out to underrepresented playwrights, including Bertram Bloch and Isabel Leighton whose *Spring Again* played Broadway for 241 performances. Nevertheless, the centerpiece of Audrey's work in the forties was four full-length plays by Tennessee Williams: the imperfect *Battle of Angels*, the inferior *You Touched Me!* with Donald Windham, and two masterpieces, *The Glass Menagerie* and *A Streetcar Named Desire.*

EMBATTLED ANGELS

Six years lapsed between the appearance of the unkempt playwright in the offices of Liebling-Wood and the arrival of *The Glass Menagerie* on Broadway. Admitting that those years were an unending struggle, Audrey tried a number of stopgap measures to sustain the playwright. She advanced small sums from the agency and encouraged modest jobs. Acting as agent, banker, and caretaker, Audrey's personal and professional stability and her reserved friendship were credited as crucial elements in Williams's maturation as a writer.[3]

At her urging, actor-director Hume Cronyn, married to actress Jessica Tandy, optioned one of Williams's short plays for production. When Cronyn decided that the play would not succeed in a commercial market, he wrote to Audrey relinquishing his option. She telephoned immediately to dissuade Cronyn from withdrawing his support, arguing her personal belief in the writer:

> Someday he's going to write great plays. I know it, and you must realize it too, from the beautiful writing in this script. I'm asking you to invest this much—the amount of another option royalty—on his future and the future of the theatre.[4]

Cronyn was persuaded and Audrey gave him six more one-acts to add to his collection. (The short plays were later published as *27 Wagons Full of Cotton*.) Cronyn did not attempt to produce the one-acts, but his investment paid off within five years when he directed Williams's short play, *Portrait of a Madonna*, with Jessica Tandy playing Miss Lucretia Collins, at the Hollywood Actors Laboratory Theatre. The short play was a touching portrait of a lonely spinster bedeviled by violent sexual fantasies and illusions of social ostracism. When Cronyn returned to New York and met with Audrey, she handed him a new script and casually asked if he knew of an actress suitable to play a character named Blanche DuBois.[5]

Tennessee Williams's first break came in the fall of 1940 when the Theatre Guild optioned *Battle of Angels* to begin rehearsals as soon as their production of *Twelfth Night* with Helen Hayes opened in November. Earlier, Audrey had submitted *Battle of Angels*, a play containing Williams's major theme—the destructive impact of society on the sensitive, nonconformist individual—to Harold Clurman for consideration by the Group Theatre, but after the failure of Clifford Odets's *Night Music*, Clurman was not interested in undertaking another large production with the Group producing. Audrey then encouraged Williams to submit the script to John Gassner, who taught a playwriting seminar with Guild administrator Theresa Helburn at the New School for Social Research. Gassner was also chief playreader for the Theatre Guild and consistently urged the board of directors to produce innovative, new talent.[6]

During the late spring, Williams made revisions to "B of A," his shorthand for the full-length play. Without notifying his agent, he pocketed an "advance royalty" check for $100 offered by Theresa Helburn as down payment on an option to produce *Battle of Angels*. When Audrey discovered Helburn's ploy, she demanded that the playwright return the check until a proper contract could be negotiated through the Dramatists Guild.

Also, without Audrey's knowledge, Williams accepted an advance of $100 from Bennett Cerf, which gave Random House the option to publish his next play. She then discovered her client collaborating with a "starving artist from Georgia," Donald Windham, to adapt a D. H. Lawrence short story ("You Touched Me") without the permission of the Lawrence estate. Audrey called the writers "naïve" and proceeded to contact Curtis Brown, Ltd. to learn that the dramatic rights were miraculously available.

The playwright's sleights of hand were motivated by his reluctance to pay his agent's 10 percent commission—a complaint echoed throughout the years of Audrey's representation.

The Theatre Guild moved into high gear that fall with preproduction plans for *Battle of Angels*. Audrey thought the Guild's codirectors were moving too quickly toward a Broadway production with their untried playwright. Even though she considered Williams's full-length play to be "far ahead of its time," she knew that it required significant revisions for a commercial production. Moreover, *Battle of Angels* contained explicit sexual scenes, religious symbolism, outspoken dialogue, and a storyline in which the heroine "indulged in extremely free roaming sexual relationships." Audrey opined, "Very strong stuff for 1940."[7]

In retrospect, Audrey considered the Guild's plan to open the play in Boston as a "manifestation of a deep collective death wish." "Banned in Boston" had long been a euphemism for censorship and recast in theater circles as "bombed in Boston."[8]

As Audrey monitored her client's rapid march to Boston's Wilbur Theatre, she learned that the Guild had engaged the Anglo-American director Margaret Webster, known for productions of Shakespeare's plays on Broadway, to stage the new script. Audrey considered the English woman an "odd" choice to stage the Southern play. Audrey also thought the subject matter unsuitable for Boston audiences. As she contemplated other tryout towns where the Guild had subscribers (Philadelphia, New Haven, and Washington, DC) as well, she thought those audiences might have appreciated the onslaught of Tennessee's bold first drama. "But Boston?" she decried.[9]

After a turbulent rehearsal period fraught with cast replacements, an insecure leading lady, unanswered calls for rewrites, and ill-managed smoke pots, *Battle of Angels* opened on December 30 for a two-week tryout in Boston and closed 13 days later. With the clarity of hindsight, the playwright later confessed that "probably no man has written for the theatre with less foreknowledge of it."[10]

On opening night, Audrey and Bill Liebling watched in amazement as subscribers hurried up the aisles when the visionary portrait of Jesus Christ with the face of the doomed fugitive kind, Val Xavier, came to their attention. At the play's end, stagehands energetically stoked the smoke pots and overwhelmed the remaining patrons with billows of smoke rolling onto the stage and coiling over the footlights. The director quipped, "The first six rows were asphyxiated, the rest fainted or fled."[11]

Critics found the play repugnant and amateurish. The critic for the *Boston Herald* called the play "one of the strangest mixtures of poetry, realism, melodrama, comedy, whimsy, and eroticism that it has ever been our privilege to see upon the boards."[12] Only the dean of Boston critics, Elliot Norton, was persuaded of the writer's merits, and, in the second of two reviews, wrote prophetically,

> Mr. Tennessee Williams need not consider his lost battle as a decisive defeat... If he can learn more of the practical side of playwriting, can keep his heart in the right place and his head clear of rubbish; if he can learn to walk with the theatre's craftsmen, he may find himself riding the clouds with the theatre's dramatists. His talent is most interesting.[13]

A CHORUS OF WOE

Years later, Audrey set down her recollections of the morning after *Battle of Angels* roared into life. In a letter to the playwright, she recounted their journey across Boston Commons following breakfast at a nearby drugstore counter in preparation for the "morning after" conference scheduled by the Guild's producers at the Ritz Carlton Hotel.[14] As they sauntered, unhurried, across the commons, she recalled that a small boy pulled the trigger of a cap-pistol and they heard a sudden pop, which seemed at the time to be "the roar of a cannon."

> We clutched at each other and you cried out, "It's the Guild. They're after me!" And we both rocked with laughter because we knew in a few minutes it was all about to begin and there wasn't time for anything other than laughter.[15]

Assembled for the meeting were a downcast Lawrence Langner, an all-business-like Theresa Helburn, and a resigned Margaret Webster. When he was told that the play was being closed after the Boston run, Williams protested and Langner made an effort to soothe his wounded feelings by promising payments of advances on royalties to ensure a rewritten script and a future production.

In the face of a theatrical flop, the playwright's tenacity surprised Audrey. During Langner's peroration that morning at the Ritz Carlton on the Guild's status as a true art institution, Audrey received a knowing wink from the playwright. She knew then that he could stand up and take whatever might befall him in the theater. Mixing up the writer's Southern lineage with his adopted name, she paid him the highest of compliments: "All writers in the theatre, should come from Indian fighting Tennessee pioneer stock. They'd last longer and so would the American theatre."[16]

With chagrin, Audrey noted the Guild's reckless abandonment of their writer. Following the closing, the Guild wrote mea culpas to their Boston subscribers in which they defended the playwright's poetic gifts and insights into a "particular American scene." The letter concluded with, "Who knows whether the next one by the same author may not prove a success?"[17] At that very moment, the next one was called *The Gentleman Caller.*

Audrey Wood never lost faith in her playwright. Nevertheless, her spirits revived in early 1944 when she received a manila envelope mailed from Provincetown containing a typewritten script now titled *The Glass Menagerie.* The bitch goddess of success opened her arms wide and embraced Tennessee Williams—along with his agent.

THE FLOWER AND THE ROCK

For the next 20 years, Audrey monitored a steadily mounting series of triumphs for her client. Although his economic stresses were obviated by royalties from his writing and options negotiated by Audrey with film companies, other physical and emotional factors became worrisome. Audrey was very much aware of her client's health issues and the dark periods during which he gave way to depression, but she was unaware of his chosen remedies.

As an agent actively engaged in her client's career, she was careful not to interfere in Williams's personal life. She read his scripts with the expertise of a dramaturg, suggested revisions, and submitted his work to producers and publishers—always mindful of the welfare of the artist and the man. Williams rewarded her with the epithet "patient Griselda" and named her his literary executor in the event anything happened to him.[18]

In an interview for *Esquire* magazine, Williams affectionately defined his agent "as a cross between a flower and the rock it sprang from." He conjectured that if someday their professional relationship came to a close, he was certain that Audrey would be the instrument of closure.[19]

During the period Williams worked as a screenwriter for Metro-Goldwyn-Mayer in the early 1940s, he submitted the draft of a screenplay to MGM's story department and discovered the script returned to his desk without comment. In the meantime, Audrey, with her usual attention to detail, filed an amended list of Williams's literary properties with MGM's legal department labeling *The Gentleman Caller* "not complete."

In her communication with her client, she pointed out that it was important to establish the fact that he had written the script before he went to MGM.[20]

Once *The Glass Menagerie* opened in New York as a smashing success, MGM claimed rights to the play. Audrey acted swiftly to answer MGM's legal department. "This is America, this is Williams' play," she wrote, "and MGM has no claim whatsoever to it."[21] The threat of litigation ended there.

Shortly before *The Glass Menagerie* opened in New York, Audrey received an outline of another play with three different titles: *The Moth, Blanche's Chair in the Moon,* and *The Poker Night.* In a letter accompanying the script, Williams explained at length:

> It is about two sisters, the remains of a fallen southern family. The younger, Stella, has accepted the situation, married beneath her socially and moved to a southern city with her coarsely attractive plebian mate. But Blanche has remained at Belle-reve, the home place in ruins, and struggles for five years to maintain the old order.

He goes on to describe the full story of *A Streetcar Named Desire*, but he had not made up his mind about the play's ending and offered three possibilities: "One, Blanche simply leaves, with no destination. Two, goes mad. Three, throws herself in front of a train in the freight-yards, the roar of which has been an ominous undertone throughout the play." He closed with a plea to Audrey to hold onto the letter since it is "my only copy of the synopsis."[22]

When the completed manuscript arrived, it was called *The Poker Night*, and the ending was resolved with a game of seven-card stud. Audrey rushed to tell Williams that his new play was stunning drama. "Wonderful," she said in recognition that he had written "a nearly complete masterpiece." Nevertheless, she had reservations about the title which, she found, suggestive of a Western action novel by Rex Beech. The playwright hinted that he had another title, but did not know if it was any good. Audrey marveled that he had a second title, *A Streetcar Called Desire*, tucked away all the time. It required the change of only one word.

In a later interview, Audrey told Lewis Funke, "I changed the 'called' to 'named' because I didn't like the two c's—but it was Tennessee's title all the time."[23] Always sensitive to the poetic value and syntax of play titles, Audrey also favored the change of title for *Chart of Anatomy* to the more appealing *Summer and Smoke*. She was constantly amused that an agent's work was never done!

Audrey set about finding a producer for *A Streetcar Named Desire* who would protect the playwright artistically and financially. "I have always proceeded on the theory that as an agent," she remarked, "I must cast the producer for a play as carefully as one would eventually cast the director, and the performers."[24] Those in consideration were Eddie Dowling of *The Glass Menagerie*, Guthrie McClintic of *You Touched Me!*, Cheryl Crawford of *Brigadoon*, and Irene Mayer Selznick of *Heartsong* by Arthur Laurents. Audrey knew that whomever she chose, she would make enemies and lose friends.

Given the success of *The Glass Menagerie*, Eddie Dowling was the logical choice, but he had alienated the Lieblings during the Chicago production by giving interviews during which he denigrated the agent and her client. Dowling claimed that he discovered the playwright at the bottom of a rain barrel. Moreover, he claimed that Williams's agent had submitted the "poor, wilted manuscript all over New York" and Dowling had rescued it from dark oblivion.[25] None of this sat well with Audrey. The truth of the matter was that Eddie Dowling had been the first (and only) producer that she had approached to handle Williams's play.

Although unknown to Broadway at the time, Irene Mayer Selznick had several qualities that swung the decision in her favor. "Not only did she have an ample bankroll," Audrey reasoned, "but she was serious and had taste."[26] Moreover, Selznick, determined to become a theatrical producer, had opened a production office in New York and was already producing Arthur Laurents' *Heartsong*. Perhaps most important in Audrey's view, Selznick had enough money (and Hollywood connections) to engage the right director, cast the play perfectly, and keep the play out of town for as long as needed.

Audrey was carefully protecting the playwright and his remarkable new script. She took the train to Philadelphia to see the out-of-town tryout of *Heartsong*, and, when she returned, sent a script to Selznick's office. She received a call the next day during which Irene Selznick asked for a few more days to make a decision about her life. Within two days the producer had made her decision.

Since the playwright and producer had never met (and his rejection by Hollywood loomed large in his memory), Audrey quietly set up an out-of-the-way meeting in Charleston, the home of her early clients Dubose and Dorothy Heyward, to avoid inquiring producers and gossip columnists. She traveled with Selznick to Charleston, checked into a hotel, and waited for Williams to arrive from New Orleans. Audrey felt like a marriage broker when she suggested that the producer and playwright "take a walk" to discuss the matter. An hour later, the two returned, the playwright signed the production contracts that Audrey carried in her briefcase, and "the marriage was a fact." To avoid the news getting out prematurely, Selznick sent a coded wire to her general manager that read: "BLANCHE HAS COME TO LIVE WITH US."[27]

Back in New York, Audrey set about persuading Elia Kazan to direct Williams's new play. Kazan initially turned down the script, but his wife, an early supporter of the playwright's career, persuaded him to meet with Audrey and Bill Liebling in their suite at the Royalton. The couple assured Kazan that he was "the perfect choice." When Kazan changed his mind, Audrey sighed with relief.[28] Liebling then functioned as casting agent, and, with Kazan's approval, assembled the stellar cast with Marlon Brando, Kim Hunter, Karl Malden, and Jessica Tandy in the central role of Blanche DuBois.

When the choice of Selznick became known, Audrey had to endure scolding from other Broadway producers for selecting an outsider—a Hollywood intruder. Some, among the Times Square insiders, indulged in rumormongering to suggest that Audrey and her husband acquired sufficient bribe money from Hollywood's powers-that-be to acquire a fashionable suburban home in Westport, Connecticut. The rumors, along with the cannelloni, were chewed over for weeks at Sardi's.[29]

Cheryl Crawford, who had emerged from the Theatre Guild and the Group Theatre to become an independent producer, summarized the prevailing feelings among Broadway's inner circles: Irene Selznick had been awarded the golden goose! As the current producer of *Brigadoon*, Crawford felt slighted and she told Audrey in a few terse words: "I think it's wrong that a new producer was handed our best playwright on a golden platter."[30]

Audrey remained calm in the face of the agitated producer. When Selznick declined *The Rose Tattoo*, calling the play a libretto, Audrey sent the script to Cheryl Crawford who subsequently produced four plays by Tennessee Williams.

In 1947, *A Streetcar Named Desire* was hailed by critics as the perfect marriage of acting and playwriting and was showered with awards—the Pulitzer Prize for Drama, the Drama Critics' Circle Award, and the Donaldson Award. Despite the clamor and months of sellout business, Audrey received no offers for screen rights. *The Glass Menagerie* had been sold to Charles K. Feldman and Warner Brothers, but there was no expression of interest in *A Streetcar Named Desire*. Audrey puzzled that perhaps Hollywood producers were timid about depicting sexual relations on screen as blunt as the ones Williams had dramatized among Stanley, Stella, and

Blanche. When she received an invitation from the playwright to attend a party in Hollywood at a Sunset Strip restaurant celebrating the start of the filming of *The Glass Menagerie*, Audrey was reluctant to travel to Los Angeles for a mere party. The pragmatic Liebling counseled: "If Tennessee wants you to be there, you should go out."[31]

Among the jewels, furs, and couturier gowns, Audrey wore her "slightly used" black dinner dress.[32] Accompanied by Tennessee Williams and his partner Frank Merlo, Audrey circulated amid a cascade of rumors that she was in Los Angeles to finalize a movie deal for *A Streetcar Named Desire.* In fact, she returned to New York with three offers for the screen rights to the play that she subsequently sold to the Feldman Group and Warner Brothers for half a million dollars and a percentage of the film's profits for her client.

Although Audrey's work was in direct support of the playwright's writing, finances, and emotional welfare, she spent an extraordinary amount of time with theatrical producers (Irene Mayer Selznick, Cheryl Crawford, Guthrie McClintic, Margo Jones, Lawrence Langer, Alfred de Liagre, Jr., Robert Whitehead, Roger L. Stevens, Charles Bowden, and David Merrick). She also negotiated film deals with Hollywood producers for *The Glass Menagerie, A Streetcar Named Desire, Summer and Smoke, The Rose Tattoo, The Roman Spring of Mrs. Stone, Baby Doll, The Fugitive Kind, Cat on a Hot Tin Roof, Sweet Bird of Youth, Suddenly Last Summer, The Night of the Iguana*, and *Boom*!

Given her workload on behalf of this one client, Audrey became understandably upset when Tennessee Williams from time to time accused her of neglecting his interests. She negotiated on behalf of her client with producers and publishers over domestic and international rights and royalties for professional and amateur rights to his plays. She paid monthly bills on his New York apartment and the house in Key West, paid his taxes and made end-of-the year charitable contributions, and monitored his sister Rose Williams's personal account. Moreover, she answered requests for photographs, autographs, appearances, and lectures often with a standard reply: "unfortunately, Mr. Williams is traveling in Europe where it is difficult for him to receive mail," or, "Mr. Williams is abroad and I have no idea when he will return."[33]

During preparations for the December opening of *A Streetcar Named Desire*, Audrey's workload for her client was intensified by a regional production of *Summer and Smoke* at Margo Jones's theater-in-the-round in Dallas. Both the playwright and the agent insisted on a change of title, and *Chart of Anatomy* became *Summer and Smoke* prior to the Dallas production in July of 1947.[34] Praised by friends, fans, and show business people, Margo Jones wanted to produce and direct *Summer and Smoke* for Broadway.

Despite her concerns that Margo Jones was incapable of producing *and* directing the sensitive play for New York critics and audiences ("an entirely different breed," according to Audrey), the agent, at the playwright's insistence, drew up a contract giving Margo Jones the rights to produce the play in New York with a production date that would be decided after *A Streetcar Named Desire* opened.[35] Williams had promised his friend that she could also direct the play and he kept his word.

Ten months after the successful arrival on Broadway of *A Streetcar Named Desire, Summer and Smoke* received a chilly critical reception at the Music Box Theatre. Margo Jones's direction was singled out as deficient and many found the play pretentious, amateurish, and unendurably lengthy. The lone voice of Brooks Atkinson praised Williams's play as "the gift of a poetic and creative writer."[36] Several years later, José Quintero's successful revival with Geraldine Page as Alma Winemiller at the Circle in the Square supported Atkinson's earlier assessment and reaffirmed Audrey's belief in the delicate play.

THE WORK SCRIPT

The 1950s were years of triumphs and failures for the agent and her famous client. Audrey signed a number of writers, including Robert Anderson, Carson McCullers, William Inge, Jane Bowles, and Maurice Valency, and began the new decade with *The Enchanted, The Member of the Wedding,* and *Come Back, Little Sheba*. She placed the first of four plays by Tennessee Williams in the capable hands of Cheryl Crawford. *The Rose Tattoo* was a romantic paean to the Dionysian element in human life with Liebling's clients Maureen Stapleton and Eli Wallach. It was awarded the Antoinette Perry ("Tony") Award for best play of the season but was followed by the critical and financial failure of the cosmic fantasy, *Camino Real.*

The opening-night party for *Camino Real* was subdued. As the reviews arrived, they were uniformly negative. One critic was puzzled by the writing ("a riddle wrapped in an enigma"); another offended by the hyperbole without significance ("an enormous jumble of five-cent philosophy"); another was revolted by the playwright's "psychopathic bitterness." In Audrey's opinion, Walter Kerr's comment was the cruelest of them all. He called *Camino Real* the "worst play yet written by the best playwright of his generation."[37]

In response to the disastrous reviews, the playwright announced that his playwriting days were over. Audrey telephoned the next morning around 11 to counsel him to reconsider his farewell to the theater. His assistant answered, "Oh, I can't disturb Mr. Williams, Miss Wood, he's working."[38] Audrey was greatly cheered that her client's writing habits were unchanged.

Within a year the Lieblings were in Rome where Williams had taken up temporary residence. He called to tell her that he was working on a new play and appeared at her hotel with a large manuscript typed on odd pages of hotel stationery. This was his "work script," as he called the jumble of mismatched pages on various hotel letterheads. (Whenever he ran out of typing paper during his travels, it was his habit to use the hotel's stationery to avoid interrupting his writing.)

Audrey read *Cat on a Hot Tin Roof* until four in the morning. When she and the playwright met the next day, she told him that it was his best play since A *Streetcar Named Desire*, and assured him that it would be a great success. Then, she gently voiced her single reservation: "It's written in two acts. You must have a third."

He countered with his decision to begin with a prologue or write a long one-act for the ending and Audrey insisted, "This play has tremendous potential, but it has to be finished. It can't end with Big Daddy's speech. You've got to work on the story by sticking with Brick and Maggie."[39] Her client balked. After she returned to New York, and many letters later, a manuscript arrived with a third act that focused on Brick and Maggie's story.

Produced by the Playwrights' Company (Cheryl Crawford had other commitments), Brooks Atkinson ranked *Cat on a Hot Tin Roof* in 1955 as Williams "finest drama," so "limpid and effortless" that it seemed "not to have been written. It is the quintessence of life."[40] Although critical praise for the play was not unanimous, Elia Kazan's direction and the performances of Barbara Bel Geddes (Maggie), Burl Ives (Big Daddy), and Ben Gazzara (Brick) were uniformly admired. Dedicated to his agent, the play ran for nearly 700 performances and received the Drama Critics' Circle Award and the Pulitzer Prize. Moreover, Audrey negotiated the film rights for $500,000 with MGM, the same studio that had declined to renew Williams's contract as a screenwriter.

Years later, when Audrey was reviewing the playwright's manuscripts housed in the Harry Ransom Humanities Research Center at the University of Texas in Austin, she came upon the script for *Cat on a Hot Tin Roof* and discovered that her client had originally dedicated the work to Carson McCullers. Carson's name was crossed out, and "For Audrey Wood" typed in.[41] Audrey realized then how close she had come to losing the dedication.

COLLISION COURSE

Beginning with preparations for the opening of *Cat on a Hot Tin Roof*, storm clouds were gathering and casting shadows over the relationship between the agent and the playwright. First, Williams had stubbornly resisted Audrey's insistence that the play required a third act. Next, Audrey compounded an already tense situation by objecting to the "elephant story," a mildly offensive story about an aroused male elephant observed by a child in the company of his mother during a visit to a zoo.

Audrey argued that the infantile joke did not belong in a play about illness and dying, but director and playwright disagreed with her. In Philadelphia, at a post-opening party, Kazan put the matter to a vote. Only Audrey and Liebling voted to cut the elephant story. As soon as she returned to New York, Audrey wrote Kazan saying that the play did not need the distraction. "I thought it was in bad taste. I thought it had nothing to do with the play and I thought it was there for shock value. I thought it was beneath Mr. Williams. Otherwise I had no reasons."[42]

A few days after the New York opening, the License Commissioner of New York arrived at the Morosco Theatre to inform the management of complaints from the audience. He decreed that the "elephant story" must be excised from the performance, or the Morosco would lose its license to operate the theater. Williams deftly removed the offending story and the play proceeded for 694 performances.

Nevertheless, Audrey's relationship with Williams was far from amicable. At the opening-night parties for *Cat on a Hot Tin Roof*, she observed that he behaved toward her and Liebling like "a child abandoned in a snowstorm by untrustworthy relatives, or hurtful friends."[43] Unknown to his agent at the time, the playwright blamed her for neglecting his career and their friendship.

INCITING INCIDENT

A telephone call from Coral Gables, Florida, in 1956 created a stir at Liebling-Wood. As Audrey listened, she heard Williams announcing that he had been working on a new play. "I haven't shown it to you yet," he said, "but it's in rehearsal down here."[44]

Astonished by Williams's announcement, Audrey exploded, "What do you mean, you have a play in *rehearsal*? How could you possibly do anything like that before I'd even read the play?" Williams explained that his friend, director George Keathley, ran a small theater in a garage, called Studio M. Playhouse, in Coral Gables. Audrey's fury grew. "What are you doing there in a *garage*?" she demanded to know.[45] Audrey then traveled to Florida to see the not-so-top-secret tryout of *Sweet Bird of Youth* attended by numerous friends, fans, and show business types. Both Cheryl Crawford and Elia Kazan were party to the secret and petitioned Audrey to allow them to produce and direct the new play.

The Broadway production took place three years later, but not without its share of *frissons*. On the first day of rehearsals, Audrey received a "panic call" to come to the Martin Beck Theatre where actress Geraldine Page, engaged to play the Princess opposite Paul Newman, was refusing to sign her contract unless she was assured in writing that she would play the lead in any future film based on the play. In Audrey's experience this was an impossible demand because film producers historically reserved the right to cast films adapted from plays with actors of their own choosing. She rushed to the theater and without preamble told the assembled cast that Miss Page's demand was unacceptable, and, if the actress refused to sign, then someone else would play the part.[46]

Faced with Audrey's no-holds-barred declaration, Page signed her contract, the rehearsal continued, and the show opened with glowing reviews for Williams's "finest drama" and "sure-fire hit."[47] Even though the weekly and monthly critics were dubious about the play's inconsistencies, the decadent subject matter, and Kazan's mannered direction, they failed to stem the tide of the succès de scandale that ran for 383 performances.[48]

The playwright dedicated the published version of *Sweet Bird of Youth* to Cheryl Crawford who had become the playwright's devoted friend and confidante, but the producer preceded Audrey into the darkness of that Dantesque wood where the playwright's discarded friends and enablers resided in his mind. She and the playwright later disagreed over the Broadway casting for *Period of Adjustment*, a bittersweet comedy about the troubled marriages of two middle-class, suburban couples. Neither audiences nor critics was responsive to the couples' domestic problems because, in Crawford's bluntly stated opinion, the "cast was too old."[49]

Williams was unhappy with Crawford's criticism, the play's reception, and the mutual decision of his producer and agent to close the floundering show. Shortly thereafter, he dismissed Crawford over her contention that an early version of *The Night of the Iguana* needed work. In the absence of Cheryl Crawford, Audrey turned to Charles Bowden, a longtime associate of the Lunts and a producer of taste who often took artistic chances, to produce *The Night of the Iguana* with the playwright's own company, called Two Rivers Enterprise.

Although the relationship with Audrey was not yet threatened, the dismissal of Cheryl Crawford foreshadowed the playwright's unexpected and venomous rejection of close associates and devoted friends. His agent would not receive the full brunt of his paranoia fueled by amphetamines and alcohol for another ten years.

During the 1960s, memorialized by the playwright as his "Stoned Age," Audrey marshaled the New York openings of *Period of Adjustment*, *The Night of the Iguana*, *The Milk Train Doesn't Stop Here Anymore* (two versions), *Slapstick Tragedy*, *The Seven Descents of Myrtle* (the rewritten *Kingdom of Earth*), and *In the Bar of a Tokyo Hotel*. Despite rumors of Williams's paranoid symptoms and dependence on alcohol and drugs, Audrey was encouraged by his seven days-a-week writing schedule and enormous output. Within the decade, she had attended six New York openings of Williams's plays and negotiated film deals for *Suddenly Last Summer* with Katharine Hepburn, Elizabeth Taylor, and Montgomery Clift; *The Night of the Iguana* with Ava Gardner, Deborah Kerr, and Richard Burton; and *Boom!* (based on *The Milk Train Doesn't Stop Here Anymore*) with Richard Burton, Elizabeth Taylor, and Noël Coward. Among the many film deals, Audrey was especially gratified by the price MGM paid to secure the screen rights for *Suddenly Last Summer*, including a percentage of the film's profits for the next two decades.

Audrey Wood observed that the 1960s was not a good decade for herself or her longtime client.[50] She had been preoccupied with her husband's failing health and the agency's future in the mid-1950s. Faced with Bill Liebling's retirement for health reasons (he had a heart condition and emphysema), they decided in 1954 to sell Liebling-Wood to the vast talent agency—Music Corporation of America (MCA). The sale startled the industry, but Liebling wanted to ensure that Audrey was protected in the business in good times and in bad.[51] Furthermore, the Lieblings made the continued employment of their staff by MCA a condition of the sale.

Audrey and her clients relocated to MCA's luxurious quarters, located on Madison Avenue at Fifty-seventh Street, complete with dusty-rose carpeting, antiques, hunting prints, and polished paneled walls. After

17 years as Liebling-Wood, Audrey confessed that it was "tough to close."[52]

As the Lieblings surmised, there were advantages to a large firm. As long as they were a two-person firm, she and Bill Liebling found it difficult to get away together, even for a holiday. "If we both disappeared, who'd mind the store," Audrey sighed.[53] Moreover, as a result of the sale of the agency at the peak of its influence, the couple was now wealthy.

Audrey was aware in the early 1960s that Williams was depending more and more upon a variety of prescription drugs. In addition, he was estranged from Frank Merlo, his friend and partner of many years, who was diagnosed with lung cancer and died in 1963. Merlo's struggle with terminal illness thrust the playwright into a period of deep depression and heavy dependence on drugs that he soon called his "Stoned Age."[54]

By 1962, two tempests disrupted Audrey's insular world: an irrepressible actress and the federal government. Despite Audrey's reluctance to cast the film star Bette Davis in the secondary role of Maxine Faulk, the rough-spoken expatriate landlady of the Mexican hostelry in *The Night of the Iguana*, she was overruled. Bette Davis signed the contracts and out-of-town tryouts began. "It was the lull before the storm," Audrey recalled.[55]

When the show opened in New York on December 28, 1961, Bette Davis made her entrance and received a standing ovation from her fans. As the curtain rose, she stood majestically in front of designer Oliver Smith's rustic hotel verandah with flaming red hair and suggestively unbuttoned blouse, raised her hands above her head, and clasped them in the classic prizefighter's victory pose, signaling her triumphant return to Broadway. Only then did she shout out, "Shannon!," and begin the show.

Despite *The Night of the Iguana*'s success, the film star developed a pattern of missed performances and ticket buyers had taken to inquiring at the box office, "Is Miss Davis playing in this performance?" Even though she had signed a run-of-play contract, Davis finally asked to leave the show and Audrey blamed herself for casting the star in an unrewarding role. Shelley Winters, Bette Davis's replacement, also became impatient and filled the long waiting periods between scenes by leaving the theater in full makeup to have a drink in a small bar across the street.

"That was another situation that called for my attention," Audrey remarked in acid tones.[56]

The Night of the Iguana was still running on Broadway, in 1962, when agency matters took an unexpected turn. The United States Justice Department charged MCA with operating in restraint of trade and a federal court ruled that the corporation had to divest itself of the agency business.

MCA's offices were quickly closed with government agents stationed by the lobby elevators to search MCA employees as they left the building to make certain no official documents were removed. The situation was especially grave for Audrey. She had contract files for clients, correspondence, stock and film deals, and foreign productions that reached back to the early Liebling-Wood years. (Friends in MCA's management eventually retrieved her files and returned them.) Most importantly, she needed to contact her clients to assure them of her continuing representation—only with another agency.

Audrey was quietly approached by Ted Ashley, who owned a mid-sized agency with Ira Steiner, and she promptly joined Ashley-Steiner (later, International Creative Management, or ICM) along with a formidable group of newly acquired agents. Audrey observed that overnight, Ashley-Steiner exploded into a major agency that housed its new agents in temporary offices in a small hotel on East Fifty-sixth Street. As usual, Audrey was sanguine: "After all my years in show business, I had long ago developed the ability to adjust. Where you work isn't important. What you do is."[57]

The unpleasantness of the MCA matter was further complicated by Tennessee Williams's reluctance to sign with the Ashley-Steiner Agency. He used the opportunity to inform Audrey that he found it necessary to disengage from all professional commitments for an unspecified time and become "a creature that acts for and decides for himself." Moreover, he informed her that he had revoked all powers of attorney, adding ominously, that he could no longer ask for service from someone no longer my representative and, quite possibly, no longer my friend and admirer.[58]

Audrey cabled immediately to assuage his distrust and implore a face-to-face meeting to assure him that her job has always been "to carry your work like a banner throughout the world and this I have done and continue to do with gusto and enthusiasm."[59]

The successive failures of six plays by Tennessee Williams in 12 years were minor distractions for Audrey in contrast to the death of her "Liebling" in December of 1969. Reflecting upon the accumulation of sad occurrences, Audrey bitterly remarked, "Nineteen sixty-nine was a dreadful winter."[60]

5. Dancing on Eggs

... an agent's job calls for diplomacy, legal skills, tact, and endless amounts of patience.[1]

As Tennessee Williams was enjoying critical and popular success with *A Streetcar Named Desire* in the late 1940s, Audrey sensed the Cold War winds of anticommunist fervor blowing across the careers of several of her writers. She represented coauthors Charles Laughton and Bertolt Brecht, the nineteenth witness in the Hollywood congressional hearings, and composer-lyricists Edgar Y. ("Yip") Harburg and Jay Gorney, who were also ensnared by conservative forces arrayed against liberals and left-wing radicals in the McCarthy era.

Originally coined to describe the anticommunist pursuits of Republican US Senator Joseph R. McCarthy of Wisconsin, "McCarthyism" soon took on a broader meaning—describing a decade of political turmoil from the late 1940s to the late 1950s characterized by heightened fears of communist influence on American institutions and espionage by Soviet agents. More generally, the term was used to describe reckless, unsubstantiated accusations, as well as demagogic attacks on the character or patriotism of political adversaries. The primary targets of government investigations lead by Senate and congressional committees were government employees, writers and artists in the entertainment industry and the broadcast media, educators, and union activists, suspected of real or supposed leftist associations or beliefs and therefore threats to America's national security.

For the most part, Audrey's playwrights and screenwriters were insulated from the so-called Red-baiting or witch-hunting of the period by their muted political interests and by the apolitical themes of their plays, including *A Streetcar Named Desire*, *The Madwoman of Chaillot*, and *Come Back, Little Sheba*. However, three of her writers cracked the door, so to speak, for their agent to peer into the political cauldron created by the anticommunist fervor that swept up writers and artists in the decade.

HARD TIMES

In Audrey's view, the charming Yip Harburg, who in 1944 returned from Hollywood to bring the popular *Bloomer Girl* to Liebling-Wood, was an amalgam of shrewd showman and political activist whose writings anticipated feminists Betty Friedan and Gloria Steinem by three decades. Harburg was born Isidore Hochberg to Russian-Jewish immigrants on the lower East Side of Manhattan, and later adopted the name of Edgar Harburg and acquired the nickname "Yip" for his terrier-like qualities.[2] Even though Harburg combined success in Hollywood and on Broadway as a book-writer and lyricist, at the core of his snappy lyrics for *The Wizard of Oz* and *Cabin in the Sky* lay a social conscience commemorated in "Brother, Can You Spare a Dime?," his Depression-era lament written with composer Jay Gorney, and "Over the Rainbow" with composer Harold Arlen, a plea for hope in hard times. His obsession with politics led him to his own post-Depression-era version of hard times when he was blacklisted in Hollywood.

In 1946, Harburg returned a second time from Hollywood to bring Audrey another book musical, cowritten with Fred Saidy with score by Burton Lane. The writers had combined two disparate stories in *Finian's Rainbow.* The first was the search by a whimsical Irishman for a pot of leprechaun gold; the second addressed racial struggles in the American South. Audrey was stunned by the originality of the piece and by the difficulties it presented. What Broadway producer in his right mind would contemplate a plot in which a Southern Senator, named Billboard Rawkins, an implacable segregationist who falls asleep and is transformed by Finian, with one magic wish, into a black evangelist? Moreover, the script also presented casting problems in the role of an ageless leprechaun (Og), the guardian of the fairy pot of gold, an elfin creature who would fall in love and sing "When I'm Not Near the Girl I Love, I Love the Girl I'm Near." It was Liebling's job to find David Wayne whose grin was just a trifle "too worldly for complete innocence," and, it was Audrey's to find two adventurous producers, Lee Sabinson and William R. Latzell, for the humorous fantasy with its underplot of social significance.[3]

Finian's Rainbow opened on January 10, 1947, the year of the United States House Committee on Un-American Activities (commonly known as HUAC) first Hollywood hearing into communist influence in the entertainment industry that ended in the Hollywood Ten's conviction for contempt of Congress. Harburg was not included among this first group of Hollywood screenwriters to be subpoenaed to testify about their known or suspected memberships in the Communist Party, their association with CP members, or support of Party beliefs. Nonetheless, Harburg's rollicking musical teased reactionaries with his thinly disguised spoof of Mississippi politicians US Senator Theodore G. Bilbo and Congressman John E. Rankin. When Finian McLonergan encounters the racist, xenophobic Billboard Rawkins, the Senator expresses his dislike of immigrants. "My whole family's hated immigrants," he says, "ever since we *came* to this country."

The Lieblings had another musical hit (725 performances) in the "raree-show enchantment, humor and beauty, to say nothing of enough social significance to hold the franchise."[4] Liebling-Wood scarcely enjoyed their triumph when Ella Logan, the female lead, renewed her demands for star billing, even though the producers had earlier stipulated that no cast member's name would be billed above the title. Despite her personal success in the role of Finian's daughter, she became obsessed with her billing and insisted that Liebling, who had cast the show and was also her agent, appeal her case to the producers. She even hired a lawyer in support of her efforts. Based upon the terms of her contract, the answer was consistently "no." Dissatisfied with the outcome of her appeals, she left the show despite excellent reviews for her beguiling performance.

Even though Audrey had been involved in "bloody contractual wrestling matches where the fine points of billing became as vital as lines drawn on a post-war peace treaty," she viewed Logan's demands and precipitous actions as self-destructive.[5] Audrey was a realist. She knew there would be other clients who would permit placement of their names in advertising and press releases to destroy their sense of accomplishment. Her job was to handle such matters with tact and diplomacy.

IMPLACABLE FORCES

One day in 1947, when *Finian's Rainbow* was selling standing-room at the box office, Audrey's telephone rang and she found herself speaking to the well-known stage and film actor, Charles Laughton. He was calling from Hollywood to announce that he had prepared an English version of *Galileo* based on the play by German émigré playwright Bertolt Brecht. Laughton told her that he was coming to New York and both writers wanted her to represent their play. He added, "Therefore, Miss Wood, I would like to arrange a meeting at which time I can read the play to you."[6]

Aware of the reputations of the German playwright and the famous actor, Audrey was flattered and agreed to represent them. She was also aware that Laughton could hold an audience spellbound by reading aloud from a telephone book. Nevertheless, she had a rule about authors reading their scripts to her and the answer was "no." By way of explanation, she told Laughton that she preferred reading scripts herself. She assured him that she trusted her eyes but not her ears.

Against her better judgment, Audrey agreed to meet Laughton at his hotel the following week. She arrived at the Gotham Hotel at the designated hour of eleven o'clock in the evening. Liebling had declined to accompany her, arguing that he needed a night's rest, and Audrey told her host that her husband was out of town. When Laughton opened the door to his suite, he was wearing an open shirt and was barefoot. He led her to a small card table, pulled over two chairs, and, seated face to face, they waited for the arrival of Orson Welles who was interested in directing the production. After a short wait, Laughton opened the script and began to read *Galileo* to his audience of one.

"It was probably the most marvelous reading of a play I've ever heard, before or since," Audrey recalled.[7] Laughton read for more than two hours, and, just as he finished, there was a knock at the door. Fresh from a long nap, Welles came in prepared to discuss the production. At that very moment, the telephone rang and Laughton handed the receiver to Audrey who listened to an outraged Liebling announcing that he was downstairs in the lobby with a taxi waiting and wanted her to come home. Without revealing that Liebling was in the hotel, she made an excuse to her hosts and said goodnight.

Back in her office the next day, Audrey faced a conflict of interest. She had another play on her desk, *Lamp at Midnight*, which also dealt with the Galileo story. Since it appeared impossible for her to represent two plays on the same subject, she called Barrie Stavis, explained the situation to him, and suggested another agent who had already agreed to represent him. Once the Stavis matter was settled, Audrey began the search for a producer for the Brecht-Laughton script with Welles as director. She began discussions with the Theatre Guild, known for their attraction to European "plays of ideas." Despite *Galileo*'s message-driven story, the Guild passed on *Galileo* for its 1947–1948 season and produced, among others, *The Winslow Boy* by Terence Rattigan and the musical *Allegro* by Richard Rodgers and Oscar Hammerstein II.[8]

The second call from Charles Laughton sent Audrey into orbit. The actor announced that he was spending the weekend in Westhampton, Long Island, and intended to read *Galileo* to a group of theater friends and acquaintances. Audrey opposed the reading and lectured Laughton on the "small, inbred world" of the New York theater. She explained that the morning after his reading each one of his listeners would be on the telephone, discussing a play that she had in submission to the Guild. "It's a very bad thing to do, believe me," she insisted.[9]

Laughton promised to reconsider her argument and Audrey put down the telephone not certain what he would do when confronted with an eager audience. Afterwards, one of Audrey's playwrights, Stanley Young, reported that for three hours Laughton read from the *Bible*! Upon hearing this, Audrey wryly remarked, "It was one of the few times I've ever given direction to an actor—and the actor took it."[10]

When a deal with the Theatre Guild failed to materialize and Orson Welles withdrew from the project to pursue other interests, Audrey turned to other producers and eventually contracted with T. Edward Hambleton, a young philanthropist with the means to finance theatrical productions, and John Houseman of "Pelican Productions" to produce *Galileo* in the small Coronet Theatre in Los Angeles in July of 1947 with director Joseph Losey. Heading the large cast were Laughton as Galileo, Hugo Haas as Barberini, and Frances Helflin as Virginia.

Examining the West Coast reviews, Audrey considered them respectful but not wildly encouraging for a transfer to New York. One reviewer complained that Laughton portrayed the legendary Galileo as "a porcine boor."[11] Others lauded Laughton's performance as a "personal triumph" and praised *Galileo* as a revolutionary production that eschewed the conventional well-made play in favor of a freer mode of presentation in 13 scenes.[12] Nonetheless, Audrey was more interested in the East Coast reviews of the Los Angeles production. The New York edition of *Variety* lauded Laughton's "personal triumph," but added that the overall impression is one "of dullness."[13] An even-handed review in the *New York Times* eased her anxieties by pointing out that Laughton "makes the scientist an appealing human figure," while, at the same time, warning that the play was outside the mainstream of American drama.[14] Despite personal reservations and mixed reviews, she worked out an agreement for the Experimental Theatre, a wing of the American National Theatre and Academy (ANTA), to showcase the New York production.

In the late summer of 1947, Audrey was swept along by two implacable forces. T. Edward Hambleton was determined to bring the production to New York, and, the United States House Committee on Un-American Activities was equally determined to root out Communists, their sympathizers, and subversive messages in Hollywood films. Foremost on the list of some 40 targets in the film industry were Bertolt Brecht and the German composer Hanns Eisler, who had written the musical score for *Galileo.* In September 1947, a month after *Galileo* closed in Los Angeles, Brecht received a subpoena to appear in mid-October before the Committee in Washington, DC.[15] At the time, Brecht and his family (his actress-wife Helene Weigel and their children Barbara and Stefan) were making preparations to return to Europe, and, Brecht, as one of 19 subpoenaed screenwriters (known as the Hollywood Nineteen and later reduced to the Hollywood Ten), was determined to separate himself from the uncooperative group to ensure his scheduled departure from the United States.

Eighteen screenwriters proposed to challenge the Committee's right to ask questions by invoking the First Amendment guaranteeing freedom of speech and assembly as a fundamental right under the Constitution. The Fifth Amendment, guaranteeing protections against self-incrimination, would be invoked by witnesses appearing before congressional committees and civil courts in the 1950s. The legal requirements for Fifth Amendment protections were such that an individual could not testify about his or her own association with the Communist Party and then refuse to "name names" of colleagues and coworkers with communist affiliations.

The 19 screenwriters were expected to draw contempt citations, lose in local and appellate courts, but prevail in the Supreme Court. Brecht disagreed with their plan, which he considered political martyrdom, and proposed through an outward show of cooperation to outsmart a powerful enemy. In effect, Brecht was siding with Schweik, his "good soldier," whose antiheroic behavior saved his own skin.[16]

Brecht set about arranging his literary affairs and preparing for the hearing. In the six days he spent in New York City at 34 West Seventy-third Street, an address given during his hearing, he spoke with Audrey about handling his literary works in America. Audrey recalled that Brecht instructed her orally before he left for Washington that her agency was to represent him, but that Ferdinand Reyher, a Hollywood screenwriter and close friend, whom Brecht first met in Berlin in 1927, was to have the final say over any arrangement she made for productions of his plays. Brecht later sent documents outlining Reyher's role as his attorney-in-fact, and granting permission for Audrey to represent both Brecht and Eric Bentley, his English-language translator in America, in future productions of *The Caucasian Chalk Circle, The Good Woman of Setzuan*, and *Mother Courage and Her Children.*[17]

Audrey was now the sole agent in America for *Galileo's* coauthors. Nevertheless, her sanguine disposition was disturbed by the ominous storm clouds gathering over Brecht's hearing and its potential repercussions for the production.

Representative J. Parnell Thomas of New Jersey, HUAC's chairman, scheduled the "unfriendly nineteen" to appear in Washington, DC during the week of October 27–30, 1947. On October 26, Brecht took a train to Washington accompanied by Losey and Hambleton, who were already preparing the New York production. Before leaving Manhattan, Hambleton booked a trans-Atlantic flight in his own name on Air France for the following Friday, October 31. The ticket was intended for Brecht who planned to leave as soon as his hearing ended. Audrey was unaware of the playwright's proposed "vanishing" act.

On the morning of October 30, Brecht followed screenwriters Lester Cole and Ring Lardner Jr. into the witness chair. Brecht had consulted with his lawyers about his answer to the Committee's anticipated sixty-four dollar question, "Are you now, or have your ever been a member of the Communist Party?" Witnesses were advised by their lawyers neither to deny that they had joined the Party nor admit that they had joined. To give a definitive answer witnesses were then faced with a choice between answering questions about other Communists or sympathizers, naming names as it were, or, being cited for contempt of Congress that, if convicted, carried a fine and jail sentence of one year. It was agreed that the European playwright, having never been a "Party" member and having no intention of remaining in the United States, should answer "no." Bertolt Brecht was Audrey Wood's only client subpoenaed to appear before a congressional committee.

There are several accounts of Brecht's testimony, including the writer's journal, that stress his evasions. As the eleventh witness of the day, Brecht was scrupulously polite, but not always entirely truthful.[18] Brecht maintained a compliant attitude of enlightened self-interest based upon Jaroslav Hašek's fictional character in *The Good Soldier Schweik* who operated on the conviction that survival and success were more important than striking heroic attitudes and making bombastic statements. To the question other witnesses had refused to answer, Brecht replied: "I am a guest in this country and do not want to enter into any legal arguments, so I will answer your questions fully as well as I can. I was not a member or am not a member of any Communist Party."[19]

Nevertheless, it was not *Galileo* that interested the committeemen. Chief Investigator for the Committee, Robert E. Stripling, asked Brecht about his "revolutionary" poems and plays, in particular, his collaboration with Hanns Eisler on *The Measures Taken* (*Die Massnahme*), Brecht's 1930

Lehrstück whose plot culminated in a murder. When asked to describe the substance of the play, Brecht referred to his adaptation of an old religious Japanese Nōh play (called his "Japanese model") that depicted devotion to an ideal until death. Confusing the endings of *Die Massnahme* with *Der Jasager,* a confusion that the committeemen were ill-prepared to sort out, Brecht mislead Stripling in his summary of the ending in which the young comrade is disciplined for violation of his comrades' orders, is shot, and thrown into a lime-pit. Brecht rejected the interpretation of the play as disciplinary murder by pointing out that it is a question of "self-extinction." In his confusion of plays and their endings, Brecht explained that the young man asked his comrades to help him die and they lead him without force to an abyss whereupon he jumped in, thereby killing himself.

In another instance of obfuscation, Brecht, upon hearing Stripling reading from his poem "Forward, We've Not Forgotten," answered the investigator's question ("Did you write that, Mr. Brecht?") with "No. I wrote a German poem, but that is very different from this."[20] Brecht had come prepared, when confronted with English versions of his poems, to argue that the translations did not duplicate the original texts. Stripling let the matter drop. After several more questions, and satisfied that Brecht's links with known Communists were principally artistic matters, Chairman Thomas thanked him as a good example to the witnesses to follow, and recessed the hearing.

From Brecht's viewpoint, the hearing was unusually polite and ended favorably without a contempt citation. He was free to continue his journey to Europe. Brecht noted in his journal that he benefited from having had almost nothing to do with Hollywood, from never having participated in American politics, and from the fact that the preceding witnesses had refused to give evidence.[21] Brecht left Washington immediately following the hearing and the next day took a flight from New York to Paris. He never returned to the United States.

Audrey was relieved that Brecht's testimony did not reach the newspapers, although his disappearance did not please her. In Brecht's absence, Audrey found it necessary to consult frequently with the remaining coauthor. Nevertheless, Laughton's ill-mannered behavior pushed Audrey Wood beyond her limits of civility. She recalled one scene, again in his hotel suite, where she knocked on the door and heard Laughton inviting her to come in. She was taken aback by the sight of the actor lying, barefoot, in rumpled trousers and unbuttoned shirt with a bowl of fruit balanced on his large stomach.

As she contemplated his rude behavior, Laughton looked at her and said, "You have either misbuttoned your coat, my dear Miss Wood, or one button is missing." Audrey's temper flared and she retorted: "Charles Laughton, I have taken a great deal from you, but I will have no criticism of the way I dress, thank you!"[22] Laughton nodded meekly, and never again brought up the subject of Audrey's clothing in her presence.

Galileo opened on December 7th, an iconic date for Americans, with Laughton in the title role and with Joan McCracken, Hester Sondergaard, and John Carradine in the large supporting cast. Despite its stirring message, the age-old story of a single man's struggle against repression, the show closed a week later. Following the opening, Audrey found that critics respected the message more than Laughton's showmanship. As Brooks Atkinson said, "The actor was a constant irradiation of expression by voice, hands, face, eyes, and shoulders."[23] Others puzzled over the polemical drama as a mix of religious masque and carnival and concluded that the play-in-performance failed to captivate audiences.

Audrey never regretted her representation of the two authors of the epic drama that, over time, became a permanent part of the Brechtian repertory revived worldwide. Even in later years, she could still hear, quite clearly in memory, Laughton's voice intoning the play's closing message: "I surrendered my knowledge to the powers that be, to use it, no, not *use* it, *abuse* it, as it suits their ends. I have betrayed my profession. Any man who does what I have done must not be tolerated in the ranks of science."[24]

While Audrey waited for Brecht to conclude his testimony in Washington and for the opening of *Galileo* two months later, she was preoccupied with blacklisted writer Yip Harburg whose *Finian's Rainbow* had opened in early January and who was writing the book and lyrics for another musical satire with the whimsical title *Flahooley*.

In June of 1950, a small booklet, *Red Channels*, later referred to as the "Blacklisters' Bible," was published by anonymous compilers calling themselves American Business Consultants who set forth the "Communist influence in radio and television." Yip Harburg was listed in *Red Channels* among 151 names of men and women with connections to organizations that the United States Attorney General had designated as communist-front groups.[25] With 22 "un-American" citations beneath his name, Harburg was no longer employable in Hollywood and returned to New York where he found work on Broadway. Broadway was largely exempt from the viral backlisting by film studios and broadcast corporations. The fact that there was no formal blacklist in the New York theater has been attributed chiefly to the independence of the producers along with their methods of financing shows. In those days, theater producers were not allied with corporate sponsors. Their funding came from moneyed backers and investors, theater buffs and speculators, who financed separate productions.[26]

It was not unusual for blacklisted writers and artists to write letters in an effort to achieve "clearances," permitting them to return to work. Harburg, whose credits included the lyrics for *The Wizard of Oz* (1939), had never belonged to the Communist Party but he did belong to and work with a number of Left-wing organizations, including many that found their way onto the attorney general's list.

When Harburg was asked by an executive of MGM to request a clearance letter to neutralize his listing in *Red Channels*, he walked a thin line between excoriating the blacklisters and exonerating his reputation without compromising himself. He wrote, "As a firm, almost fanatical believer in democracy, as a proud American, and as the writer of the lyrics of the song 'God's Country,' I am outraged by the suggestion that somehow I am connected with, believe in or am sympathetic with communist or totalitarian philosophy." He explained that by joining such organizations as the National Council of Soviet-American Friendship, the Hollywood Writers' Mobilization, and the League of American Writers he had hoped poets might succeed in their attempts at peace where politicians had failed. Reasoning that his songs "speak for themselves as well as for me," he appended copies of his lyrics for "God's Country" and "Brother, Can You Spare a Dime?" to his statement.[27]

Known as one of the most dedicated Left-wingers in the business, Harburg waged his campaign with letters, lunches, and petitions to Kenneth Bierly, a former FBI agent who had a company called the Research and Security Corporation and who for a fee would check out a person's record. If there was no evidence of Communist Party membership, Bierly provided a clearance letter for the "innocent" or "duped," permitting them to work again.

Unlike his creative collaborators Burton Lane, Harold Arlen, Ira Gershwin, and Jay Gorney, Harburg was obsessed with politics and wrote message-driven songs and musicals. Whereas the clumsy analogies to American politics in *Finian's Rainbow* were tolerated in early 1947, the jabs at capitalism in *Flahooley* were perceived as anti-American in 1951. Once Harburg found himself on the Hollywood blacklist as a result of belonging to and working with liberal organizations, his Left-wing activism was characterized as un-American and a menace to national security. Unlike Hollywood film companies and the broadcast media, Broadway's independent producers freely ignored the blacklist. Nevertheless, theater producers were rumored to maintain "graylists" of undesirable artists that usually ignored the artist's politics but selectively ruled against unruly temperaments, difficult performers, and waning talents.

By the mid-1960s, the songwriters who emerged in the late 1930s along with their book musicals were replaced by anti-Semitic themes in faraway pogroms (*Fiddler on the Roof*), stories on the hedonistic and amoral Berlin of the Weimar Republic (*Cabaret*), a stagestruck young woman's hard climb to a successful showbiz career (*Funny Girl*), and Stephen Sondheim's music and lyrics for the Roman slave's antics (*A Funny Thing Happened on the Way to the Forum*). Moreover, the peace movement and civil rights marches, the free speech movement and the hippie drug culture, found new voices to express the antiestablishment protests of the times in the tribal love-rock musical *Hair*.

SURVIVING

Jay Gorney (born Abraham Jacob Gornetzky in Bialystok, now Poland) emigrated with his parents in 1906 to Detroit, Michigan, to escape the pogroms of Eastern Europe. His father was hired as an engineer by the newly formed Ford Motor Company and his son worked his way playing the piano through the University of Michigan and its Law School. As a talented young musician, composer, and songwriter, he made his way from the mid-west to New York's Tin Pan Alley, an area of the city where music publishers set up shop with tinny pianos to promote popular music. There, he met lyricist Yip Harburg and a singing-actor by the name of Bill Liebling. Over time, the Liebling-Wood Agency became Gorney's agent and Harburg became his collaborator on musical revues, films, and radio shows. Their greatest success in the 1930s was "Brother, Can You Spare a Dime?," a torch song about a man down on his luck, was featured in producer Lee Shubert's musical *Americana*.

After the modest success of *Americana*, Gorney moved on to Hollywood where he became a successful composer and lyricist for cinematic musicals, but returned to Broadway in the 1940s with his wife Sondra and two young children to compose music with various lyricists for twelve Broadway musicals.

On the cusp of the virulent blacklist, Jay Gorney wrote music for *Touch and Go* with lyricists Jean and Walter Kerr.[28] While working on *Heaven on Earth* earlier, Gorney was recruited to teach and administer a new department, called "Writing for Musical Theater," where German émigré director, scenic artist, and writer Erwin Piscator had established the Dramatic

Workshop under the auspices of the New School for Social Research in Manhattan.

Nevertheless, politics was entering the creative lives of screenwriters and artists (and their agents) in the late 1940s and the Gorneys found themselves on the outer fringes of the Peekskill riots organized against actor-singer and political activist Paul Robeson who had recorded Jay Gorney's song, "The Four Rivers," from the popular Broadway revue *Meet the People.*

Soon after the Gorneys relocated to New York City in 1947, the composer received a call from Audrey Wood who announced that she had an assignment for him. Jean and Walter Kerr were in the drama department of Catholic University in Washington, DC, and wanted a composer to set their lyrics to music for a revue, then titled *Thank You, Just Looking* (later *Touch and Go*). Gorney discussed the project with his agent who assured him, perhaps disingenuously, that from time to time hit shows came to Broadway from Catholic University.

Audrey was troubled by a report in *Life* magazine about a meeting of Hollywood studio heads at New York's Waldorf Astoria Hotel on the same day that HUAC won contempt citations against the Hollywood Ten, and less than a month before *Galileo* opened. The Hollywood producers issued the "Waldorf Statement" to pacify uneasy investors, declining profits, and protests against immoral films. The two-page statement affirmed that the studios "will not knowingly employ a communist or a member of the party or group which advocates the overthrow of the Government of the United States by force or by any illegal or unconstitutional means."[29] The Hollywood blacklist had begun and Audrey Wood was nowhere naïve enough to think that her voluble screenwriters and their New York projects would be untouched.

Touch and Go proved Audrey's earlier assertion about Catholic University. With enthusiastic reviews for the "easy-going revue" with its "cheerful" score, the show played at the Broadhurst Theatre for 176 performances.[30] Nevertheless, the composer remarked that the Kerrs's warmth and friendship evaporated with the changing political times and they behaved as though no one had written the music for the show.[31]

By 1950, Jay Gorney had become a visible target for the anticommunist hunters. That year, he was hired by CBS-TV as a producer-writer-composer for a talk show that aired for several weeks. As soon as it was announced in trade publications that he had joined the CBS staff, Gorney was attacked as a "Red" in the September 22, 1950, issue of *Counterattack: The Newsletter of Facts to Combat Communism*, an anticommunist publication aimed at exposing Communism in American business, including the film industry and the broadcast networks.

Gorney was accused of sponsoring the Waldorf Peace Conference, of signing the statement of the National Council of Arts, Sciences and Professions calling for the abolition of the United States House Committee on Un-American Activities, and for working for a "Red" organization, namely, the Dramatic Workshop. Now labeled a "Red," he was fired by CBS, his coauthored scripts for ABC and CBS were bought but never televised, and two years later he was dismissed by the Hunter College School of General Studies where he was teaching another course on writing for musical theater.

All of these accusations and reprisals preceded the subpoenas for Jay Gorney and his wife delivered by FBI agents to their apartment on West 86th Street. As they witnessed friends and associates being brought before HUAC, they proceeded to hire their good friend and noted civil-rights attorney Bella Abzug to represent them. Both husband and wife had been falsely "named" by other screenwriters as members of a Hollywood "communist cell." Arguing against summoning both parents of two small children, Abzug arranged for the FBI to allow Jay Gorney's subpoena to stand and to retract his wife's subpoena.

On the morning of May 6, 1953, the Gorneys, accompanied by their attorney, went to Foley Square in lower Manhattan where the hearings were being held. The soft-spoken Jay Gorney gave the appearance of a docile witness until the committee chairman asked the $64 question: "Are you now, or have you ever been a Communist?" Like most witnesses in the 1950s, Gorney, in consultation with his attorney, had, unlike the Hollywood Ten, invoked the Fifth Amendment asserting his constitutional protections against self-incrimination. Invoking the Fifth kept him out of prison, but lost him a thriving career for, in his wife's words, "the rest of his life."[32]

It would be eight years before Jay Gorney and Yip Harburg recovered their reputations to the degree that they had another musical on Broadway. *The Happiest Girl in the World*, with music adapted from Offenbach by Jay Gorney and lyrics by Yip Harburg, opened on April 3, 1961, and played for 97 performances. The reviews were mixed and congratulations were muted. Even though they had survived the McCarthy years, witch hunts, and committee hearings, *The Happiest Girl in the World* was their last collaboration—and Jay Gorney's final Broadway show. It was also the final year that Audrey Wood provided representation for the composer who found that Hollywood's doors remained closed to blacklisted composers whose musicals on Broadway could not be sold to film studios.

Even as she represented the blacklisted Yip Harburg and Jay Gorney, Audrey's politics remained unknown. Sondra Gorney described the agent as "all business" in her dealings with her clients.[33] Audrey did not engage in small talk or comment on her own political leanings or her clients' politics. Her mother, who was from Wisconsin, was perhaps a Republican and most likely the Lieblings from New York City were Democrats, but Audrey's impeccable manners and strict business persona were such that she betrayed no political partisanship while handling her temperamental clients.[34] National politics were nowhere in evidence at Liebling-Wood when Audrey represented her writers in the marketplace.

While he waited to be cleared from Hollywood's blacklist, Yip Harburg returned to New York and Audrey welcomed the creator of the new musicals *Flahooley* with Barbara Cook that reached Broadway in 1951, and *Jamaica*, featuring Lena Horne, in 1957. Nonetheless, these shows were not as promising as Yarburg's earlier musicals *Bloomer Girl* and *Finian's Rainbow*. Harburg remained on the blacklist for another ten years and Audrey was gratified when his contributions to American music were recognized by his peers in 1972 and he was inducted into the Songwriters Hall of Fame.[35]

Like others connected with Broadway, Audrey was insulated from the political havoc of the 1950s by her independent agency, her neutral politics, her relentless work ethic, and by the talents of her clients. At the same time that she represented the elusive Bertolt Brecht, the voluble Yip Harburg, and the soft-spoken Jay Gorney, her clients by the names of William Inge, Robert Anderson, and Tennessee Williams dominated Broadway's stages and Hollywood's screens for the remainder of the decade.

6. Personal Monsters

Remember nobody asked you to be a playwright.[1]

Two years before *Galileo* arrived in New York, Audrey Wood learned of a playwright by the name of Robert ("Bob") Anderson who was writing plays on a battleship in the Pacific. From a naval ship in the Gulf of Leyte, *Come Marching Home*, Anderson's drama about a returning serviceman and the problems he encounters in civilian life, reached Audrey's desk the same year that *The Glass Menagerie* opened on Broadway. Thus began a 35 year relationship that found agent and playwright at Broadway openings of *Tea and Sympathy*, *You Know I Can't Hear You When the Water's Running*, and *I Never Sang for My Father*.

Born in New York City, Anderson wrote his earliest plays at Phillips Exeter Academy in New Hampshire and continued writing poetry, essays, and plays at Harvard where he graduated magna cum laude. He continued postgraduate studies in Harvard's English Department before enlisting in the US Navy. He also married local Cambridge director (and later literary agent) Phyllis Stohl, ten years his senior, whom he met when he acted in plays that she staged at Radcliffe College. With her husband on a ship in the Pacific, she became the emissary between her husband's plays and his newly acquired agent, Audrey Wood.

By the time Audrey received *Come Marching Home*, Phyllis Stohl Anderson was working in Manhattan as a script-reader for ABC radio, a playreader for the Theatre Guild, and soon-to-be literary agent with MCA. With a discharge from the Navy and a prestigious Rockefeller award in his pocket, Anderson studied playwriting with theater historian John Gassner at the New School for Social Research. While he worked on his plays, he wrote radio and television scripts for "live" dramatic shows, including the Theatre Guild on the Air.[2]

In 1954, with the sale of Liebling-Wood to Music Corporation of America, Audrey realized that she and Phyllis Stohl were working in the same agency. Audrey suggested that Phyllis might prefer to represent her husband, but Audrey's offer was refused outright.

When Audrey received *Tea and Sympathy*, she considered the play extremely well-written, but acknowledged that the provocative play would be a tough sell. On Broadway in 1953, adultery was a rare onstage occurrence, homosexuality a forbidden subject, nudity unheard of, and the sex act between adults a well-kept secret. At this juncture, Audrey had two scripts written by her clients (*Tea and Sympathy* and *Cat on a Hot Tin Roof*) that revealed the dark side of marriage and exposed homosexuality heretofore kept tightly locked in dramatic closets. In addition, *Tea and Sympathy* contained a thematic caution about the Red-baiting McCarthy era that failed to tolerate and respect "differences" in people.

Aware of the potential for controversy twice over, Audrey set out, while Williams was still working on *Cat on a Hot Tin Roof* in Key West, to cajole reluctant producers to consider Anderson's drama that dealt with the anguish of a young adolescent in a boys' prep school where his peer group suspects him of being a homosexual. Tom Lee is isolated in real and imagined *differences* brought about by the prejudices of his classmates.[3]

Bob Anderson had given his agent five bound copies of the play. As she stared at four rejected scripts, Audrey invited the discouraged writer to lunch at Sardi's to remind him that one copy was still in the hands of the Playwrights' Producing Company created in 1939 to produce plays by its founding members—Maxwell Anderson, S. N. Behrman, Sidney Howard, Elmer Rice, Robert E. Sherwood, and John F. Wharton. By the 1950s the group, joined by producer Roger L. Stevens, had become a major producing force in the American theater. Audrey had turned to them in her efforts to find congenial producers for *Tea and Sympathy*.

Several days after her lunch with Anderson, the telephone on her desk rang and she picked up the receiver to hear the magic words: "Audrey, we want to option Bob Anderson's play for a Broadway production."[4]

Audrey's work now began in earnest. Elia Kazan was hired to direct, whereupon he cast Deborah Kerr, an actress of "immaculate delicacy" fresh from her role in the film *From Here to Eternity*, as the sympathetic wife and young John Kerr (no relation to the actress) in the role of the troubled student.[5]

As the curtain fell on the final scene during the play's first tryout performance at New Haven's Shubert Theatre in September 1953 with Deborah Kerr slowly unbuttoning her blouse preparatory to the boy's sexual initiation, Audrey recalled that the audience, lulled by the familiarity of a prep school scene in the headmaster's living room, was caught completely off guard by the emerging sex scene between a mature woman and a 17-year-old young man. They were shocked into silence by the unanticipated scene that ended with what was to become the play's most famous line: "Years from now, when you talk about this—and you will—be kind."[6]

Audrey held her breath during the wait before applause erupted from a deeply moved audience.

The producers, director, playwright, and the Lieblings assembled for the postmortem at the Taft Hotel following the performance. The discussion of production problems quickly focused on the final scene that some called too literal or too bold. As he listened to the arguments that the final scene might offend, Elia Kazan who believed that Anderson's play was a truly felt work and flawlessly constructed, stood up and announced, "Over my dead body. If it's cut I leave the play."[7]

Audrey agreed with Kazan. She admired the director's efforts to avoid sensationalizing the ending with heavy-handed theatrics. In truth, Audrey had only praise for Anderson's script and for Kazan's handling of a potentially charged scene depicting an adolescent unsure of his sexuality in a judgmental male world intolerant (both on stage and off) of homosexual impulses. She was also aware that the play implicitly touched upon the McCarthy-era witch hunts that caught up film and stage artists in its congressional nets. The previous year, Kazan had been called before the United States House Committee on Un-American Activities. During his second hearing in April of 1952, he cooperated with the committeemen as a "friendly" witness, and, for years thereafter, his name was synonymous with stage and film celebrities who named names.[8]

Audrey and Bill Liebling were prepared to stand by Elia Kazan as he denounced any attempt to revise the ending of *Tea and Sympathy*, but the producers intervened before they could voice their opinions and agreed that the play required no further revisions. The play proceeded to Broadway with strong out-of-town notices that assured audiences that they were about to see a hit at the Ethel Barrymore Theatre where another play represented by Audrey Wood had opened six years earlier—*A Streetcar Named Desire*.

Reviewers assured audiences that *Tea and Sympathy* was a delicate play staged with great skill and beauty.[9] Anderson's play stayed in the venerable theater for two years and transitioned into a prosperous national tour. Robert Anderson was elected to membership in the Playwrights' Producing Company where he found enthusiastic support for his work for the next seven years.

Before Audrey could fully enjoy the fact that she had another major playwright in her circle of clients, a charge of plagiarism was brought against the playwright. The charge was doubly shattering because Anderson's wife was drawn into the dispute. The plaintiffs alleged that they had submitted a script to Phyllis Stohl at MCA and that she, in what is legally known as a "breach of trust," had shown it to her playwright-husband. They further alleged that Robert Anderson had copied their manuscript under the title *Tea and Sympathy.*

The irrefutable fact, later proved in court, was that Anderson's play had been written *before* his wife received the script. When confronted with the evidence, the plaintiffs withdrew their suit but not before the author and the Playwrights' Company had incurred considerable legal fees. As one of the founding partners, John Wharton commented: "If you ever have the good fortune to write a successful play and the bad fortune to be sued for plagiarism, you will be surprised by the amount of shock it produces."[10]

The stress of the lawsuit was compounded by the playwright's grief over learning of his wife's terminal illness. Nothing had prepared him for the shattering news that she had incurable cancer and for her death two years later. Following the loss of his beloved partner in 1956, Anderson struggled to regain his footing as a writer. It would be six years before he had a play on Broadway again. In the interim, Audrey brought good news when she announced the sale of *Tea and Sympathy* to MGM for a "whopping sum." Anderson wanted to write the screenplay himself but was cautioned by the studio heads that movies were a totally different medium. They were mistakenly advising an individual who had written television scripts from the time he left the US Navy.

Anderson persisted and wrote a first draft for the purpose of solving the censorship problems that the Breen Office, the industry's censorship agency charged with monitoring questionable language and morality in Hollywood films, would likely present over the use of such words as "homosexual" and "queer," coupled with a film that ended with the seduction of a teenage boy by the headmaster's wife. For the screenplay, Anderson used less explicit language and retold the story in a flashback that presented Tom Lee as a happily married husband and father, thus satisfying a pre-Stonewall generation of filmgoers and studio heads. With the release of the film in 1956, Anderson became a bona fide screenwriter and followed *Tea and Sympathy* with film treatments of *Return to Paradise*, *The Nun's Story*, and *Sand Pebbles.*

Forty-eight hours before Phyllis Stohl died, she asked Audrey and another MCA agent, Kay Brown, to come to her hospital room. She reviewed her list of clients and their considerable traits and problems—creative and financial—with the two agents and asked them to take over the writers' future representation. Satisfied that her "brood" was in capable hands, Phyllis handed the list to her two friends. As she left the hospital room, Audrey knew that she was saying farewell not only to a remarkable friend but also to one of the best agents in the business for unearthing and encouraging new talent.[11]

From a distance, Audrey observed Robert Anderson literally write his way out of grief. For the next three years, he concentrated on adapting literary works for film and Audrey quietly monitored the contracts for his screenwriting. He wrote screenplays based on a story taken from James A. Michener's novel *Return to Paradise*, and *The Nun's Story*, a mega-success adapted from Kathryn Hulme's book and starring Audrey Hepburn and Peter Finch. During his sojourn in Los Angeles, he described his screenwriting as a crutch to keep occupied through his grief over his wife's death and until he could work again on his own plays.[12]

By 1958, he had finished a new play, a gentle love story dealing with two lonely people who converge in a small New England inn on Christmas Eve. In *Silent Night, Lonely Night*, he wrote about middle-aged loneliness and diminishing possibilities, familiar motifs in modern American drama from Eugene O'Neill to William Inge.

Anderson's new play generated interests from actor Henry Fonda and also from the Playwrights' Producing Company in support of its newest member. As rumors of Fonda's enthusiasm spread to Broadway offices and Hollywood film studios, Audrey was thrown into a dizzying round of contract negotiations. There was one glitch, however, that threatened to topple Audrey's house of cards. Reserving the right to do its own casting, the major studio, that had offered a preproduction deal before rehearsals began, refused to star Fonda in the future film version.

It fell to the playwright to tell his friend that the studio's position was nonnegotiable. The actor instantly felt betrayed. Caught in the middle, Audrey gave Fonda the opportunity to try to package a deal for the screen rights that included his services. He turned to Universal only to learn that the studio, where he had previously made such deals, was not interested. Audrey proceeded with contracts for the stage production in the knowledge that half a million dollars had vanished into the night. Anderson's new play went into rehearsal with Peter Glenville directing and Barbara Bel Geddes, star of *Cat on a Hot Tin Roof*, playing opposite Fonda.

Not only had the film deal vanished, but Fonda's enthusiasm had also waned. Audrey, who watched such things with a keen eye, detected the sea change in the actor's demeanor during rehearsals. Moreover, the playwright expressed concern that Fonda's performance was "dry and reserved and remote" and not the least conveying the deeply lonely man who conquers his loneliness by loving and caring for another person.[13]

When *Silent Night, Lonely Night,* a star vehicle for two major performers, opened in December of 1959, Audrey found the production only half a success. Despite the efforts of Barbara Bel Geddes, the spark needed to win over critics and audiences was absent. The play received indifferent notices ("slow and ruminative," "uneventful," "excessively verbose") and closed after 124 performances.[14] Audrey had little time for "what if's" as she juggled Broadway productions of *Sweet Bird of Youth* and *A Loss of Roses* with an increasing number of films by her clients, including *The Fugitive Kind, Suddenly Last Summer*, and *The Nun's Story.*

Six years after its tepid reception on Broadway, *Silent Night, Lonely Night* found another life as a two-hour prime time holiday film for television, starring Shirley Jones and Lloyd Bridges. Audrey was sanguine about the modestly priced option that was far below the original six-figure offer for the film rights. Much to the playwright's annoyance (and his agent's), *Silent Night, Lonely Night* kept reappearing at Yuletide on America's television sets long after the writer's royalties for reruns had ended. Audrey recalled that Bob Anderson, now married to actress Teresa Wright, said to her, "Audrey, if I ever decide to write a film about the Easter Bunny, promise me we'll keep a large piece of it!"[15]

In the mid-1960s, Anderson dropped by Audrey's office at the Ashley-Steiner-Famous Agency (shortly to become the International Famous Agency) on Madison Avenue to tell her that he intended to try his hand at writing comedy. When she expressed surprise, he described his new project as something for Saturday-night audiences, explaining that he had noticed during the run of *Tea and Sympathy* a waning of enthusiasm for the play on Saturday nights. He told his perplexed agent that he had made up his mind to write a play that would sustain audiences during the week but also keep the Saturday-night crowd happy.

Audrey was delighted with the results: a quadruple bill of plays of various lengths—a farce, a short drama, and two brief comedies—and on subjects he had never "tackled" before. When she caught her breath, Audrey remarked, "One thing's sure, you've certainly written a different sort of something."[16]

Audrey's early enthusiasm was curbed by her knowledge that short plays, even in combination, were not to be found on Broadway in the early 1960s unless they were musical revues or written by British playwrights or

European absurdists. Although Anderson insisted that his plays were for Saturday-nighters, Audrey was chiefly concerned that producers and audiences would not accept a fragmented evening of one-acts.

She submitted Anderson's script to established producers but found no takers. Just as she began to despair, two young men came to her office looking for a property to produce on Broadway. Jack Farren and Gilbert Cates were unknown in commercial theater circles. Their prior experience as producers was in commercial television, but their enthusiasm won the day with the empty-handed agent. She called Anderson to seek his advice and he answered, "What have we got to lose?" Audrey took his answer at face value. They had nothing to lose and a great deal to gain in their "remarkable gambling house of a business."[17]

Audrey's untried producers optioned *Four Plays for Saturday Night*, as the show was then called, and set about engaging Alan Schneider as director and actors Martin Balsam, George Grizzard, Melinda Dillon, Joe Silver, and Eileen Heckart as the cast for the quartet of plays. The title was changed to *You Know I Can't Hear You When the Water's Running* and found audiences for 775 performances, including Saturday nights.

When he wrote his memoir, director Alan Schneider, an early interpreter of the plays of Samuel Beckett and Edward Albee, cited the importance of Anderson's short plays for theater in America. He credited the production with lowering barriers on one-acts as potential Broadway properties as was shortly proved by Neil Simon's *Plaza Suite*, three plays set in the Plaza Hotel.

Schneider also credited *You Know I Can't Hear You When the Water's Running* with being the first play on Broadway to concern itself seriously with the issue of nudity, although no actor appeared completely nude at the Ambassador Theatre in 1967. In the opening one-act, called *The Shock of Recognition*, Martin Balsam, playing an actor desperate for a part and auditioning for the playwright, delivered the play's title as he emerged not quite-in-the-altogether from a bathroom while shaving. Shortly after the show closed, critic Walter Kerr cited Anderson for encouraging a spate of shows with nudity, including the rock musical *Hair* and *Oh, Calcutta!*[18]

Despite the break up of MCA and Tennessee Williams's progressive mental instability, 1967–1968 was a very good season for Audrey Wood and the long-serving Bob Anderson whose plays walked "a tightrope between realism and sentimentality."[19] Anderson followed *You Know I Can't Hear You When the Water's Running* with a strongly autobiographical play, *I Never Sang for My Father*, about the relationship between a domineering father and his son who, for his entire life, has felt inadequate in his father's judgment. Audrey had high hopes for the play and was enamored for personal reasons with the repetition of the play's first line at the close: "Death ends a life but it does not end a relationship, which struggles on in the survivor's mind toward some final resolution... which it may perhaps never find."[20]

It is likely that her fervor for the sentiments of Anderson's play was influenced by the declining health of the love of her life, dearest Liebling, who was seriously ill from heart disease. To address his medical crisis, the couple had leased an apartment, two years earlier, on Sands Point Road in Sarasota, and completely furnished it, adding two sets of Audrey's "best" dishes, her "most favorite typewriter," Liebling's "loved electric blanket," and memorable show posters from *Room Service, The Visit, The Killing of Sister George*, and *You Know I Can't Hear You When the Water's Running.*[21]

Audrey intended to commute regularly to and from New York City to attend to the needs of Liebling and her clients, but from time to time her stays in Florida were extended by her husband's deteriorating health. As she sat in the Longacre Theatre in late January of 1968 listening to the beginning and closing lines of *I Never Sang for My Father*, she was already preparing to endure the painful struggle with the absence of Bill Liebling from her life after 31 years.

Despite Audrey's admiration for Anderson's play and its topflight cast (Hal Holbrook, Alan Webb, Lillian Gish, and Sloane Shelton), critics did not admire the show. Clive Barnes wrote a lukewarm review in which he dismissed the play as soap opera, both sentimental and maudlin.[22] The gentlemanly playwright was uncharacteristically overwrought that Barnes, his contemporary, was so dismissive of his Laurentian theme about fathers and sons. Nevertheless, two years later, the playwright, his play, and his agent rebounded when a film version featuring Melvin Douglas and Gene Hackman became a minor classic revived intermittently by film societies and art houses.

When Audrey pondered the writer's resiliency through his creative ups and downs and dry spells, she concluded that his calm temperament and wry sense of humor sustained him. She praised Bob Anderson as "a remarkable example of a professional—and I use that word in its best sense."[23]

Anderson's final play on Broadway was *Solitaire/Double Solitaire*, another mix of one-acts—one an ironic science-fiction fantasy and the second a grimly realistic portrait of a disintegrating marriage. Directed by Arvin Brown, then artistic director of the Long Wharf Theatre in New Haven and originally staged there, *Solitaire/Double Solitaire* played to lukewarm reviews for a disappointing 36 performances. The play opened in 1971 and Anderson lived another 36 years writing novels, screenplays, and television scripts.

Invited to membership in the Playwrights' Producing Company following the success of *Tea and Sympathy*, Robert Anderson never fulfilled the group's hopes for his talent that combined realism and sentimentality. Moreover, he was out of step with the postwar theater in America. Unlike Arthur Miller and Tennessee Williams, who began to write in the Depression-era of the 1930s in response to the fragility of the social and financial world and its toll on dignity and self-assurance, Anderson filled Broadway's stages with middle-class concerns for loss of innocence, the stability/instability of marriages, and familial tensions between fathers and sons, husbands and wives. Unlike his more famous contemporaries, Anderson came from financial security (his father, self-made and self-reliant, was successful in the insurance business). His Ivy-League education further isolated him from the protest writing of the 1930s best exemplified in the Federal Theatre's "Living Newspapers" and the Group Theatre's protest plays demanding that activists *awake and sing* when confronted with the world's ills.

Caught between the economic concerns of the Depression years and the global threats of the nuclear age, the post-war American theater responded in the forties and fifties by turning to intensely psychological concerns. Anderson's postwar writing exemplified this national turn toward "psycho-biography," as C. W. E. Bigsby labeled the playwright's work.[24] As he pursued familiar psychological landscapes, Anderson never strayed far from home and hearth, from marriage between two emotionally unsuited people, from the onset of middle age with its diminishing possibilities, and from the eternally unresolved father-son conflict.

Always a good-spirited citizen, Anderson was a founding member of the New Dramatists Committee (shortened to New Dramatists) as a workshop for young playwrights and served in the early 1970s as president of The Dramatists Guild established to protect the rights of dramatic authors for US productions of plays and musicals. During one of his talks to Guild playwrights, he closed with these words:

> In the middle ages, the mapmakers drew in the world as far as they knew it, and around the edges of the known world, they wrote in big letters. BEYOND HERE ARE MONSTERS. Well, playwrights are always venturing into that world of monsters... personal monsters, to find out what they didn't know they knew, and often what they didn't know they felt. That can be frightening, and healthy, for playwrights.[25]

Audrey was always clear-sighted about the personal monsters, to the degree she knew them, endured by her clients at their typewriters, in bars, and on the mean streets of America's towns and cities. While Anderson sublimated his monsters in the muted interplays he conjured between husbands and wives, fathers and sons, Audrey grappled from a distance with the monsters of depression and despair that afflicted Tennessee Williams and William Inge. The muted tones of Robert Anderson's intimate dramas and the angst-free translations of Maurice Valency were often welcome respites from the sturm und drang of the creative decline of Audrey's quasi-sons from Mississippi and Kansas.

THE TRANSLATOR'S AGENT

When the soft-spoken Maurice Valency, wearing a tweed jacket and bowtie, appeared in Audrey's office with his English Version of *The Madwoman of Chaillot* by the postwar French playwright Jean Giraudoux, he seemed an odd candidate for Audrey's attentions. Her other clients dramatized familiar American scenes of Southern plantations, New England prep schools, and small mid-western towns. On the surface, Valency's adaptations of modern European plays appeared peripheral to Audrey's world. Nevertheless, for 20 years, she attended to the increasing volume of his work that moved at a steady pace to include *The Enchanted*, *Ondine*, *The Apollo of Bellac*, and *The Visit*. The translator's English versions of French and German plays by Giraudoux and Friedrich Düerrenmatt evolved into Broadway productions, musicals (*Dear World*, based on *The Madwoman of Chaillot*, with composer-lyricist Jerry Herman), and films of *The Madwoman of Chaillot*, *Ondine*, and *The Visit*.

Audrey engaged in an assortment of deals for Valency's uniquely adapted foreign works for English-language stages. She worked on stock rights, foreign production contracts, and film and television sales for the Columbia University professor. She also found herself briefly on the edge of the opera world when a composer approached her about a production of an opera based on *The Madwoman of Chaillot.*

Valency insisted that his adaptations were not translations with faithful line-by-line readings of the original texts. Referring to his English versions of Giraudoux's plays, he explained, "... none of these is, strictly speaking a translation. All were made with a definite end in view, that is, production on the American stage." He argued that his Americanized versions were only an approximation of Giraudoux's voice and concluded, "This is about as much as translation can hope to accomplish in the theatre."[26]

In her new role as "adapter's agent," Audrey nurtured her client's angst-free career until she also represented actor Mel Ferrer as part of the *Ondine* package. The troubled production of *Ondine* encapsulated almost every theatrical cliché known to Audrey's world: difficulties casting a mermaid, absent producers, and a litany of complaints from the leading man about his director, dressing room, costumes, and reviews.

Ondine was ready for Broadway early in 1954. Following unflurried productions of *The Madwoman of Chaillot* with Martita Hunt as the Countess Aurelia and *The Enchanted* directed by George S. Kaufman with his actress-wife Leueen MacGrath as the charming, but spirit-obsessed, Isabel, Audrey anticipated another trouble-free production. At the outset, *Ondine*, the fairytale story of a beautiful mermaid and the prince who falls in love with her, was beset with problems. The Playwrights' Company, with Robert Sherwood and Roger L. Stevens producing, hired Alfred Lunt to direct the romantic fantasy. The various chiefs-in-charge spent weeks trying, without success, to find the right actress for the ethereal mermaid.

Like the producers, Audrey was in a quandary when a magical theater moment occurred. She received a telephone call from actor Mel Ferrer inquiring if "Miss Wood" had any ideas for a play suitable for film and stage stars like himself and his fiancée Audrey Hepburn. As she talked with Ferrer, she was staring at the unfilled cast list for *Ondine*. Audrey knew instantly that the beautiful star of *Roman Holiday* was the perfect mermaid. She mailed scripts to the actors in Paris, and they agreed to join the cast as Ondine and the Prince. Hepburn signed on the condition that her (less talented and experienced) husband-to-be play the romantic lead. In addition, Ferrer asked Audrey to represent him in the United States and she agreed.

With the casting dilemma solved, Audrey was untroubled by the fact that she was now representing the translator and the leading actor. Kay Brown represented Audrey Hepburn and therein hangs the tale of two agents teaming up to troubleshoot the daily crises of the pre-Broadway tryouts in Boston.

Despite the stellar cast (Anne Meacham, Marian Seldes, John Alexander, and Alan Hewitt), Audrey Wood was catapulted into one crisis after another by Ferrer's frenetic behavior. He made outrageous demands on the producers, translator, director, designers, and his agent. Even though Audrey patiently explained that she had no artistic control over such matters, Ferrer insisted that his costumes had to be exact replicas of the authentic armor on display at the Metropolitan Museum of Art, and, in violation of all rehearsal protocol, he disregarded the director's authority. Ferrer was convinced that Alfred Lunt's ideas were stale and his direction unimaginative. Lunt's biographer, Jared Brown, added that Ferrer also resented the fact that Lunt's seasoned actress-wife, Lynn Fontanne, was frequently present during rehearsals.[27]

During one blow-up, Lunt packed his suitcase and went home to Wisconsin. As president of the Playwrights' Company and the show's lead producer, Robert Sherwood intervened and refused to allow Valency to expand Ferrer's role by altering the script, persuaded Lunt to return to Boston, and convinced Hepburn, who was fearful that she would alienate her fiancé, to stay with the show.

Despite the sound and fury, the Boston tryout was a critical and financial success largely due to Audrey Hepburn's star status, the allure of Alfred Lunt, who had played Boston many times with Lynn Fontanne, and Jean Giraudoux whose previous works were familiar to them in Valency's adaptations. Even though Ferrer believed Boston audiences were flocking to see his performance, his agent was not convinced that he was the draw.

Once *Ondine* arrived at Broadway's Forty-sixth Street Theatre, Ferrer's demands continued to aggravate the situation backstage. He summoned his agent to the theater to take note of the unsatisfactory state of his dressing room. All Broadway show people were aware that dressing rooms had never been spacious in the older Broadway theaters, and, upon inspection, Audrey observed that Ferrer's quarters were less "opulent" than Hepburn's, but so be it. To the agent's astonishment, the producers ordered that Ferrer's dressing room be repainted and refurbished to the actor's satisfaction.

As rumors spread throughout the theater community, the actor decided to make a speech on opening night to allay the gossip about this unprofessional behavior. As the audience cheered Hepburn, resplendent in her Valentino gown, during the curtain call, Ferrer held up his hands to signal for silence and proceeded to thank Alfred Lunt for being a splendid director. Audrey Wood reported with some amusement that the critics had already left the theater to meet their deadlines and missed Ferrer's beau geste, but, within a week, *Variety* reported the entire backstage story as front-page news and Audrey Wood received another summons to attend Ferrer in the Palm Court at the Plaza Hotel.

Ferrer made two demands: he wanted an apology from *Variety* and he wished his agent to have the story "properly reported" by the press. Audrey took a deep breath, held up ten fingers, and counted off, one by one, each instance of his unprofessional behavior, including his demands to have Valency revise the play to lessen Hepburn's role, and, lastly, his insistence that he share the final curtain call with the actress. Ferrer listened to the litany of his abuses and never again mentioned *Variety.*

Nevertheless, Alfred Lunt, not the *Variety* reporter, had the last word. At the opening-night party, a patron amazed Lunt by asking if he had learned anything from working with Mel Ferrer. "Yes, madam," Lunt brusquely replied. "I learned that you cannot make a knight errant out of a horse's ass."[28]

The delicate fantasy, populated by sprites and knights errant, with music by Virgil Thomson, settings by Peter Larkin, and costumes by Richard Whorf (with the exception of Miss Hepburn's gowns by Valentino), opened to nearly unanimous praise: "ideal literature," "ideal acting," "ideal theatre." The theatergoing public clearly agreed with Atkinson's undimmed praise: "As a work of theatre, *Ondine* is perfect. It is all imagination which is the genius of the stage... Under Alfred Lunt's skimming direction, it emerges as a fully wrought work of art composed of dialogue, music, pantomime, and spectacle."[29]

Audrey Hepburn received the Antoinette Perry ("Tony") Award for best performance by an actress in a nonmusical, and Alfred Lunt received the award for best direction. There was not an available seat in the theater when Ferrer decided to leave the cast and Hepburn followed him to Italy where they were married. Deciding that their mermaid was irreplaceable, the producers closed the show.

In 1957, the Lunts chose a translation by Audrey's client of a play by Friedrich Dürrenmatt for what became their farewell performance on Broadway. *The Visit* fell under Audrey's maxim that "each property has to find its proper niche." "Often the timing is wrong," she mused. "A great deal of theater history is made by *being there at the right moment, with the right people.*"[30] The agent's Olympian view proved auspicious when the macabre Swiss play in Valency's translation and the fabulous Lunts joined forces to make stage history.

The famous theater couple had traveled to London to discuss *The Great Sebastians* with British producer Binkie Beaumont, but, en route, the Lunts became entranced with a strangely ironic play called *The Old Lady Pays a Visit.* Audrey was not part of the Lunts's circle and did not learn of their interest or of Valency's new translation until she was asked to draw up contracts for the London production.

In the early 1950s, a quartet of playwrights occupied Audrey's attention. Time after time, "Represented by Audrey Wood" appeared in playbills for *The Member of the Wedding, Come Back, Little Sheba, The Rose Tattoo, Camino Real, Tea and Sympathy, Picnic, Bus Stop*, and *Cat on a Hot*

Tin Roof. So intense was Audrey's work that she attended openings during the same month for Inge's *Bus Stop* and Williams's *Cat on a Hot Tin Roof.*[31] Within three years, Audrey would be seated in the newly named Lunt and Fontanne Theatre with Broadway's peerage to witness theatrical history in the making.

By 1957, it was clear that the famous theater couple would not be "physically capable of performing on the stage for very much longer."[32] Lynn Fontanne was in good health, but nearly 70, and Alfred Lunt, five years younger than his wife, was plagued with various illnesses. Since their next play to follow *The Great Sebastians* would likely be their last, they were determined to settle upon a play that would counter the criticism that they always appeared in fashionable drawing-room comedies. They wanted a work that would offer depth, richness, and opportunity to display their histrionic abilities.

At first, the Theatre Guild answered their call. During a respite at their home in Genesee Depot, Wisconsin, prior to their London appearance in the Lindsay-Crouse comedy, the Guild sent *The Old Lady Pays a Visit*, adapted by Maurice Valency, to the Lunts's friend and legal counsel Donald Seawell, owner of the *Denver Post*, who at the time was screening scripts sent to the Lunts for consideration. Intrigued by the play, Seawell made a special trip to Genesee Depot to hand (literally) the script to the Lunts.

Dürrenmatt's play was a powerful indictment of the way people allowed money to control their lives and alter their values. It told the story of Claire Zachanassian, one of the wealthiest women in the world, who returns to the small, poverty-stricken town in Central Europe where she grew up. The townspeople, hoping the elderly Mme. Zachanassian will pay to refurbish their village and their lives, welcome her. She consents to give then a billion marks with one condition: they must agree to kill the grocer Alfred Ill who seduced her many years before and abandoned her when she became pregnant. At first, the townspeople react to the proposal with horror and outrage but shortly begin an inexorable passage from righteous indignation to equally righteous participation in the murder of the grocer.

Troubled by the intermingling of the comic and tragic views of life, frequently mistaken for nihilism or confused playwriting in the popular mind, the Lunts declined the script and the Theatre Guild cancelled their option to produce *The Old Lady Pays a Visit.* Roger L. Stevens spoke with Audrey and obtained the rights for the Producers' Theatre, a creation of producers Roger Stevens and Robert Whitehead and real-estate mogul Robert W. Dowling. Again, the Lunts declined the Dürrenmatt play.

During their voyage to London to present *The Great Sebastians*, the subject of the Swiss play came up again and again. Later, as the Lunts sat in Binkie Beaumont's office, they learned that the London producer had recently discussed the play with gifted British director Peter Brook. Beaumont proposed that the Lunts talk with Peter Brook, and, if the three wanted to consider the Swiss play, he would seek Dürrenmatt's permission to coproduce the play in Valency's translation in Great Britain with the Producers' Theatre. All parties knew that *The Great Sebastians* would have to be postponed, or cancelled altogether.

It so happened that Dürrrenmatt gave carte blanche to Valency and Peter Brook to make script changes. The major alteration was in the physical appearance of Claire Zachanassian. In the original script, she was described as disfigured and severely crippled, requiring an ivory hand and wooden leg. In the new version, she became a physically attractive woman whose grace and beauty masked her insanity.

Audrey was not apprised of the intense discussions taking place in London and Paris that involved her client. She would not be included until Valency's final script (there were four versions), retitled *The Visit*, was optioned for British and American productions. Nor did Audrey give a great deal of thought to her missing translator as she negotiated contracts for *The Square Root of Wonderful*, *Orpheus Descending*, *Garden District*, and the Pulitzer Prize-winning *The Dark at the Top of the Stairs*.

As Audrey tracked the pre-London tour of *The Visit* in December of 1957 through British towns, Edinburgh, and Dublin, she found the reception disheartening. The tour started in Brighton where the play was advertised as high comedy. (This was wholly beyond Audrey's belief!) Critics and audiences expressed shock and outrage over the harsh view of humanity represented in the play starring their beloved Lunts.[33] By March, Audrey was not surprised to learn that Binkie Beaumont had decided not to open *The Visit* in London.

The story of *The Visit* might have ended in Newcastle-on-Tyne had Roger Stevens not flown to Dublin. He found the production magnificent and the Lunts's performances unforgettable. Backstage, he told the couple that he remained enthusiastic about bringing *The Visit* to New York.

Once committed to Broadway, Stevens faced serious marketing problems. There were no splendid reports of the production's success elsewhere as a means of interesting New York theatergoers, but the solution was at hand. In previous years, Stevens's organization had bought the Globe Theatre, built in 1910 on West Forty-sixth Street with a grand Beaux-Arts façade and a second entrance on Broadway. The theater was converted into a movie house in 1931. Under new ownership in 1957, the Globe was already being reconverted into a beautiful Broadway theater with a new entrance on West Forty-sixth Street, and, in the spring of 1958, the refurbished theater needed a new name.

When Stevens solicited ideas for an opening-night gift for the Lunts, Charles Bowden suggested that he name the theater for the beloved actors.[34] Now, Roger Stevens had his marketing strategy: the first production in the Lunt-Fontanne Theatre would feature the Lunts in the New York premiere of *The Visit.*

With *The Visit* on America's shores, Audrey represented Maurice Valency's interests for Broadway and a national tour. The play opened on Broadway in early May and laid to rest anxieties about negative reactions to the production and also dampened protests against the Lunts playing distasteful people. That same year, Valency dedicated his published edition of four plays by Jean Giraudoux to his agent in acknowledgment of her steady behind-the-scenes guidance.

The New York opening was a mélange of dedication ceremony for the refurbished theater, a gala occasion to celebrate the return of the Lunts after a two-year absence, and the once-in-a-lifetime event of opening a new theater named for them. The first-night audience was composed of well-known figures in society, politics, and the arts. Against all tradition, champagne flowed and cigar smoke wafted from the mezzanine lobby before and between acts. Audrey wore her "slightly used" black dinner dress for good luck.

Reviewers cast aside their chiding of the Lunts for their earlier choices of mannered plays. Glowing words dominated the newsprint: "superb performances," "devastating drama," "ingenious directing," "unforgettable," "brilliant." Alfred Lunt was described as "the master of wordless eloquence" and Lynn Fontanne as a remarkable combination of "irony and grandeur." "But that is not what she had in mind," Brooks Atkinson continued, "the grandeur becomes power. The coolness disguises ferocity. Reserved, detached, elegant, responsive, intelligent, Miss Fontanne gives a superb performance."[35]

Audrey took delight in the all-round praise for the translator, the play, and the Lunts. As she monitored Valency's royalties, she turned her attention to *Sweet Bird of Youth*, *A Loss of Roses*, and *Silent Night, Lonely Night*, and the film versions of *Suddenly Last Summer* and *The Nun's Story.*

Whereas Jean Giraudoux had the talents of director Louis Jouvet and his Paris-based company at the Théâtre du Vieux Colombier, Maurice Valency's adaptation of *The Visit* benefited from a number of theatrical forces: the gifted Lunts, the remarkable Peter Brook, and the persistent Roger L. Stevens. Audrey Wood, with her own forcible talent, guided the business of her translator during those years, along with the careers of Robert Anderson, William Inge, and Carson McCullers.

7. Darkness in the Heartland

In the theater, what seems a rational solution often does not apply to the emotional problems of creative people.[1]

With a recommendation from Tennessee Williams, an early play of William ("Bill") Inge reached Audrey Wood's desk in 1945. Audrey's client had returned from the Chicago tryout of *The Glass Menagerie* in late 1944 to his family home in St. Louis and consented to an interview with a local reporter originally from Independence, Kansas. The playwright and the journalist struck up an intense friendship (some allude to a brief sexual affair) based on mutual interests and shared lifestyles.[2] Within a month, Inge attended the Chicago opening of Williams's new play and was inspired to pursue playwriting as a career.[3]

Although Inge had already tried his hand at writing plays without success, he responded to the way Williams fashioned *The Glass Menagerie* out of the inner emotions and aspirations of unheroic people occupying an apartment in a St. Louis tenement. Inge credited Williams with showing him the way into the American heartland as dramatic landscape.

THE HEARTLAND AS SETTING

When his work on the newspaper lessened that spring, Inge sat down at his typewriter to write his own memory play crafted from his childhood remembrances of his family in Independence where he was born and grew up. Earlier, at the Chicago premiere of *The Glass Menagerie*, he met Williams's friend, director-producer Margo Jones, and, within three months, sent a script to her in Dallas where she was starting a professional theater. It so happened that Williams was visiting Margo Jones when Inge's play arrived. They liked *Farther off from Heaven* and Williams telephoned to say that Margo wanted to open her new theater-in-the-round, called Theatre '47, with Inge's play.

Williams also saw to it that two copies of *Farther off from Heaven* reached Audrey Wood. Although she recognized Inge's talent, she did not find the play "saleable," but, nevertheless, attempted to encourage him in a telegram.

> READ YOUR PLAY WITH GREAT DEAL OF INTEREST OVER THE WEEKEND ENORMOUSLY ADMIRE WRITING AND CHARACTERIZATION BUT EXTREMELY SKEPTICAL CONCERNING PLAY'S COMMERCIAL VALUES WANT TO BE HELPFUL BUT DON'T BELIEVE CAN HANDLE PLAY DESPITE MY BELIEF IN YOUR WRITING ABILITY IF YOU DO COME TO NEW YORK WOULD LIKE TO TALK TO YOU SORRY SHOULD I HOLD SCRIPTS ADVISE.[4]

Inge replied in the first of many letters written in anger and disappointment, but Audrey answered with practiced equanimity: "I simply wanted to re-iterate the fact here that I do think that you write above the average and that you have an unusually superior sense of characterization."[5]

Two years later, *Come Back, Little Sheba* arrived at Liebling-Wood and Audrey signed William Inge. With new client and script in hand, Audrey's difficulties began. Representing an unknown playwright made the task of finding a producer, never easy under the best of circumstances, extremely difficult. Audrey turned to Phyllis Stohl, head at the time of the Theatre Guild's playreading department, who proved influential in persuading the Guild to option *Come Back, Little Sheba* for Broadway.

Inge arrived in New York in 1949 to meet with his agent for the first time. There's no record of their initial meeting, but, given their history as agent and client for the next 25 years, Audrey won his confidence and they discussed *Come Back, Little Sheba* with an eye toward its preproduction phase.

After a delay of several months, the Theatre Guild decided to give the play a tryout at Lawrence Langner's Westport Country Playhouse in Connecticut in the late summer. The schedule was not auspicious. Inge's play was booked for a week following the close of the Playhouse's subscription season. Despite the risky schedule, Audrey persevered.

Although unknown on Broadway at the time, Daniel Mann's background at the Actors Studio made him an ideal choice to direct a play grounded in the emotional realities of unremarkable lives. At Langner's suggestion, Shirley Booth was cast as Lola, the garrulously affectionate wife. A fine comedienne, she had appeared in *Three Men on a Horse*, *My Sister Eileen*, and *The Philadelphia Story*, but she was reluctant to take a dramatic role and declined.

Persuaded that Shirley Booth was absolutely the right actress for the role, Audrey, after consulting Langner, telephoned the actress who, years earlier, had been an ingénue in her father's stock company in New Jersey. Audrey reached Shirley Booth at her farm in Pennsylvania and made an impassioned speech on behalf of her client and the play. The actress told Audrey that she would rethink the offer, and, several days later, telephoned Langner to say that she had changed her mind.

On a cold night in late September, the Westport Country Playhouse opened *Come Back, Little Sheba* for a dress rehearsal with a "papered" house of Westport businessmen and their wives along with friendly locals. The Lieblings huddled together "like refugees on a sinking ship" in the drafty auditorium.[6] Audrey felt that the audience's reaction to a crucial scene in the second act (the mid-western chiropractor, played by Sidney Blackmer, suddenly goes off the wagon, and, threatens to kill his wife), would signal whether or not Bill Inge had written a viable play.

To Audrey's great relief, the audience of strangers and nontheatergoers stopped breathing, or so it seemed, during the startling scene between Blackmer and Booth. When she could not hear a sound in the drafty theater, she knew that Inge's play worked.

The official opening the next evening seemed almost anticlimactic. Audrey recalled the wild applause, the loud cheers, and the stomping of feet as the final curtain fell. She sat back and assessed the long odds over which they had triumphed in their gambling house of a business: two performers cast against type, a director given his first major job, and a play by a hitherto unknown author.[7]

Rehearsals for *Come Back, Little Sheba* began, again, in New York with Shirley Booth and Sidney Blackmer in their original roles. Much to Audrey's chagrin, the Guild's producers ignored the play's pre-Broadway tryout in Wilmington, Delaware, to attend the opening of Katharine Hepburn's debut as Rosalind in *As You Like It*. The *Come Back, Little Sheba* company sent a congratulatory wire to their absent producers and collectively signed it, "From the Dark Horse."

The absence of the Guild's powers-that-be spared the company the ritual part of out-of-town openings with the customary second-guessing and late-night conferences, but Audrey soon confronted another too familiar problem experienced by many creative people under pressure. William Inge had long been an alcoholic, and, like his character Doc, conspicuously fell off the wagon in the face of the pre-Broadway tryouts. Fearing the possible failure of his play and the loss of his newfound life as a playwright, Inge had concealed his alcoholism and his sexual orientation. Nevertheless, when faced with the mounting pressure of the Broadway opening, he got drunk and cruised the streets around Times Square.[8]

Casting about for a solution to her own fears for the fate of her newly minted playwright in the hypertense atmosphere of a Broadway opening, she turned to Paul Bigelow, who worked for the Theatre Guild and was aware of Inge's drinking problem. He arranged for Inge to enter a sanitarium in Connecticut where he was treated with Antabuse, a relatively new drug treatment for alcoholism. From the sanitarium, Inge compulsively revised his play and sent weekly rewrites to Audrey. With plays by Tennessee Williams, Carson McCullers, and Maurice Valency requiring her immediate attention, Audrey finally sent a telegram, saying, "NOW JUST STOP. I CAN'T BEGIN TO READ YOUR PLAY EVERY WEEK"[9]

Come Back, Little Sheba opened on Broadway in February of 1950 to critical praise for its simple honesty. One critic commented that the play could have been "more skillful drama," but the praise for Booth's and Blackmer's resourcefulness and veracity was unanimous.[10] Audrey was gratified by the fact that the play, which dealt with the agony and remorse of two ordinary people, established William Inge as an important American writer.

Audrey exulted in the successes of her clients' plays in the 1950–1951 season: *The Enchanted, The Member of the Wedding, Come Back, Little Sheba*, and *The Rose Tattoo*. Ever vigilant on behalf of her clients' interests, Audrey negotiated the sale of film rights to *Come Back, Little Sheba* to Hal B. Wallis and his partner Joe Hazen for a reported $150,000. Ketti Frings, another of Audrey's clients who had adapted *Look Homeward, Angel* for the stage, wrote the screenplay, but, when the time came for casting, Hollywood stars declined the role of Lola in favor of the only actress suitable for the part. Wallis and Hazan offered a contract to Shirley Booth to recreate her original role, but remained nervous about the lack of a "name" to ensure ticket sales. They offered Burt Lancaster, from the recent film *Sorry, Wrong Number*, the part of Doc. At the Academy Awards that year, Shirley Booth won the Oscar for best performance by an actress and Audrey was gratified that sometimes life was far more interesting than fiction or Hollywood endings.[11]

Tennessee Williams arrived in New York to see *The Member of the Wedding* that opened a month before *Come Back, Little Sheba*. Everyone spoke of Carson McCullers and Bill Inge as Williams's protégées since he had recommended both writers to Audrey Wood. While his relationship with McCullers remained that of the protective, older sibling, his friendship with Inge cooled with the success of Inge's *Picnic*, the same year Williams's struggled with *Camino Real* and the rewrite of *Battle of Angels* under the title *Orpheus Descending*. The source of disaffection on Williams's part was attributed by friends to jealousy and an overriding sense of competition as a result of the mid-westerner's rising fame. When *Picnic* opened in 1953, it ran for 477 performances, won the Pulitzer Prize, and the New York Drama Critics' Circle Award. Opening a month after Inge's play, *Camino Real* received only lukewarm praise and endured for 60 performances.

Donald Spoto remarked upon the "quiet contest" between the two playwrights that involved Audrey as the keeper of their careers. She was most likely aware of the tensions between her longtime client and her newly acquired one. If she was unaware, she became fully informed when friends reported Williams's public statement that "Inge may be Audrey's gentleman playwright, but I prefer to remain her degenerate playwright."[12]

ON A TIGHTROPE

Audrey walked a tightrope between her volatile clients and tried to give equal time to the troubled *Camino Real* and the beguiling *Picnic*. She was taken with the sensitive, moving evocation of Inge's mid-western background as a prime example of what Brooks Atkinson referred to as Inge's "dramas about the private dilemmas of obscure people."[13]

As Audrey observed during rehearsals and director Joshua Logan, known for his staging of *South Pacific*, *Mister Roberts*, and *Wish You Were Here*, confirmed that *Picnic's* ending was too depressing for audiences to accept. The downbeat ending in which the proper girl is deserted by the braggart drifter and remains behind to suffer the tongue-wagging and jeers of the townspeople was Inge's effort to avoid pandering to the public's desire for a happy ending.[14]

The reaction of out-of-town audiences was the "deciding factor." Also as coproducer with the Theatre Guild, Logan demanded that Inge rewrite the ending so that Madge followed the drifter away from the small town. Inge complied, but the play still failed to receive a warm reception in tryouts. Stymied, Logan, searching for a means of transforming the virile drifter into a sympathetic character, persuaded Inge to provide a missing piece of exposition to explain that the vagrant's overbearing manner was a defense mechanism spawned by his insecurities. The new ending worked. New York critics praised *Picnic* as "an original, honest play" and "a highly satisfactory evening," and it won the Pulitzer Prize for Drama.[15] Audrey negotiated the sale of the film rights to star William Holden as the drifter and Kim Novak as the alluring hometown girl. She was satisfied that the sale was substantial enough (by one account $350,000) to afford financial security for the playwright in the years to come.

Despite the praise, Inge always thought that *Picnic*'s "happy ending" pandered to commercial interests. When the opportunity presented itself 23 years later, he rewrote *Picnic* as *Summer Brave* and restored his original ending to prove he was right. "Alas, he was wrong," Audrey quietly recalled.[16]

Two years later, observers declared *Bus Stop* the finest play of Inge's career. Marooned in the middle of the night by a snowstorm somewhere in a small Kansas town, passengers from a bus take shelter in a dingy café. The comic and often poignant story involved an impromptu romance between a third-rate nightclub singer, a tongued-tied cowboy, and a tough-talking cafe and bus stop manager. Audrey and Inge took the play to Robert Whitehead and Roger Stevens, who, aware of the success of *Come Back, Little Sheba* and *Picnic*, were delighted to produce, and Harold Clurman, who had staged *The Member of the Wedding*, agreed to direct. Much to Audrey's relief, no problems surfaced in the preopening preparations for *Bus Stop* to derail the playwright's emotional stability.

When the show opened in the Music Box Theatre in 1955, *Bus Stop* became Inge's third consecutive success on Broadway. Critics and audiences responded with warmth and amusement to Inge's comedy that looked at salt-of-the-earth mid-westerners stranded with their hopes, dreams, and foibles within the warm interior of a rundown diner surrounded by a wintry landscape. Kim Stanley played the nightclub singer, Albert Salmi the cowboy, and Elaine Stritch the acerbic bus stop manager. Critics praised the artistic and intellectual maturity of Inge's new play and summed up his comedy about ordinary people as "humorous, simple, steadily entertaining and vastly endearing."[17]

After the triumphant opening and the rave reviews, especially for Kim Stanley's nightclub singer, Audrey scarcely had time to savor her client's triumph. She was soon called backstage to encounter a display of emotional difficulties that would plague the remarkable actress throughout her career. Audrey remarked that it was enormously sad to see the actress, plagued by emotional difficulties, unable to leave her dressing room.

Attending to the backstage trauma masked by the highly successful onstage *Bus Stop*, Audrey reflected upon the peculiar nature of the agent's business characterized by "a certain amount of success, many disappointments, and often disaster."[18] With long experience of skirting disasters, Audrey picked up the telephone and negotiated with Barbara Baxley, Inge's longtime friend, to replace Kim Stanley as Cherie.

In the mid-1950s, Inge experienced a significant personal loss. Margo Jones accidentally inhaled fumes from a poisonous cleaning fluid used on the carpets in her Dallas apartment and died of kidney failure on July 24, 1955. In response, Inge turned to writing a homage to his lost friend who had believed in his talent. He reworked *Farther off from Heaven* as *The Dark at the Top of the Stairs*. Nevertheless, there was a foreboding side to his renewed effort. Since Audrey had originally declined the play, she had become, in Inge's mind, a questionable sounding-board for the revision.

Audrey was not troubled by the fact that Bill Inge seemed to ignore her. She was occupied in the mid-1950s with the sale of the Liebling-Wood Agency, an outcome of Bill Liebling's concern for his wife's welfare following his retirement. While Audrey was engaged in the move to MCA's offices, she continued negotiating for productions and films by Michael V. Gazzo, Maurice Valency, Rube Goldberg, Robert Anderson, Jane Bowles, Carson McCullers, and Tennessee Williams.

When Inge's completed script arrived in the summer of 1957, Audrey carried it to Sarasota where Bill Liebling was comfortably housed. Her seven-page, typewritten response to Inge's script revealed not only her meticulous understanding of stagecraft but one of the chief reasons she proved invaluable to her clients.[19]

Audrey began with the observation that Inge had written a "company play," not a play for "stars." Within the context of a play built around a group of characters, she examined storylines, scenes, and characters that required further development. She referred to herself in the third person as "the reader" and likewise addressed Inge in the third person as "the author." The purpose of this distancing effect was to make her comments less personal and the material easier for the playwright to view from a new perspective.

Audrey's analysis embraced nine points over the play's three acts. In the first Act, she wanted the small boy's "fears" of the neighborhood bullies and the teenage girl Reenie's fear of her peer group further amplified. "Does the author mean that her lack of security comes from some relationship between the father and mother?" Audrey wanted to know.

Audrey was careful to offset what could be taken as negative criticism by using such phrases as, "I am now speaking as a woman!" or "Please remember, I am just asking for a scene, not a complete rewrite." From time to time, she softened the impact of her comments with, "I am not sure I am right but . . . " To lessen the impact of her concerns, she reminded the author that for a long time *Picnic* had no love scene between Madge and the stranger who comes to town. "Ultimately, there was a beautifully written scene," she recalled, "which turned out to be one of the most touching moments of the play."

At the end of her comments, she assured "the author" that her suggestions in no way changed his play. "It is simply a further examination in terms of DEPTH." Even in the coda to her remarks, she continued in the third person: "Mr. Inge knows these people better than anyone else walking around the world today, and if Mr. Inge is induced to probe further into the lives of the characters he has written this can truly be an important American play."

Audrey turned to Arnold Saint-Subber to produce Inge's new play and Elia Kazan to direct. Kazan had staged Robert Anderson's *Tea and Sympathy* and Tennessee Williams's *A Streetcar Named Desire, Camino Real*, and *Cat on a Hot Tin Roof.* Moreover, he was one of the cofounders of the Actors Studio and his connections with the Studio's psychological realism appealed to Audrey and the playwright. As it developed, Kazan directed the last two successes of Inge's career: *The Dark at the Top of the Stairs* and *Splendor in the Grass.*

Nevertheless, Kazan was not overly excited by what he discerned as "conventional mid-America stuff," but he was finally persuaded by the exceptional opportunities in Inge's script for gifted actors.[20] Kazan assembled the remarkable talents of Pat Hingle, Eileen Heckart, and Teresa Wright for *The Dark at the Top of the Stairs* that opened in late 1957. Once again, Inge demonstrated the realist's urge to tell small, even terrifying, truths culled from his memories of childhood (the "dark" at the top of the stairs) that expand into adult fears in the face of an unknowable future. On this occasion in a small town in Oklahoma, Inge's characters (children and adults) become victims of their loneliness, confusions, and frustrations, along with their palpable needs for social acceptance, financial security, and solid marriages.

Critics and audiences responded to the power in Inge's work that emerged from his respect for the details of daily living and the modest needs of ordinary people. Praising the direction, acting, and Inge's "quick and poignant glances into the privacy of hearts and souls," Brooks Atkinson declared *The Dark at the Top of the Stairs* Inge's finest play. Other first-night reviewers concurred with "deeply moving," "wonderfully evocative," "unpretentious," and "very gifted writing."[21]

As fine as *The Dark at the Top of the Stairs* was, it betrayed Inge's reluctance to drive his familiar world beyond the mundane into a larger social or metaphysical universe. The small towns remained small towns and Inge failed to enlarge upon their universal tropes. As he shaped the stories of ordinary mid-western lives, his conservatism never allowed him to attain the stature of Eugene O'Neill or Arthur Miller or his now remote friend Tennessee Williams.

With the success of *The Dark at the Top of the Stairs*, Audrey turned to negotiating screen rights with Warner Brothers and a contract with Random House to publish the play. Neither of these assignments was out of the ordinary for the agent until the editor at Random House wanted Tennessee Williams to write an introduction to the published version of Inge's play. Even though the writers had not spoken for a number of years, Inge had dedicated the play to Williams, and, once again, Audrey was placed in the position of negotiating between her clients. Donald Spoto reported that Williams, working on a number of plays and screen treatments at the time, was lukewarm to the suggestion. He had experienced the failure of *Orpheus Descending* that season as well and was concerned about the fate of his newest plays opening Off Broadway as *Garden District*.

"Audrey," Williams told her when she telephoned him, "it is one thing to type three words—'For Tennessee Williams'—on a dedication page. It's quite another thing to write several pages of introduction."[22]

Audrey persevered and Williams wrote three pages, titled "The Writing is Honest," tinged with an aroma of jealousy. He suggested that the gentleman from Kansas had a "peculiar" talent for frequently uncovering a secret world beneath the genial surface of ordinary American life without the usual melodramatic tools of hidden corpses or bloody axes. He further suggested, somewhat cryptically, that Inge's personal odyssey was a drama as yet unwritten.[23]

ASSIGNING BLAME

Although Inge was at the peak of his fame on Broadway in the 1957–1958 season, the muted praise of Tennessee Williams foreshadowed what was to come in the critical rejection of Inge's last plays. Within the year, Audrey was taken aback by an acerbic attack on her client by a fast-rising young drama critic who wrote a critical repudiation of Inge's four celebrated plays.[24] In an effort to offset the personal damage inflicted by Robert Brustein's assessment of Inge's writing as a "fiddle with one string," playwright and close friend, William Gibson, disclosed how Inge's emotional and creative equilibrium had been shattered by the critic's harsh criticism.[25]

For almost ten years thereafter, Audrey watched Inge's career move steadily away from the seven lush years of successes and devolve into four consecutive failures with *A Loss of Roses*, *Natural Affection*, *Summer Brave*, and *Where's Daddy?* She was a helpless onlooker as the writer exchanged the down-to-earth people of his mid-western settings for big-city streets and urban notions of sex and violence. Moreover, she was not surprised when he also exchanged her in the 1960s for another MCA agent (Bridget Aschenberg), moved to Los Angeles where he eventually lived with his sister Helene Inge Connell, and found satisfaction in teaching and writing screenplays and novels. Nevertheless, Inge found no escape from his clinical depression.

As critics rejected his plays one by one, Inge was increasingly unable to cope with failure. *A Loss of Roses* quickly lost its bloom during rehearsals. Not even the firm directorial hand of Daniel Mann could steady the situation. Shirley Booth, playing the mother opposite Warren Beatty as the son trapped in an Oedipal relationship, repeatedly called for script changes and threatened to leave the show before the New York opening. Audrey was caught in a three-way dilemma, admittedly, of her own making. She represented the playwright, the director, and the leading actress. Observing the fractious rehearsals, she realized the depth of her mistake. "As it turned out," she consoled herself, "no single agent, no matter how strong, could ever cope with the stresses and strains that developed."[26]

Faced with the star's ultimatum, Audrey conceded to the breaking of Booth's run-of-the-play contract. Audrey knew that no legal recourse would ameliorate the situation. Betty Field, who had appeared in the film versions of *Picnic* and *Bus Stop*, replaced her.

Embarrassed and furious with herself, Audrey resolved never to get into a no-win situation again with her clients. She concluded upon reflection: "In the theater, what seems a rational solution often does not apply to the emotional problems of creative people."[27] Audrey was about to experience this lesson in spades.

As the production struggled in tryouts, Audrey became convinced that *A Loss of Roses* would not succeed on Broadway in its present state. She suggested to producers Arnold Saint-Subber and Lester Osterman that they cut their losses. She supported her argument with the fact that Twentieth Century Fox had already paid for the screen rights, so there would be no loss to them (or to Bill Inge), but actually a profit. The producers agreed and she turned to Inge to urge him to agree to the closing. As a principal ("silent") backer, Inge held the power of the final decision. He told Audrey that he wanted to think about it, and, Audrey, who had followed a policy of allowing her clients to make the final decision in such instances, replied, "Of course, Bill, it's your play."[28]

The next day, Inge rejected the advice of his agent and producers. *A Loss of Roses* opened in the iconic Eugene O'Neill Theatre to indifferent notices. Critics complained that Inge had written a "dull, poor and purposeless play."[29]

Despite enduring indifferent-to-hostile notices and a show that lasted 25 performances, Audrey received *the unkindest cut* from the playwright. In an interview for *Theatre Arts*, Inge blamed his *agent* with the self-serving remark that Audrey should have been "firmer" with him.[30] Asked about Inge's comment, Audrey responded in acid tones: "Do I have to explain any further how difficult it is to be an agent?"[31]

When Lewis Funke inquired how Inge reacted when Audrey suggested that *A Loss of Roses* close out of town, she was forthright about the matter: "It's their work and you have to let them go. I've always said, 'If I were you, I'd do thus and so, but you don't have to do it. It's your play.'" Funke then asked if she ever felt guilt over not seeing the script's problems that later manifested themselves on stage. "No. No, I can only do what I can do and people listen or they don't listen. I think you have to tell the truth," she replied.[32]

With *A Loss of Roses* behind her, Audrey paused to consider the delight critics seemed to take in "dragging down creative talents who have heretofore been successful." With William Inge and Tennessee Williams in mind, she observed,

> No matter how well established the playwright's previous work, or how good the past body of produced plays, each opening night is yet another obstacle course, one that grows tougher, not one whit easier, to navigate. Instead of cherishing our talents and encouraging them, critics seem often to relish demolishing them.[33]

Audrey continued to represent Inge with the sad knowledge that he was a deeply wounded man. Although he had the prospect of writing his own screenplay for *Splendor in the Grass*, to be directed by Kazan, with a small role for himself in the film—all negotiated by Audrey on his behalf—he could not shake-off the critical rejection of *A Loss of Roses* and the bitter fact that he had gone against the advice of his agent for the first time—and failed.

Within a year, Inge severed ties with Audrey and she turned her attention to new works by Robert Anderson, Tennessee Williams, and recently acquired client Arthur Kopit. She was, therefore, surprised when, several years later, Inge called from the West Coast to announce that he had decided to "come back to your family." Without hesitation, she reassured him, "Bill, you know I never left you."[34]

Audrey thought Inge might change his mind within a few days and wrote him a tongue-in-cheek note saying, "Dear Bill, if you still feel the way you felt this morning, I am enclosing agency contracts."[35] He returned the signed contracts and remained her client for the last few years of his life. Nevertheless, she found there was little interest in his new plays, namely, *Natural Affection* and *Where's Daddy?*, nor did Inge ask for her guidance as he struggled to be "modern" in his writing to make a comeback on Broadway. In effect, he blamed her for discouraging him and boasted that he did not care if she liked his new work, or not.[36]

Natural Affection staged another Oedipal conflict. In addition to its sensationalism that ended with the graphic murder of a mother-surrogate, and a lexicon of four-letter words, Audrey believed that the launch of the play, directed by Tony Richardson with Kim Stanley as the mother and Gregory Rozakis as the delinquent son, was doomed to failure by external circumstances. A citywide newspaper strike prevented reviews from reaching potential theatergoers. Nevertheless, the comments published at the conclusion of the strike set aside any notion that the reviews would have changed the play's reception. Critics surmised that Inge, in an effort to prove that his work was not old-fashioned and sentimental, was attempting to exceed the shock value of recent plays by Tennessee Williams and Edward Albee.[37]

Audrey was by no means obtuse. She did not discount the fact that Inge's own Oedipal rage, to some degree, touched upon her position as a surrogate mother who nurtured the careers of her clients with a "nurse-like concern" and often watched over their finances, paid their bills, and answered their mail. Robert Anderson talked about Audrey's "mothering" to Donald Spoto with the disclaimer that her manner was not entirely exceptional in the 1940s and 1950s when an agent's function was more personal. It was also reported that when asked by another client if she had any children, her answer was swift. "No, dear, I have authors," she said.[38]

In her memoir, Audrey affirmed the view of herself as a mother-figure:

> I've never had children, but I suppose being an author's representative is a little like having a child. You decide to take on a writer and you take on a tremendous responsibility. You handle all the details of his business life—his contracts, his whole financial present—and, perhaps, his future.[39]

There is no doubt that Audrey saw herself as the guardian agent of her clients' careers and their personal welfare.

Within the context of Audrey's hands-on guardianship of her clients, Tennessee Williams discussed his ambivalence toward his agent. He granted that the difficulty lay in the fact that, "like all mother-image people, Audrey Wood, whether she knows it or not, has a will to manage, to control her sometimes recalcitrant son-or-daughter images." He confessed that he had reached an age where too much domination and care-taking was oppressive.[40]

Despite the sometimes difficult relationships, Audrey's playwrights attributed their early successes to their powerful and shrewd agent with the uncanny sense of not only what was good in their writing, but also what would succeed in the hard business of the commercial theater.

Inge's last play on Broadway, *Where's Daddy?*, continued the "change" (Inge's word) in his writing in the 1960s that moved away from the materials and language closest to his creative vision, that is, the American heartland.[41] The play's modish themes, drawing on psychoanalysis, parenting, and racism in America, were shoveled, as one critic said, into an "old-fashioned domestic-comedy container." Other mainstream critics found the play "preposterous," "gross and unattractive," with Walter Kerr writing the harshest assessment. "I don't care where daddy is," Kerr lamented, "where's William Inge?"[42]

With sporadic consultations between them, Audrey continued to oversee the publication of Inge's plays and monitor the contractual agreements regarding residuals from films and royalties from amateur and professional revivals of his earlier successes, namely, *Come Back, Little Sheba*, *Picnic*, *Bus Stop*, and *The Dark at the Top of the Stairs*. By 1968, Inge was called America's "most ignored dramatist."[43]

In the mid-1960s, producer Leland Hayward, with Joshua Logan directing, attempted without success to transform *Picnic* into a musical called *Hot September*. During the pre-Broadway tryout in Boston, Hayward sought Audrey's advice. "It's hopeless. There is nothing you can do," she told him. Expanding upon the agent's dilemma, she added: "Sometimes there are moments when you can do work on something and fix it but there are other moments—in this case, it was so out of bounds—the woman character has the hit song and not the young people whom the play was about."[44]

Audrey saw Inge for a final time in April of 1973 during a trip to Los Angeles to negotiate a contract for her client James Costigan's television play *Love Among the Ruins*. She was shocked to see that he was grossly overweight, drinking heavily, and largely uncommunicative. When she returned to New York, Audrey reported to Inge's friends that it was painfully obvious that he was on a self-destructive path that could have drastic consequences. She was not surprised, then, to learn in early June that he had closed himself in a car in the garage attached to the house where he lived with his sister, turned on the ignition, and died inhaling exhaust fumes. He was 60 years old when he was buried in his boyhood hometown of Independence, Kansas, on June 11, 1973.

Three decades after the premiere of *Come Back, Little Sheba*, Bridget Aschenberg walked into Audrey's office and handed her several bound copies of Inge's early play published in an African language. Audrey held in her hands the tangible evidence that Inge's sympathetic portraits from the American heartland were reaching audiences in distant lands.

8. Iron Butterflies

[Being an author's agent] is a peculiar line of work, precarious, filled with a certain amount of success, many disappointments, and often disaster.[1]

As the daughter of the Palace Theatre manager, Audrey Wood was in the business of representing playwrights whose work was commercial. For her, the cold reality of the agent's business was finding a well-written drama that affirmed the writer's talent and the script's commercial value. The next step was to sign the playwright, find producers with money, bring them together with the writer, marry both parties with contracts, and apply endless amounts of patience to the many complications that preceded opening night.

When Audrey started out in the 1920s, women were not considered "money-writers" by male producers, even though a number of women were making names for themselves as playwrights: Rachel Crothers, Zona Gale, Zoë Akins, Anne Nichols, Edna Ferber, Susan Glaspell, and Sophie Treadwell. The percentage of women writing produced plays was relatively small and obstacles to success in the Broadway theater, dominated by the Selwyn Brothers and the Shuberts, were daunting.

The American commercial theater has been a hard business for women authors, and remains so today. In 1922, when Audrey was 19, Anne Nichols had to rent a theater and produce her own play, *Abie's Irish Rose*, to convince the Selwyn Brothers that she was a viable commercial writer. After 2,327 performances and an intake of one million dollars at the box office, the gentlemen-producers conceded that Anne Nichols was a force to be reckoned with.

When Audrey placed her name on the door of the Audrey Wood Agency in the mid-1930s, women playwrights, while not legion in numbers, were present on the great white way, for example, Dorothy Heyward with Dubose Heyward (*Porgy*), Sophie Treadwell (*Machinal*), Lillian Hellman (*The Little Foxes*), and Edna Ferber (*Dinner at Eight*). By the time Audrey's career ended, she had represented a proportionate share of women authors during her 40-year career. However, it cannot be said that Audrey favored women writers over men, or vice versa. The script's *commercial* potential was paramount in her decision to represent the writer. When *Mamba's Daughters* and *The Member of the Wedding* arrived at Liebling-Wood, Audrey without hesitation accepted them as commercially viable plays.

NO MODERN-DAY HEROINE

What separated Audrey Wood from the power brokers and commodity merchants of her Broadway world, was not only her gender, but her keen eye and taste that informed her choice of scripts and subsequently her choice of clients. She was quick to say that she did not think of herself as a modern-day heroine, breaking down doors to invade male territory. "I was too busy looking for a way, any way, to get myself a job," she recalled of her early interviews before securing a position with the Playwrights Company. She found her niche as an "author's agent" and parlayed her reputation at Liebling-Wood into that of super agent, thought of by those she represented as "intimidating," "powerful," "inexhaustible." Described variously as having a needle-sharp quickness of wit and burning enthusiasm combined with a taste for frankness and a combative spirit (the iron-fist in the velvet glove), she stood in the company of Hallie Flanagan, Theresa Helburn, and Cheryl Crawford—accomplished, pioneering women whose visions and energies shaped the American theater in the mid-to-late twentieth century.

Tennessee Williams called his miniscule agent an *enigma*, going so far as to suggest that she displayed male and female attributes. He found that she had a "male" preoccupation with plays that would prove successful in the marketplace. Her feminine side nurtured her writers as talented, contentious "children," and she spoke of "giving birth" to a play on opening night. Audrey accepted her femininity by dressing conservatively as a no-nonsense business woman with the mandatory hat and the classic brooch pinned to the shoulder of her dress or jacket. She made her bones, as the gamblers say, a generation before the feminists championed the "second sex."

When Audrey reflected upon her public image, she emphasized that she was a small woman with "a quiet, well-bred voice" in a male-dominated business. She told Max Wilk during the writing of her memoir, "Being a woman isn't something I work on. It's just something I am." She added,

"It's hard for men to compete with this," meaning, the conservatively dressed, soft-spoken, assertive woman whose keen eye for a script often out-paced her male cohorts.[2]

Neither the gender of the writer nor his/her sexual orientation was of concern to Audrey. She accepted the fact that most playwrights were men and had no compunction discarding the weak play regardless of the prestige of its author. She told the author of *The Glass Menagerie*, *A Streetcar Named Desire*, and *The Rose Tattoo* not to show *Camino Real* to anyone until he had reworked it. When *Mamba's Daughters*, *The Member of the Wedding*, and *In the Summer House* arrived on her desk, she responded typically with three questions: Is the author talented? Will the play offer something of interest to producers and audiences? Will the playwright persevere once she entered the marathon that is the commercial theater? Even as she responded to her intuitive instincts—the green lights flashing—she was forever sanguine about the outcome. She realized that whether or not the play and its author would go the distance to the finish line was, in every instance, the gambler's long shot.[3]

A number of her clients did not reach the finish line or went to Hollywood as screenwriters and never returned. Nevertheless, Audrey's intuition flashed green when, first, *Porgy* and, then, *Mamba's Daughters* arrived from South Carolina's resident writers, Dorothy and DuBose Heyward.

GREEN LIGHTS FLASHING

The Heywards became a very young Audrey Wood's clients while she was honing her agent's skills at the Century Play Company. As a husband-and-wife team, Dubose Heyward supplied the stories from his novels and Dorothy crafted the narratives into dramatic form. As a student at Radcliffe College, Dorothy Hartzell Kuhns of Canton, Ohio, had enrolled in George Pierce Baker's English 47 Workshop at Harvard where she strengthened her skills in dramatic technique. She wrote five plays between 1924 and 1948, and famously created dramatizations of her husband's novels *Porgy* and *Mamba's Daughters.* Whenever Gershwin's masterwork *Porgy and Bess* was produced under Audrey's watchful eye, it carried on the title page the legend "based on the play by Dorothy Heyward and DuBose Heyward."

Dorothy Heyward is credited with recognizing the potential of her husband's novel for the stage. While he worked for United Artists on the screenplay of Eugene O'Neill's *The Emperor Jones* to feature Paul Robeson, Dorothy set about secretly adapting *Porgy*. In earlier discussions about the novel's potential for the stage, DuBose Heyward had argued that the events of the novel were not stageworthy. When George Gershwin contacted the novelist with the idea of making *Porgy* into an opera, Dorothy showed her husband her unfinished adaptation. Upon reading his wife's script, he recognized the stageworthiness of the novel's events, and, together, husband and wife worked on a revision in the summer of 1926, whereupon they asked George Gershwin to postpone his plans for an opera until they could get *Porgy* produced.[4]

Dorothy Heyward's revised the novel's ending that had closed on a melancholy note without hope that Porgy would ever reclaim Bess, who vanished with Sportin' Life under the mistaken impression that Porgy has been jailed for killing Crown. Instead, the authorities had taken Porgy to identify the villain's body. When he returned to Catfish Row in the novel's original ending, Bess is missing and Porgy's future uncertain. Dorothy changed the ending to show Porgy leaving Catfish Row in pursuit of his beloved Bess. The Heywards brought their play to Audrey who placed the script with the Theatre Guild.

Few serious plays with all-black casts had been produced on Broadway before the 1926–1927 season. Paul Green's *In Abraham's Bosom* with a mixed cast of white and black actors struggled to find an audience in 1926 until it won the Pulitzer Prize. With *Porgy* in hand, Guild producer Lawrence Langner turned to in-house director Rouben Mamoulian, who staged the Heywards' play in October of 1927 with Frank Wilson as Porgy and Evelyn Ellis as Bess, aided by the talents of Rose McClendon and Jack Carter in a cast of 24.

The drama presented an original and sensitive portrayal of blacks working on the docks of Charleston and living in Catfish Row, an old mansion reclaimed by blacks as a communal home for their families. One critic described the Heywards as "observers, rather than polemicists," who looked sympathetically upon the residents of Catfish Row, noting their humanity, their hardships, their loves, and sorrows.[5] The successful run on Broadway established the love story of the disabled Porgy and the drug-using Bess as serious drama for African American actors and as the future sourcebook for George and Ira Gershwin's *Porgy and Bess*.

While George Gershwin (described by Audrey as "a young girl's dream gent come to life") fulfilled other commitments, Dorothy Heyward turned to other collaborators to continue her Broadway career and wrote two plays.[6] Before Moss Hart launched a successful career with George S. Kaufman, he teamed with her on *Jonica*. She wrote the libretto for the musical comedy about a naive young woman's adventures between leaving a convent and her engagement to a former boyfriend in New York City. The musical opened at the National Theatre in Washington, DC in 1930, and later arrived on Broadway for 40 performances. Critics called *Jonica* "a moderately pleasing but undistinguished pastime."[7] A second play, *Cinderelative*, written with Dorothy de Jagers, possessed a comic plot arising from a daughter's search for evidence of a father's love. The comedy was dismissed as a "flight of vagrant fancy" and closed within a week.[8]

When George Gershwin became available, Audrey took contracts to the composer that set forth the terms of the collaboration among all parties, including Ira Gershwin, to write the lyrics with DuBose Heyward. When Gershwin completed the seven hundred-page score with orchestrations, Audrey estimated that, uncut, the renamed *Porgy and Bess* would take four and a half hours to perform.

Gershwin's operatic version was produced by the Theatre Guild in 1935 at the Alvin Theatre with Alexander Smallens conducting and Rouben Mamoulian directing. Despite reviews praising the melding of storyline and music, the hybrid musical ground to a halt, slowed down by "gobbits of opera," and lost its $70,000 investment.[9] Both DuBose Heyward and George Gershwin died without an opportunity to see the compressed revival in 1942, produced by Cheryl Crawford with original conductor Alexander Smallens and with Todd Duncan and Anne Brown recreating their roles as Porgy and Bess. The revival earned *Porgy and Bess* its reputation as the Gershwins' most enduring work in theaters and opera houses and a source of royalties for Dorothy Heyward who lived another 19 years.

In 1938, Audrey, now a partner at Liebling-Wood, received a second dramatization from Dorothy Heyward, based upon her husband's novel *Mamba's Daughters*, a strong and moving drama of a black matriarch and her struggles to raise her family. From the moment Guthrie McClintic, whose major successes were *Winterset*, *Candida*, and *No Time for Comedy* and was married to actress Katharine Cornell, optioned *Mamba's Daughters*, Ethel Waters entered Audrey's life in a serious way.

In 1939, Ethel Waters, known as a headliner in nightclubs, vaudeville, and musical revues, had become an exciting stage personality and celebrated jazz singer. She had introduced Irving Berlin's "Heat Wave" and "Supper Time" in his show *As Thousands Cheer*. Audrey was aware that audiences accepted the remarkable actress as an entertainer, but, Broadway producers even in the late 1930s had not offered serious roles to black performers. Audrey was concerned that ticket buyers might not support the play.

Despite Audrey's reservations, audiences hailed Ethel Waters as the first African American actress to star in a dramatic role on Broadway. However, while praising Ethel Waters's performance, critics objected to the Heywards' heavy-handed melodrama and overt sentimentality, and *Mamba's Daughters* closed a financial failure four months later.

DuBose Heyward died of a heart attack the next year and Dorothy Heyward wrote two more serious plays. The first, *South Pacific* (no relation to the successful Richard Rodgers and Oscar Hammerstein II musical), written with Howard Rigsby, about two sailors of different races shipwrecked on an island, and, *Set My People Free*, based on the slave uprising of 1822 in Charleston. Both plays dealt with the issue of race that had been the centerpiece of Dorothy Heyward's work from the time of her first dramatic collaboration with her husband on *Porgy*.

Mamba's Daughters remained a landmark production for Liebling-Wood for reasons other than the contributions of Dorothy and DuBose Heyward. Within two years, Ethel Waters played the lead in the first musical comedy represented by the agency. *Cabin in the Sky* with book by Lynn Root and score by Vernon Duke and John LaTouche assured the actress an enduring reputation on stage and in film.

A decade later, Audrey encountered Ethel Waters a final time when Carson McCullers brought *The Member of the Wedding* to the agent and Audrey was involved in the casting of the play's maternal symbol—Berenice Sadie Brown.

THE FRAGILE CHRYSALIS

When Carson McCullers tried her hand at dramatizing her critically acclaimed novel about identity and the universal need to belong, Tennessee Williams, who had encouraged his friend to adapt her novel for the stage, offered to introduce her to his agent. McCullers declined out of loyalty to Ann Watkins, who had been her agent for three years. Audrey would not receive the script of *The Member of the Wedding* for another four years.

In the summer of 1946, Tennessee Williams invited "Sister-Woman," his term of endearment for his Georgia friend whose warmth and fragility reminded him of his sister Rose, to be a guest in a rented two-story frame house on Nantucket with him and his companion Pancho Rodriguez. The two writers were drawn together by their shared sensibilities about the South. Moreover, Carson's unassuming warmth and affection won the hearts of her hosts who had corresponded with her but did not come face to face with the novelist until the tall woman wearing slacks and a baseball cap, exhibiting a "delightful crooked-toothed grin," stepped off the island ferry.[10]

Carson McCullers had seen no more than a handful of plays in her entire life and had little understanding of dramatic structure, but Tennessee Williams, convinced that her writings would make "strong theatre," acquired a portable typewriter for her use that summer.

Each day the two writers sat at opposite ends of a long dining-room table and Williams worked on *Summer and Smoke* while McCullers worked on her adaptation. When queried about his part in her dramatization, Williams insisted that "Carson accepted almost no advice about how to adapt *The Member of the Wedding*." He did acknowledge to Virginia Spencer Carr, McCullers's biographer, that he suggested she adapt her book as a play, and, was gratified when she finished the first draft while seated at the large table on Nantucket.[11]

Later that summer, Carson gave the script to Ann Watkins with instructions to find a Broadway producer for the play. That November, the novelist and her husband, Reeves McCullers, departed for Paris where Carson became seriously ill and doctors diagnosed two severe strokes—the second impaired Carson's vision in her right eye and left her partially paralyzed. This medical onset was attributed to the tensions between the married couple, to their excessive drinking, and to Carson's distress over the perceived rejection of her play.[12]

The novelist had received a letter from Ann Watkins saying that the agent had approached the Theatre Guild who agreed to produce the play but with conditions. They wanted Carson to consent to work with an experienced playwright to revise her script. Upset and disappointed, Carson agreed and signed a contract with Greer Johnson, whom the Guild recommended to cowrite the revision. Once the revision arrived during the fall of 1947, Carson failed to see how the new manuscript had improved her solo efforts. Before she could sort out her next step with the adaptation, she suffered a third stroke. She and her husband returned to their residence in Nyack, New York, where she began a period of recuperation during the winter and spring of 1948.

Audrey learned through the Broadway grapevine that Carson McCullers had refused to allow the Theatre Guild to go forward with a production of the cocreated script and Greer Johnson was threatening to sue for loss of royalties. Audrey took note of the rumors of Carson's demand for the return of her dramatic rights, Johnson's suit for $50,000, and the submission of the disputed contract to the American Arbitration Association for settlement. Tennessee Williams appeared as Carson's chief witness and spoke eloquently on behalf of the novelist's rights to her creative property. The court ruled on November 8, 1948, that "the contract for dramatization of the novel is in full force and effect for one year—subject to the assumption that the Theatre Guild, if it produces the play, will use the joint script prepared by both parties."[13] Nevertheless, the Theatre Guild, largely discouraged by Ethel Waters's rejection of the central role of the cook, failed to exercise its option, and the ownership of the disputed script reverted to McCullers.

Before the lawsuit developed, the novelist had been dictating a revised script to a part-time secretary (a manual typewriter was now impossible for her to use). Her husband gave her an electric typewriter that required little pressure from the fingers of her afflicted left hand. She finished the play in scarcely two months and discontinued her association with Ann Watkins, who also represented Greer Johnson.

When she turned to Williams's agent, Audrey hesitated to sign the novelist because she feared that her representation might lead to a conflict of interest with Tennessee Williams. Nevertheless, he assured Audrey that he had no intention of collaborating with any writer and she proceeded to sign Carson McCullers in 1948. Audrey never learned how much advice Williams had given his friend in the writing of her play, but she knew that he had provided invaluable assistance by sitting with her day after day and demonstrating the kind of focus required to write a play. "If he hadn't," Audrey surmised, "it's safe to say there might never have been a finished play."[14]

When Audrey met with the novelist to talk about her script, she realized that the talented writer had no concept of how much time and work would be involved in a professional production, how complex the preparations, and how difficult the production process could be. "To put it mildly," Audrey reflected, "Carson was naïve and charmingly innocent about the theater."[15]

A SPECIAL PRODUCER

With the sensitive coming-of-age story of the adolescent girl, Frankie Adams, on her desk, Audrey confronted the enormous problems the script presented. The agent never voiced her trepidations to the fragile writer but they were threefold: the play's subject matter about an adolescent's rite of passage that did not fit the requirements of the commercial theater for large scenes, a cast requiring exceptional actors that did not fit Broadway's idea of a "star" cast to attract audiences, and, a special kind of producer for both play and playwright.

Audrey was most anxious to identify a producer who was knowledgeable about the theater, had great taste, and the necessary boldness to produce the unusual play. Most importantly, Audrey wanted a producer who would be sympathetic to the gifted woman on her first venture into writing for the stage.[16]

Audrey approached 33-year-old Robert Whitehead who had begun his producing career with *Medea*, starring Judith Anderson, the previous year. He was an associate of Roger L. Stevens and was shortly to engage in founding the Producers' Theatre and later the Repertory Theatre at Lincoln Center. Audrey gave a copy of McCullers's script to Whitehead who agreed to bring *The Member of the Wedding* to Broadway with Harold Clurman directing.

Audrey gathered her entourage, with director Harold Clurman chief among them, and drove to Nyack in upstate New York on the western shore of the Hudson River, to spend several hours discussing the play with the writer. Audrey's recollection of McCullers on that day is a lasting portrait of the charmingly innocent playwright, wholly unprepared to imagine or engage in the demands of a Broadway production. Audrey, exhibiting her motherly side, described her client in this way:

> Dear Carson, lanky, her hair cropped short, smiling, almost childish in her enthusiastic responses to the professional discussion which dealt with casting, scenery and costumes. She approached it all with the anticipatory glee youngsters have when putting on a play in the attic.[17]

Later, during their drive back to Manhattan, Clurman, who had directed plays by Clifford Odets and Irwin Shaw for the Group Theatre (and later Inge's *Bus Stop*), turned to Audrey and asked in a quiet voice, "Audrey, what do we do if we get into trouble in Philadelphia?" Understanding his suggestion about the naïveté and questionable stamina of their playwright during tryouts, Audrey suggested *prayer*.[18]

Whitehead and Clurman cast the three leads in the play that took place in a small Southern town in 1945. After a face-to-face meeting in Nyack with the playwright, Ethel Waters, having her demands met to alter a few lines and interpret the role herself, agreed to play Berenice Sadie Brown; a young Julie Harris was Frankie Adams, a gangly girl of 14, who aspired to be a member of the wedding; and Brandon de Wilde, making his stage debut at age seven, played Frankie's cousin, John Henry West.

Rehearsals were trouble free and all went well until the dress rehearsal at the Walnut Street Theatre in Philadelphia attended by friends, staff, agent, the playwright, and her husband. Performances were shaky and there were problems with the scenery and lighting. When the curtain fell, Audrey remarked with unadorned candor that she had just suffered through one of the worst theatrical evenings she had ever experienced. The only levity came when the tall, wavering figure of Carson McCullers stood up in the gloom of the houselights and cheerfully announced in her Southern drawl, "It was just lovely. I enjoyed every minute of it. Now if you all will excuse me, I'm going back to my hotel and get a night's sleep."[19]

The professionals in the house (agent, producer, director, production staff, and designer Lester Polakov) were amazed that their playwright did not have the slightest clue that the final rehearsal had been dreadful. Nevertheless, opening night in Philadelphia reaffirmed their belief in the gentle play. The audience responded to the humor, childish audacity, and tenderness of the play's inner life. There were no further crises, but the play took four hours to perform. To shorten the running time, McCullers was asked to remove a barroom scene that seemed superfluous. She agreed and excised the scene with the deftness of a surgeon, Audrey reported.[20] When the show arrived at Broadway's Empire Theatre, Carson McCullers had not been required to rewrite a single line of dialogue. Mother Audrey was astonished and proud.

The Member of the Wedding opened on January 5, 1950. Reviewers skipped over the lack of unconventional play structure to praise McCullers's masterly writing that brought insight, grace, and beauty to the stage. Brooks Atkinson called McCullers's literary style "deft and spinning" and her characterizations of the people in the ramshackle kitchen "superb pieces of work." Other reviewers were equally ecstatic for the "mood" play that held its audience spellbound.[21]

At the invitation of *Theatre Arts*, Carson responded to the observation that *The Member of the Wedding* was not "exactly a play." She wrote:

> *The Member of the Wedding* is unconventional because it is not a *literal* kind of play. It is an inward play and the conflicts are inward conflicts. The antagonist is not personified, but is a human condition of life: the sense of moral isolation. In this respect, *The Member of the Wedding* has an affinity with classical plays—which we are not used to in the modern theatre where the protagonist and antagonist are present in palpable conflict on the stage. The play has other abstract values; it is concerned with the weight of time, the hazard of human existence, bolts of chance.[22]

The play and its playwright garnered multiple awards, including the New York Drama Critics' Circle Award for "best first play by an author to be produced on Broadway" and "best play of last season." Although Carson had hoped to receive the Pulitzer Prize, she was aware that the award was reserved for an "original" American play and her adaptation, based on her novel, kept her out of contention. The Pulitzer went to *South Pacific.* New Directions published the play (dedicated to Reeves McCullers) and *The Member of the Wedding* was listed as one of the top ten plays of the year and included in *The Burns Mantle Best Plays of 1949–1950.* Audrey quickly sold film rights to Stanley Kramer, who, within three years, made it into a film with Ethel Waters, Julie Harris, and Brandon de Wilde repeating their performances under the direction of Fred Zinnermann.

Carson McCullers's debut as a playwright qualified as a painless process and uneventful experience. Audrey was amused by the mental image of Carson receiving a boat-load of royalty checks in her mailbox in Nyack. Audrey chortled as she imagined Carson saying to herself, "This is for sure a simple way to earn a living!"[23]

During the year *The Member of the Wedding* opened, Audrey marshaled Valency's *The Enchanted* and Inge's *Come Back, Little Sheba* onto Broadway stages and negotiated film rights for *Summer and Smoke, The Member of the Wedding,* and *Come Back, Little Sheba.* While she waited for Carson's health to permit the writing of another play, Audrey's plate was full. During the seven-year hiatus between *The Member of the Wedding* and *The Square Root of Wonderful,* Audrey handled new plays (and film contracts) for Maurice Valency, William Inge, Tennessee Williams, Michael V. Gazzo, and Jane Bowles.

By her own admission, Audrey always tried to work with writers whose quality of work and literary style she admired. Jane Auer Bowles, married to composer and author Paul Bowles, was a rarity in the 1950s as the third woman during the decade to be represented on Broadway by Audrey Wood.

At the same time Audrey represented her novel *Two Serious Ladies* and her shorter prose pieces, she encouraged Bowles to complete her script of *In the Summer House* about the struggle between a domineering mother and her colorless daughter who finally breaks free from the matriarch's control. Oliver Smith optioned Bowles's play and renewed his option year after year before the play was finally produced by the designer and the Playwrights' Company. Even with Judith Anderson giving a towering performance and stage veterans, Mildred Dunnock and Jean Stapleton, in the supporting cast, the play, directed by José Quintero, failed to connect with audiences in 1953, and lasted only 55 performances. Praising Bowles's writing as sensitive and gem-like in its use of words, Brooks Atkinson concluded that the material about neurotic people residing in a vulgar world had not been molded "into anything of real value."[24] Another producer, Hale Matthews, optioned the screen rights, but the screenplay adapted by Nora Johnson proved a hard-sell in Hollywood.

Audrey took pride in the fact that she never gave up on a playwright whose writing she admired. She negotiated publication of *In the Summer House* and worked toward a regional production of the play in Michigan with a revised script, known as the Ann Arbor version.

In 1963, shortly after Audrey began her tenure at Ashley-Steiner, two producers came forward to stage an Off Broadway revival of Bowles's play. With Bowles in Tangier, Morocco, recovering from a stroke, Audrey shared her confidence in correspondence with the writer that the play with Estelle Parsons and Leora Dana would receive "the mature and sensitive production it richly deserves."[25] However, the play was not well-received and Audrey reluctantly wrote to Bowles, describing the unenthusiastic reviews from "second-string" reviewers. (The tactful agent did not tell the writer that her play opened opposite Jule Styne's *Funny Girl* which received the full attention of the major reviewers.) Audrey closed with, "Regardless of what happens, it was a beautiful production, and one I feel which does your lovely play real justice."[26]

As usual, Audrey was resigned to the difficulties she encountered promoting Bowles's work, despite its originality. Each property has to find its "niche," she remarked, reflecting upon those that did not find a place in the commerce of Broadway.[27]

LOST CAUSES

Audrey often referred to Carson McCullers as a "gallant lady," but Audrey was dealing gallantly with health issues of her own in the summer of 1951. As an individual who had never been seriously ill, surgery for an appendectomy and a slow recuperation were unexpected setbacks. During her convalescence at her house in Westport, she wrote to Carson that she felt "like Atlas must at the end of a long day in front of 630 Fifth Avenue." Nevertheless, she wanted her client to know that she continued to work on contracts for the film of *The Member of the Wedding*, television rights for *The Ballad of the Sad Café*, and publication of the complete *The Ballad of the Sad Café and Other Works*.

Audrey-the-patient closed her letter on an endearing note of concern for the novelist's health: "Take good care of yourself, Carson, my dear," she wrote. "No one in the world quite understands as much about certain humans as you do and it's important that writers like you keep us close to the men and women you choose to write about."[28]

Prior to her second and final appearance on Broadway, Carson McCullers reeled emotionally from the death of her mother in Nyack and the suicide of her husband in a Paris hotel. Moreover, with *The Square Root of Wonderful*, she experienced her first significant encounter with failure that required an emotional and mental strength that her close friends doubted she possessed. Earlier, Tennessee Williams had warned his Georgia friend that it takes "a tough old bird to work in the theatre."[29]

In the mid-1950s, Audrey learned that McCullers was working on a new novel *Clock Without Hands* and a romantic tragicomedy called *The Square Root of Wonderful*. Audrey was aware that the writer had become involved with Arnold Saint-Subber, the successful producer of *Kiss Me, Kate* and the early Neil Simon hits *The Odd Couple* and *Barefoot in the Park*. She also understood that Carson's health was deteriorating (her paralyzed left arm had become increasingly painful), but Saint-Subber encouraged her by promising to produce her play. Monitoring her health and progress with her writing, Audrey found that Carson "worked bravely," and the script was finally completed in 1957.[30]

Saint-Subber first hired Albert Marre, who had successfully directed *Kismet* and *The Chalk Garden*, to work with Carson to revise the script and also to stage the play. Marre admired Carson's charm, grace, and keen sense of humor, but knew that their work on the play was far from finished when Saint-Subber announced that he had booked theaters for tryouts and Broadway. At the time, Marre was committed to Jean Anouilh's *Time Remembered*, which he had optioned and had ready for production, so he bowed out and Saint-Subber hired José Quintero, who had launched the Circle in the Square, an off Broadway theater, in 1951 and directed definitive productions of *The Iceman Cometh* and *Long Day's Journey into Night*. He brought the director to Nyack to meet the playwright. Audrey described the meeting as "love at first sight." Fascinated by the darkly handsome Quintero, Carson became so enthralled that, when the director admired an oriental rug in one of the rooms, she promptly gave it to him. Then she changed her mind and Audrey received almost daily telephone calls that became long conversations during which Carson eventually announced that she dreamed that Quintero returned her rug. Later, Audrey reported Carson's prophetic dream to the director who vigorously rejected the suggestion to give up the rug![31]

Quintero struggled to make *The Square Root of Wonderful* a workable vehicle for Broadway. After the curtain came down on the pre-Broadway tryout in Princeton, he asked Audrey to take a walk with him through the campus. Quintero, who had directed *Summer and Smoke* and was now a client at MCA, quietly announced to Audrey that he could not go further with the play. In defense of his seemingly abrupt decision to withdraw from the production, he argued that he had nothing more to contribute. Despite Audrey's arguments to the contrary, Quintero was adamant.

Audrey had little influence on the developing situation, although many close to the play's source were advising that *The Square Root of Wonderful* should not open in New York. Having promised to produce Carson's play, Saint-Subber commuted to Nyack for three years where he stayed with Carson as friend, lover, play-doctor, and producer. He credited her with enriching his life even as he worked tirelessly to extract a workable play from her.[32]

After Quintero's departure, Saint-Subber brought in Joseph Mankiewicz whose firm Figaro, Inc. became a coproducer, but the film director also concluded that the play was unworkable. By now, Audrey knew deep in her heart that *The Square Root of Wonderful* was a "lost cause": There had been too many script-doctors, too many directors, and a playwright whose illness made it impossible for her to throw away the many revisions and return to her seedling version.[33] Moreover, in the many drafts, Carson had not recaptured the other-worldliness of her best writing nor had she created uniquely original characters to flesh out the story of a young woman, twice divorced from an irascible writer, who has fallen in love with an architect.

Tennessee Williams suggested hiring George Keathley, who had staged *Sweet Bird of Youth* the previous year in Florida. Keathley presided over the insertion of a new third act and stayed with the play through its Broadway opening in October of 1957. Brooks Atkinson expressed the critical dissatisfaction with the play: "Very little of Mrs. McCullers' odd genius has gotten into the fabric of this frail, delicate, though listless, play."[34]

After the disaster with *The Square Root of Wonderful*, the writer, who was known to exhibit professional jealousies and to reject well-meaning friends for imagined slights, cast out her agent of ten years. Unable to fault her producers and multiple directors for the play's failure, she blamed Audrey for the disappointing outcome—attributed to the "impasse of her creativity."[35]

In the early 1960s, she turned for representation to Robert Lantz, who had given up his literary agency to become part of the Figaro producing group. He believed that, with time to work on *The Square Root of Wonderful*, it could have been a better play.[36] Lantz remained Carson's agent in his new agency until her death, following an irreversible coma at the age of 50.

Three decades later, Audrey recalled the fragile writer of *The Member of the Wedding* watching her characters on stage, playing out their stories, just as she had imagined them. Audrey expanded the remembrance in her memoir to include the sound of Ethel Waters's vibrant voice as she held Julie Harris on her lap, cuddled Brandon de Wilde close to her, and sang the spiritual "His Eye Is on the Sparrow, and I Know He Watches Me." This memory stayed with Audrey as an iconic moment in the theater and one of the many reasons she remained *stagestruck* throughout the years.

9. An Accidental Career

But I have been an agent for a long time now and I intend to continue for as long as my sense of humor stays with me.[1]

By the 1960–1961 Broadway season, Audrey Wood had been a successful agent for almost 25 years. Her morning routine rarely varied. Whether she was traveling from her house in Westport or from the Royalton Hotel on West Forty-fourth Street, she arrived at her office at MCA where she put down her briefcase filled with scripts that she had read the previous evening. She returned "urgent" calls, read letters and contracts demanding her "immediate" attention, and noted "requests" for meetings during the day. The most time-consuming of these routines were the contracts that required careful study. She read and initialed each page and promptly returned them to the agency's legal department. Then she turned her attention to her clients' productions that were in various stages of preparation for Broadway.

Following the disappointments of *The Square Root of Wonderful*, *A Loss of Roses*, and *Period of Adjustment*, the new decade held great promise for Audrey's new and continuing clients. In addition to negotiations for film and television contracts for *The Dark at the Top of the Stairs*, *Summer and Smoke*, *West Side Story*, *Silent Night, Lonely Night*, *Period of Adjustment*, and *Splendor in the Grass* (Inge won the Academy Award for best original screenplay), Audrey also represented another Broadway-bound play by Tennessee Williams—*The Night of the Iguana*. Unknown to Audrey at the time, a new playwright was waiting in the wings.

A SERIOUS MAN

Twenty years earlier, a lanky Harvard engineering graduate by the name of Arthur Kopit had appeared in Audrey's office at the urging of producer Roger Stevens. Born Arthur Lee Koenig, the young boy received his stepfather's name when his divorced mother Maxine was remarried to George Kopit and the family lived in an affluent suburb of Long Island.

Arthur Kopit began a playwriting career as an undergraduate with short plays staged at Harvard's Dunster House by his college dramatic group. His talent won him a postgraduate fellowship to travel in Europe during the summer of 1959. He finished a long one-act in Scandinavia and submitted the script to a playwriting contest sponsored by Harvard's Adams House. Directed by his classmate Michael Ritchie (later a successful film director) while Kopit was far away in Spain, *Oh Dad, Poor Dad, Mama's Hung You in the Closet and I'm Feelin' So Sad* was given a production at the Agassiz Theatre in Cambridge. Critics pronounced the play with the longest title ever to grace a theater marquee in Boston the best play of the season and Roger Stevens, hearing absurdist echoes of Eugène Ionesco in Kopit's bizarre title and madcap surrealism, decided it might be a good bet for Broadway. The producer contacted Kopit's parents to option the rights to their son's play as soon as he returned from Europe and urged them to encourage him to secure an agent to protect his interests. Stevens suggested Audrey Wood, saying, "You must have her because she's hell with producers, but great for playwrights."[2]

Of all the words written about Audrey by her clients, Arthur Kopit captured the play agent's strategies and verbal endearments (some called them irritants) in dialogue written for *End of the World* about the threat of the nuclear arms race to humankind. As a secondary thread, he wove into the play his concern for the survival of serious playwrights on Broadway. In an early scene, Audrey West (aka Audrey Wood) dispenses advice to her client Michael Trent (aka Arthur Kopit):

> *Audrey*: Dear, I checked him [the producer] out. He's legitimate, he has the money. So I'd say you've got a deal.
> *Trent*: Audrey, his idea is terrible!
> *Audrey*: Then don't take it.
> *Trent*: How can I not take a deal like this? This is a definitional sweetheart deal, this is the deal of a lifetime!
> *Audrey*: Dear, what do you want me to do?
> *Trent*: ADVISE me!
> *Audrey*: Take the deal.[3]

When Kopit recreated his agent as a dramatic character, he captured Audrey's astute business sense exercised on her client's behalf, her mannered way of talking with "dear" and "darling" sprinkled throughout her conversation, and her unabashed concern for the playwright's artistic and financial welfare.

Oh Dad, Poor Dad's journey to Broadway began in 1960. When Kopit returned from his travels abroad, Audrey had read his script and was convinced that it demonstrated remarkable talent. She appreciated the young writer's superb sense of comedy, at times surrealistic, and his bizarrely original outlook on life. Most likely, she was highly amused by the allusions to *The Rose Tattoo* (Rosalie, the girlfriend-seductress) and to *Suddenly Last Summer* (menacing Venus fly-traps). Nevertheless, Audrey was not fully convinced that a hit in Cambridge among the groves of academe would necessarily succeed within the mean streets around Times Square.[4]

Convinced that she wanted to represent the writer, she invited him to lunch at Sardi's. With little understanding of her early representation of Tennessee Williams and Robert Anderson, Kopit was indecisive about the famous agent having sufficient time to represent an unknown writer. As they left the restaurant, he told her that *Oh Dad, Poor Dad* was to be produced in February at the Loeb Theatre in Cambridge. She congratulated him and returned to her office with nothing settled about the writer's future representation. Hearing rumors of other literary agents flocking to Cambridge to woo the playwright, she sent him an opening-night wire in which she said that she hoped she would be the one to "get the brass ring." Still, she received no response from Kopit. Instead, she had a call from Arthur Wang, head of the publishing-firm Hill and Wang, who wanted to print the text of Kopit's play before it reached Broadway. Audrey explained that she had nothing to do with the play or its author. Wang's response confirmed that she had, indeed, captured the brass ring. "That's strange," Wang replied, "I just spoke to Kopit up in Cambridge about publishing his play, and he said, 'Call Audrey Wood; she's my agent.' "[5]

Reflecting upon the first year of Arthur's Kopit's career, Audrey described them as heady days for a young writer. "Barely out of college," she recalled, "he had a Dramatist's Guild contract, a first-class producer, and a potential future as a professional playwright."[6] Nevertheless, the path to success was not easy. At the outset Roger Stevens decided *Oh Dad, Poor Dad* might have greater appeal to British audiences. In his view, the favorable reception on London's West End of Samuel Beckett and Harold Pinter and the thriving experimental theater scene there seemed congenial for the unusual play with its provocative title.

With Audrey's and the playwright's approval, Stevens made a deal with British producer Binkie Beaumont to mount the play in London. With dispensations from British Equity, the Actors Studio's Frank Corsaro was hired to direct and play the lead and the legendary Stella Adler was cast as the flamboyant Madame Rosepettle.

Audrey and Bill Liebling went to England to attend the pre-West End opening in Cambridge. Pleased with the enthusiastic reception for Kopit's play, they returned to New York confident that the play would be a hit in London, but were soon disappointed. The London audience at the Lyric Hammersmith had no idea that it was attending a comedy and the London critics, with the exception of Kenneth Tynan, savaged *Oh Dad, Poor Dad, Mama's Hung You in the Closet and I'm Feelin' so Sad.*

AN UNUSUAL CLIENT

Given the play's history thus far, Audrey was surprised when she received a call about Kopit's play from the director-choreographer Jerome Robbins, who, earlier, had been represented at MCA on a one-time basis. Robbins called before Kopit's play was produced in London, asking to direct it, but Frank Corsaro had already been signed. After the British disaster, Robbins spoke to Audrey a second time and told her he would still like to stage the play. Having proven successes in ballet and musical comedy, he turned to straight plays to make a contribution to the artistic fermentation occurring in the theater and dance worlds of the 1960s.

In one sense, Audrey inherited the choreographer of *Call Me Madam*, *The King and I*, *Peter Pan*, and *West Side Story.* She was surprised when an MCA executive asked her to take Jerome Robbins as a client, urging that it would be the ideal marriage of agent and talent. Audrey was not convinced. She had never worked with a choreographer and did not think her background was right to represent Robbins, but she agreed to have lunch with him at Dinty Moore's, a famous theatrical restaurant on Forty-sixth Street across from the Lunt-Fontanne Theatre, where he was in rehearsal. She knew that Robbins was difficult to pin down, often mercurial, and accustomed to total authority on all projects. Moreover, she did not think he would accept the agency's offer of a relationship with their diminutive literary agent who had not previously represented a choreographer.

Robbins was so engrossed in a rehearsal with his company, "Ballets: U.S.A.," that he either ignored or forgot their appointment even though Audrey was seated in the empty theater waiting for him to take a rehearsal break. Finally, she asked the stage doorman to tell Mr. Robbins that Miss Wood was across the street, if he wished to join her when he finished rehearsal. They had a hurried conference in Dinty Moore's during which

Audrey assured Robbins that she would be willing to represent him, if he agreed.

Much to Audrey's amazement, Robbins signed the contracts for his representation and returned them accompanied by his business card and a box of yellow roses. Not to be outdone, she returned his copy of the contracts, accompanied by her business card and a box of red roses.

Their first project, however, was not the Kopit play. Robbins was offered the task of transferring his choreography to the film version of *West Side Story* and Audrey found her client reluctant to make the commitment. As Audrey listened, Robbins laid out his concerns: producer Leland Hayward had offered him the opportunity to direct *Gypsy* on Broadway and was advising him not to take the film of *West Side Story*. Hayward argued that Robbins would find directing the film artistically frustrating as a result of the financial controls put in place by the film company.

Audrey listened to her client in the full knowledge that MCA had executives in California close to the film company; moreover, she was aware that the deal had already been negotiated for Robbins to direct the film version with his choreography. He only needed to agree to the deal that was in place. When Robbins finished laying out the pros and cons of his choices in the matter, Audrey spoke truthfully to her client in tone and words similar to the dialogue recreated by Kopit for his fictional agent in *End of the World*. The real Audrey Wood told her client:

> Jerry, if you really feel you cannot go through this sort of anxiety—if you really feel you can live through someone else reproducing your choreography on the screen, it's fine with me. Obviously, you don't need the money, you're well off, so if you decide against it, I'll go along with your decision.[7]

She waited almost a full day for his decision. When he telephoned, Robbins's advised her that he had decided to do *West Side Story*—and *Gypsy*. Despite the pressures that the agency would have exerted on their agent if Robbins had declined the film, Audrey had astutely surmised that Jerome Robbins would not place his choreography in another's hands.

Soon after *West Side Story* went into production, Audrey took contracts for Robbins's employment to the site of the new Lincoln Center where he was filming among vacant lots piled with rubble. Audrey was not pleased that the filming had moved ahead of contractual agreements. She found Robbins high on a camera crane rehearsing (and filming) a scene with the Jets, the street gang, dancing down the street in search of the rival Sharks. Even though he was already filming sequences with the dancers, Audrey urged him to sign the contracts to protect his interests, including his royalties and film credits as codirector and choreographer.

The film was released by United Artists in 1961, four years after the musical of *West Side Story* opened on Broadway, but the film, as predicted by Leland Hayward, had been a brief, frustrating stint for Robbins. Once the film was over budget and behind schedule, the producers fired Robbins and the film was finished by codirector Robert Wise who continued to consult with the choreographer during the editing. Wise had worked on the book scenes and Robbins had rehearsed the dances and musical numbers in advance of filming and together they collected Academy Awards for Best Motion Picture of 1961 and shared the Best Achievement Award in Directing. Gene Kelly of *Singin' in the Rain* fame presented Jerome Robbins with a special award for choreography.

With little interest in surefire comedies and modern realistic dramas, Robbins found Kopit's unconventional play attractive because it "presented the preposterous as everyday occurrences that lent themselves to choreographic staging."[8] Robbins's second call to Audrey about the availability of *Oh Dad, Poor Dad, Mama's Hung You in the Closet and I'm Feelin' So Sad* was fortuitous. Despite the mixed reception in London, Roger Stevens remained interested in a New York production.

Marketed as a "pseudoclassical tragifarce," *Oh Dad, Poor Dad* was staged Off Broadway at the Phoenix Theatre, comanaged by founders Norris Houghton and T. Edward Hambleton. Kopit's play was staged by Robbins, with Jo Van Fleet as Madame Rosepettle, Austin Pendleton as her neurotic son, and Barbara Harris as his hapless girlfriend. Since *Oh Dad, Poor Dad*'s running time was only one hour and twenty minutes, a decision was made to add Kopit's *Sing to Me through Open Windows* to precede the main event. Whether it was the enigmatic ending (declared a downer by some) or the over-long set change between the two plays, *Sing to Me through Open Windows* was eventually dropped.

An Off Broadway sensation, Kopit's tragifarce captivated audiences with two Venus flytraps, designed by William and Jean Eckert as puppets that growl and snarl and reach out with their branches to capture people, a snapping silver piranha, named Rosalinda, who prefers Persians to alley cats, and two corpses that litter the apartment. (Rosalie has been smothered and Dad's embalmed corpse has fallen out of the closet.) As Madame Rosepettle returns to behold her dazed son and disordered apartment, she delivers the closing line, "As a mother to a son I ask you. *What is the meaning of this?*"[9] A fast blackout follows and then the houselights come up.

The play was celebrated as the arrival of the American version of the Theatre of the Absurd. In *Oh Dad, Poor Dad,* Kopit revealed an ability to make grotesque fun of popular psychological ideas about American society (mothers and sons, wives and husbands, household plants and closeted corpses).

Audrey monitored her client's theatrical success: a solid hit, accolades in the press, and weekly royalty checks. At 23, Arthur Kopit's career had gone into orbit with Audrey Wood piloting the spaceship—more likely *clinging* to the controls. She was very much aware that it was customary for young writers to be seduced from the legitimate stage by Hollywood film studios and television companies waving lucrative contracts for their writing services. She had watched the careers of Yip Harburg and others swerve into the money pots and one-way streets of Hollywood where a return to the legitimate theater rarely occurred. Over the years, she had watched those talented men and women return to Manhattan, talk wistfully of "knocking out" that second play or musical-comedy libretto, only to turn westward again to the next well-paid assignment, never to write again for the legitimate theater.

Envisioning the loss of another unusual talent to Hollywood, Audrey discussed her worries with Kopit in the knowledge that the theater would be a difficult workplace for him because his idea of a family play was a synthesis of serious, comic, and grotesque elements. Moreover, she knew that it was unbusiness-like of her to shield him from Hollywood. Audrey was relieved when he agreed that he should stay in New York and write plays. She was confirmed in her assessment when Robbins restaged *Oh Dad, Poor Dad* for Broadway with British comedienne Hermione Gingold as Madame Rosepettle and reviewers found the play "original and fresh."[10]

Following his work on *Oh Dad, Poor Dad,* Jerome Robbins left MCA and Audrey regretted that their professional relationship had been brief. In a rare moment of nostalgia, she said, "I would be proud to work once more with so gifted an artist."[11]

In 1965, Arthur Kopit's short plays, *The Day the Whores Came Out to Play Tennis* and *Sing to Me Through Open Windows,* were produced Off Broadway without success. Undaunted, her client returned to his typewriter and Audrey sold the film rights for *Oh Dad, Poor Dad, Mama's Hung You in the Closet and I'm Feelin' So Sad* to Paramount for Rosalind Russell as Madame Rosepettle with Robert Morse and Barbara Harris, as the son and girlfriend. Even though the film script was faithful to Kopit's play, the absurdist take on life without Jerome Robbins's inventive staging, did not amuse filmgoers and the film quickly disappeared from view.

Always sanguine about flops, Audrey diagnosed *satire* as "the most fragile of commodities."[12]

During the five years Audrey waited for Kopit to write another play, her days were consumed with new works by a troubled Tennessee Williams, a struggling William Inge, and a complacent Robert Anderson. In this waiting period, Audrey was honored by New Dramatists, a service organization for playwrights, during an annual luncheon in recognition of the literary agent's "extraordinary dedication" to the special requirements of playwrights and her "exclusive concern" for their development, their interests, and the quality of their productions for more than 30 years. In the time between *Oh Dad, Poor Dad* and the full-length *Indians,* Kopit told journalist Don Shewey that he spent a lot of time "waiting for something to seize me."[13] What sparked his imagination was a newspaper item about a shooting incident in Saigon that fueled his impression that the Vietnam War was a continuation of deadly cowboy-and-Indian games on another continent. He conceived Buffalo Bill's Wild West Show as metaphor for the good-guy versus bad-guy mythology that often disguised the greed and genocide with which the American West was won.

As she experienced the erosion of Williams's talent in the late 1960s along with the winding-down of Inge's career, Audrey was cheered by the fact that her youngest client had written a major theatrical piece for the stage. Audrey was captivated by the political ramifications of a play that explored the long, anguished history of Native Americans in the American West. She and Roger Stevens set to work arranging a production of *Indians* with the Royal Shakespeare Company in London. As she read the many tributes from British audiences and critics, she called the London opening a "wise decision."[14]

At this point, Kopit's agent and his producer pooled their collective experiences and made another judicious decision. Motivated by sheer prudence, Audrey advised her client that the complex play with the large cast should be introduced out-of-town at one of the regional theaters where production costs would not derail the venture at the outset. She turned to Zelda Fichandler, producing director of Washington's Arena Stage, who had guided Howard Sackler's *The Great White Hope* from the nonprofit theater to commercial success in New York during the previous season.

As previews began in the nation's capital, Audrey received a call from film and television producer David Susskind wanting to buy the film rights to *Indians* before the show opened in New York. In a moment of sheer intuition, Audrey declined Susskind's offer. When Bill Liebling asked his wife how much the producer had offered, she told him that Susskind had offered $150,000. Liebling questioned her decision but Audrey persisted, "No, I'm sorry, but I think this property is worth much more."[15]

Audrey reopened negotiations with Susskind, but the producer wanted to read the script. Again, Audrey was reluctant. She was convinced that few people, not even famous producers, had the gift of being able to read a script and make an informed judgment on how it will play on stage. Audrey's adage of many years had held her in good stead: "A good play is not meant to be read; its worth can be easily misjudged."[16]

With the playwright's consent, she made a counter-offer. If Susskind truly wished to buy *Indians* before it opened, he must sign a letter of intent to secure the play. Roger Stevens's earlier depiction of Audrey as "hell for producers" proved prophetic once again.

At the time, Stevens strengthened his argument on behalf of the invaluable Miss Wood by describing a replica of a dinosaur bone that sat on his desk in Washington. The replica featured several small dinosaurs clustered beneath the larger bone. When he showed the object to show business visitors, he cheerfully referred to the display as "Audrey Wood protecting her young."[17]

Audrey reinforced her legendary reputation as she drew up the letter of intent for Susskind's signature. As she waited for his office to return the contract, she confessed to being nervous about the sight-unseen deal, but Susskind had already discussed the project with Paul Newman who wanted to play the legendary Buffalo Bill Cody in the film version of Kopit's play. With the stage and film star committed, Susskind was secure in signing the letter of intent.

As it turned out, the American production of *Indians* was an artistic success but not a commercial one. In Audrey's view, the show was overproduced and overwhelmed by the sounds of horses' hooves wafting continuously through the speaker system. She recalled Stacy Keach, as Buffalo Bill, waiting patiently on stage for the sound effects to be tuned properly—and retuned and tuned again. Audrey sensed that it was not an easy time for the leading actor and the large cast. "Whatever the cause, mechanical or human," she pronounced of the message-driven play, "the flaws were glaring."[18]

Audrey tiptoed around David Susskind who was not pleased with his sight-unseen investment. About a year passed before he asked her to lunch to discuss another project. Somewhat ruefully he said, "You know, Audrey, I will never, never forget what you did to me. You taught me a lesson. I will never pre-buy a play." She replied, "David—*you* called *me*, remember?"[19]

THEATER MATTERS

Seated in Boston's Wilbur Theatre during the tryout of Kopit's *Wings*, Audrey mentally revisited the scene of the final-act conflagration created for Tennessee Williams's *Battle of Angels* thirty-eight years earlier. She had returned to the Wilbur many times since 1940, but no matter how many years passed, she still recalled the smell of the smoke created by the overzealous handlers of the smoke pots drifting across the stage and the sounds of first-nighters leaving their seats in outrage, holding scarves and handkerchiefs to their faces, as they exited through the aisles.

This time was different. Wilbur audiences applauded the stunning performance of Constance Cummings as Emily Stilson, the gallant woman struggling to recover from a stroke in Kopit's play informed by the clinical facts and emotional truths experienced by victims of aphasia. With excellent reviews in her briefcase, Audrey returned the next day by train to New York's Grand Central Station and her office confident in Kopit's play but guarded about future audiences at Broadway's Lyceum Theatre. Even though there were rapturous out-of-town notices for Constance Cummings's performance and excellent word of mouth for the play, Audrey knew the unpredictability of commercial success. Nevertheless, she reminded herself that, if one is looking for security, one does not seek it in the theater.[20]

Wings had a three-year journey from a radio station in Minneapolis to Broadway's Lyceum Theatre. Audrey was first approached by producer Howard Gelman and British director John Madden, to discuss the interest of her clients in writing original plays for radio. *Earplay*, as the program was called, was to be produced with assistance from National Public Radio and also sold to European stations at the same time. Audrey's attention was riveted when she was assured that writers would receive *advances*.

Arthur Kopit, who had not written a play since *Indians*, was uppermost in Audrey's mind during the discussion. The playwright was grieving over the death of his father and Audrey was searching for a way to motivate him to return to his writing. She arranged for Gelman and Madden to meet the writer. Audrey's timing was perfect. Kopit had begun to germinate an idea to write about the clinical and emotional truths surrounding his father's severe stroke that resulted in irreversible brain damage.[21]

Eventually, Kopit's one-hour radio play dealt with a middle-aged woman who in her youth had been an aviator (a wing-walker or barnstormer) and experienced a stroke later in life. She undergoes the frightening experience of attempting to recover from the effects of aphasia, especially the loss of speech. The title and central metaphor for *Wings* were derived from a photograph Kopit saw during a visit to a rehabilitation center. The woman in the photograph was a wing-walker in her twenties standing on the lower wing of a biplane with silk scarf around her neck, goggles set high on her leather helmet, wearing jodhpurs, boots, and a leather jacket. He described the woman's face in the photograph as "lean and handsome and imperious. Her eyes seem on fire; they are filled with an unquenchable eager passion."[22]

The playwright coined the term "autobiographical format" for his new work. His research took place at the Burke Rehabilitation Center in White Plains, New York, where his father had been transferred after hospitalization. There, Kopit met three women, one a therapist and two with varying degrees of aphasia. As he engaged with the clinical and emotional truths of brain damage, a composite character (Emily Stilson) became central to Kopit's play about language disorder along with the isolation and terror experienced by stroke victims. Avoiding a documentary or clinical approach to dramatizing a medical condition, Kopit's radio play took place in Emily Stilson's mind and dealt with the tedious and painful stages of her slow recovery—to the moment of her death.

Kopit's universal landscape was not the clinical condition but the fortitude and spirit exhibited by human beings thrust into an existence without language, mobility, or means of escape.

When *Wings* was produced for *Earplay* in May 1977 with Mildred Dunnock playing Emily Stilson, Audrey found the piece affecting and often thrilling drama. Although reviews were excellent, Audrey was aware that the market for radio plays was limited. She was, therefore, startled when Robert Brustein, dean of the Yale School of Drama and producing director of the Yale Repertory Theatre, called to discuss the possibility of turning Kopit's radio play into a theater piece.

Mildred Dunnock's health did not permit her to reprise her role and recasting the central actress seemed daunting until John Madden journeyed to London where he approached Constance Cummings, most recently seen as Mary Tyrone in *Long Day's Journey into Night* with Laurence Olivier. Once the actress read the script, she was excited by the challenge and traveled to New Haven, where she played with a supporting cast of Yale drama students. Cummings received rave reviews, but the general consensus was that the subject matter was too offbeat for Broadway.

Nevertheless, *Wings* developed a momentum of its own. Joseph Papp invited the Yale Repertory Theatre to restage the play at the New York Public Theatre in lower Manhattan for a limited run in the spring of 1978.

Again, it met with rave reviews and Audrey encouraged Roger Stevens to see the show since he had been Kopit's commercial producer from the beginning. Stevens called the next day to tell Audrey that he thought *Wings* was Kopit's best writing and intended to bring the show to the Kennedy Center and then to Broadway.

The early reception at the Kennedy Center was mixed. Audrey received reports that audiences were puzzled by the ending. She traveled to Washington to scrutinize the play's final moments during which Emily, prone on her bed and soaring off on imagined wings on a terrifying flight at night, dies and the stage is thrown into total blackness to indicate her death. By sitting in different places in the theater, Audrey realized that, from certain seats, the audience could see the actress walking off in the darkness after the blackout. Madden restaged the ending to mask the actress's exit.

Reflecting upon the variety of endeavors that inform an agent's life, Audrey concluded, "Such are the sometimes peculiar functions which concern a playwright's agent."[23]

Wings soared into the Lyceum Theatre in January 1979. Constance Cummings was honored with the Tony award for Best Performance by a Leading Actress and Audrey was convinced that Arthur Kopit had written a play of lasting value.

THE CUSTOM TAILOR

Within 18 months, Audrey was negotiating contracts for her client to write the book for the musical *Nine*, based on Federico Fellini's semiautobiographical cinematic masterpiece *8 ½*, with staging by Tommy Tune and choreography by Thommie Walsh. She was also monitoring the progress of Robert Anderson's *Free and Clear* under option for a commercial production at the Kennedy Center and Ruth Wolff's *Sarah in America* at the American Shakespeare Theatre, Stratford, Connecticut, with a transfer to the Kennedy Center. In addition, she attended weekly writing conferences with Max Wilk on the manuscript for her memoir. The year was 1981.

Nine opened in May of 1982, but Audrey Wood, stricken by a massive stroke a year earlier, was no longer available to advise her clients or attend the Tony Awards where Arthur Kopit had been nominated for Best Book of a Musical. Kopit continued to work on *Nine* to accommodate the cast changes for the national touring company, namely the replacement of Raul Julia in the role of the womanizing Italian director trying to make a film while experiencing a midlife crisis. The script had to be altered to suit the personality of Sergio Franchi, the new leading man, and cuts were needed to reduce the running time of the show for out-of-town audiences.

Seated in the back of the Lunt-Fontanne Theatre during rehearsals for the touring company, Kopit pronounced himself "a custom tailor." During an interview with Don Shewey, the playwright remarked on the challenge to suggest ways to move the narrative forward through music, staging, lighting, or costumes because there was never enough time for language. His job was to be invisible in the structure of the show, hence, a custom tailor.[24]

"What is it that makes Arthur Kopit," Don Shewey asked the writer, "still willing to buck the odds by dealing with serious themes on Broadway?" He received Kopit's concise answer: "Theater matters."

> When you ask an audience to pay money and sit in a theater, you've got to do more than just delight them. Television can do that. Movies and musicals can get by just with glitz, dancing, entertainment, sheer technical excellence. In the theater, you must feel and think also. It has to do with why theater has always existed in civilization. Theater matters.[25]

When Kopit wrote *End of the World With Symposium to Follow* (the published script was dedicated to his agent) in 1984, he included a parallel argument for the writing of serious drama. The play's autobiographical material was derived from Kopit's objection to his government's escalation of the nuclear arms race, his personal interviews with politicians and military personnel on nuclear arms policy, his experience of producers throwing money at writers to promote their causes, and his recollections of conversations with his agent over the creative process and unfortunate play titles, such as *End of the World.*

End of the World (the title was shortened during tryouts) also began as an accidental project. Kopit was teaching a playwriting workshop at the City College of the City University of New York when an insurance millionaire approached him with a four-page outline (a futuristic scenario about the specter of nuclear holocaust and global doom) and proposed that the writer create a full-length play based on his scenario about a Soviet-American showdown. He offered Kopit, who was then supporting his family with grants and royalties, the considerable sum of $30,000 for researching and writing the play.

Kopit accepted the commission and started research on thermonuclear weapons but quickly discarded the millionaire's scenario as unworkable.

He focused instead on his own inability to come to terms with the horrifying reality of nuclear weapons—thus, calling it an "autobiographical format."[26] Kopit conceived of a two-pronged detective story that set forth modern-day Faustian arguments for global annihilation (and survival) together with a personal exploration into his own creative and destructive impulses as a writer.

Consigned to a Connecticut nursing home three years before *End of the World* opened, Audrey was not available to argue the importance of previewing the apocalyptic play in a nonprofit regional theater where the financial stakes were lower and critical pressures minimal. The progress of *End of the World* from typewriter to Broadway production, staged by Hal Prince of *The Pajama Game* and *Damn Yankees* fame, was, in hindsight, ill-advised. When the play opened in Broadway's Music Box Theatre on May 6, 1984, after a four-week commercial tryout in Washington, DC, with Linda Hunt, the Oscar-winning actress from the film *The Year of Living Dangerously* in the role of "Audrey West," one critic pronounced the "over-explicated parable about mankind's universal capacity for evil" an aberration in the career of a talented writer.[27]

It is appropriate to give the accidental playwright, who studied engineering and captured the attention of a famous producer and a prestigious agent with a whacky play, a final word on his agent of two decades. When asked to write a tribute to his agent for publication in her memoir, Kopit joined with nine other notables to provide insight into the wise, witty, and enduring Audrey Wood.

Arthur Kopit chose to reflect upon the vast number of *paperweights*, a lifelong collection spread across the tabletops and desks of her office and home. Curious about the lure of these smooth, finely painted stones, he surmised that Audrey identified with them. "She, like these smooth stones, held things together," he wrote. "Did so without fuss. Did not crumble under pressure. She was what we knew we could always count on. She was *immutable*."[28]

10. Irish Fictions

But in order to survive this endless obstacle course, a playwright must try to write something of lasting value.[1]

By the 1978–1979 Broadway season, Audrey Wood for over forty years had taken great pride in spotting the true gifts of hitherto unknown playwrights. She had taken chances on the early writings of Tennessee Williams, Robert Anderson, Carson McCullers, William Inge, and Arthur Kopit. Waiting in the wings that season were *Faith Healer*, the sixth play by Irish playwright Brian Friel to be represented by Audrey in North America. *Wings* by Arthur Kopit, A *Meeting by the River* by Christopher Isherwood and Don Bachardy, *G. R. Point* by David Berry, and *Knockout* by Louis LaRusso were also set for production. In Audrey's estimation, the hypnotically appealing *Wings* and the popularly conventional *Knockout* took second and third place in the Broadway obstacle course to Friel's enduring *Faith Healer*.

AN IRISH SENSIBILITY

Twelve years earlier, Audrey represented Brian Friel for the American production of *Philadelphia, Here I Come!*, the story of a young working-class Irishman, frustrated by the relationship with his father and his drab village life, who decides to emigrate to an American city with a musical name. Friel's play opened in February of 1966, and, almost immediately, Audrey received a call from producer David Merrick, famously known for his publicity stunts to sell his shows. He had recently produced *Hello, Dolly!* and *Marat/Sade* (*The Persecution and Assassination of Jean-Paul Marat as Performed by the Inmates of the Asylum of Charenton under the Direction of the Marquis de Sade*) and had agreed to produce Friel's second play in America, *The Loves of Cass McGuire*, about a woman, returning home from self-imposed exile in America and finding herself exiled a second time by an imprisoning family and by her own delusions. Following on the heels of the bright success of *Philadelphia, Here I Come!*, American audiences were not comfortable with Friel's harsh depiction of the returning exile and her retreat from reality.[2]

Weeks before the Boston tryout, Audrey sent David Merrick the Dramatist Guild contracts that covered the production of her client's play. The night she attended the Boston opening, Merrick had still not returned the signed copies. Although she had talked by telephone with him on several occasions, she met the producer for the first time at a post-opening party at the Ritz-Carlton Hotel. Annoyed by Merrick's dismissal of protocol, Audrey was in a take-the-bull-by-the-horns mood. She looked up at the statuesque producer who towered over her and said, "David, now that you've actually produced the play, why don't you go up to your room and bring me the contracts—*signed*."[3] He disappeared and returned with a small envelope and handed it to her with a smile. Thereafter, Audrey was never certain whether he signed the contracts before or after the show opened in Boston.

Whatever happened at the Helen Hayes Theatre in New York, Audrey was confident that night in Boston that she had twice introduced the enduring Irish playwright to American audiences.

Described as a medium-sized man with a direct blue gaze and slight Northern-Irish lilt, Brian Friel, a graduate of St. Patrick's College, Ulster, exchanged his early plans to join the priesthood to work as a teacher in Derry, while writing short stories and plays for radio and the stage.[4] Noted for his interest in rural Irish life and history and his use of lyrical dialogue and poetic metaphor, he created a mythical town, Ballybeg (meaning small town) in County Donegal in Northern Ireland as his semi-fictional landscape peopled with working-class characters living out their self-deceptions, regrets, frustrations, betrayals, and disappointments. Gradually, his themes of dislocation and intimations of loss enlarged to examine the interaction between the Irish character and a variety of institutional failures, including family, class, government, and the Catholic Church. The playwright became known for taking the "spiritual pulse of the Irish people," and finding the dramatic form that rendered their condition one of "universal interest."[5] This was the kind of serious playwriting Audrey Wood applauded.

By 1962, encouraged by the reception of his short stories at the *New Yorker* magazine, Friel had become a full-time playwright. His early plays produced in Belfast and Dublin won the attention of stage director Tyrone Guthrie, who lived in County Monaghan and was known for his work at London's Old Vic and the Stratford (Ontario) Festival Theatre. Guthrie invited Friel to accompany him to his new repertory theater (the Guthrie Theater) in Minneapolis to increase his knowledge of stagecraft. Friel's experience at the Guthrie resulted in the humorous and sensitive coming-of-age story about a young Irishman, longing for a faraway city with an exotic name, who is conflicted about his decision to leave the drab village of his loneliness and frustrations. *Philadelphia, Here I Come!* was first produced in Dublin in 1964 and then in New York and London.

With plans underway for a Broadway production, Friel's London agent contacted Audrey Wood and she entered the Irishman's life as his North American representative and remained so for the next 15 years.

TRIUMPHS AND FAILURES

Critics celebrated the arrival of Friel's "funny, prickly, and affecting" play about a youth's projection of happiness and fulfillment in a new kind of Promised Land.[6] Despite the overwhelming reception of *Philadelphia, Here I Come!*, Brian Friel had little success on America's stages in the late 1960s and early 1970s with *The Loves of Cass McGuire*, *Lovers*, *Crystal and Fox*, *The Mundy Scheme*, and *The Freedom of the City*. The most politically engaged of the five, *The Freedom of the City*—about three civil rights marchers who stumble into the violent event, called "Bloody Sunday," in Londonderry, Northern Ireland—had productions at Chicago's Goodman Theatre and Washington's Kennedy Center and reached Broadway's Alvin Theatre in 1974 for a mere nine performances.

The potential for the success of Friel's plays was abbreviated by lukewarm-to-hostile reviews by New York critics. Despite excellent casts, which featured at different times Ruth Gordon, Art Carney, Jack Cassidy, Lenny Baker, and Kate Reid, critics faulted the playwright for predictable scenes and flawed craftsmanship.[7]

While Audrey waited patiently for Friel to repeat the popular success of *Philadelphia, Here I Come!*, she received a call from another London agent, Leah Salisbury, asking her to represent David Storey and his play *Home*, transferring from London's Royal Court Theatre to Broadway's Morosco Theatre. The 37-year-old Yorkshireman, a graduate of London's Slade School of Fine Art, used his working-class and professional rugby League experiences as background to his novels and plays about family and class conflicts in which sports metaphors served to depict the rage, savagery, and violence embedded in such civilized institutions as family, educational institutions, and professional sports. Audrey looked at Storey's plays as allegories of families and nations.[8]

New York producer Alexander H. Cohen, who was known in the 1960s for transferring London productions of *Beyond the Fringe* with Alan Bennett and Dudley Moore, *The Ages of Man* with John Gielgud, and Harold Pinter's *Homecoming* to Broadway, agreed to finance the transfer of Storey's *Home* from London's Royal Court Theatre to Broadway for a limited engagement. Audrey's job was uncomplicated. She did not have to search for a producer, director, or star-actors. Stage and film director Lindsay Anderson had been closely associated with the development of Storey's plays at the socially conscious Royal Court Theatre in Sloane Square and restaged the play for Broadway. Audrey had only to oversee the contracts for the writer whose play was arriving with its notable cast of British actors (John Gielgud, Ralph Richardson, Mona Washbourne, and Dandy Nichols) for a November opening in 1970.

Despite its fragmented dialogue, abrupt exchanges, silences, and non sequiturs, *Home* proved a star vehicle and a late triumph for the two knights of the British stage. It gradually emerges in the storyline that Harry and Jack (first names only) are on the grounds of a mental hospital where, lodged deep within their gentlemanly understatements, jokes, and card games, lie despair and unstated reasons for their incarceration. The second act introduces other patients who become the means of their redemption. Storey's play further addresses the state of the British nation during which ironic symbolism (the mental institution) is confirmed by a closing eulogy on the achievement of "this little island."

New York critics declared *Home* "vastly original," "strange and extraordinary" in its "quiet vaudeville." They compared Storey to Samuel Beckett and Harold Pinter and one critic summarized the play as written in an elliptical style wherein the characters touch on the weather, on their youth, on their marriages, and on the "disintegration" of the world around them.[9] Audrey basked in the kudos for the flawless production and the sheer perfection of the acting.

With 110 performances in its limited run, *Home* set the stage for the favorable New York reception of David Storey's plays for the next three years. In *The Changing Room*, a provincial Rugby team engages in locker-room banter and offstage efforts to beat the opposing team. Storey crafts the situation into an allegory of national character, frustration, humiliation, and longing for personal triumph over a rugby opponent where, unlike in the game of life, the rules are clearly defined.

The Changing Room premiered in the United States at the Long Wharf Theatre in New Haven in December of 1972. The splendid reviews ("finest new play seen on the North American continent this season") enticed Audrey to seek out producers interested in transferring the play to Broadway.[10] With 22 men in the cast, producers hesitated to step forward and Audrey puzzled over the matter, but not for long. She firmly believed that agents often had to do the work of producers. Her to-do list, as she explained to Lewis Funke, included coming up with directors' names, submitting scripts to directors and leading actors, and shouldering the ultimate responsibility for bringing in investors' money.[11]

Even though Charles Bowden, who had produced *The Night of the Iguana* and *Slapstick Tragedy*, expressed interest in *The Changing Room*, she was aware that he did not represent the total monies needed for a New York production. She decided to introduce Bowden to two women who had expressed interest in producing. In Audrey's view, Lee Reynolds and Isobel Robins represented the additional monies to capitalize the New York run of Storey's play. She invited the three to her office and later described the meeting as "weaving a beautiful piece of golden cord together." The outcome on stage was a critical success ("stunning work," "formidable accomplishment") and a New York Drama Critics' Circle Award for best new play of the season.[12]

Storey's third play in America, the class-conscious *The Contractor,* introduced to Manhattan's Chelsea Theater Center a gang of laborers engaged in putting up, then taking down a wedding tent. During their onstage labors, the significance of working and the triviality of the work are mirrored in the constant construction and deconstruction of the temporary shelter for the privileged wedding guests.

David Storey recalled his "redoubtable" agent at breakfast in the Savoy Hotel where she was staying during a trip in 1967 to see the London premiere of Tennessee Williams's *The Two-Character Play* (later *Out Cry*). As she talked with her new client, she continuously smoothed the linen tablecloth with the side of her hand, creating the impression of someone with "a forceful and likeable nature."[13] Just as she smoothed the wrinkles in the tablecloth, she gave the impression that she was also smoothing away the playwright's anxieties over his forthcoming Broadway debut.

Despite the modest-to-dismal track record of Brian Friel's four plays on regional and New York stages, Audrey persevered in her representation of the Irish writer with, as Friel described, "unusual probity and unswerving loyalty."[14] *Faith Healer* struck a deeply personal chord with Audrey.

She was fascinated by the play's experimental form (four monologues) and moved by the emotional examination of the artist's (read "healer's") struggle with his calling. Each of Friel's three characters has a separate scene written as a long monologue: the itinerant faith healer travels from village to village working minor miracles on the physically ill; his wife travels with him in their derelict van; and his enduring manager arranges appearances in run-down churches and ill-kept town halls for small donations. The three scenes are followed by a fourth in which the healer returns to reflect upon his profession, his unrewarding travels, and his anticipation of a violent death.

Nevertheless, it was more than the unusual weaving of monologues to tell the end-story of the faith healer and his acolytes that captivated Friel's American agent. When she first read his script, Audrey admired the play about the healer (substitute artist or writer) and the periodic loss of his ability to practice his craft. Nevertheless, she knew that finding a Broadway producer for a quartet of monologues, along with a star-quality actor for the central role of the healer, would prove a daunting task. Although she had launched a star-search many times since Bill Liebling's death almost ten years earlier, she still felt his loss when she was required to undertake the job that he had accomplished time after time for many Broadway casts and now-famous actors, including Marlon Brando, Eli Wallach, Maureen Stapleton, Paul Newman, and Julie Harris.

Audrey squared her shoulders to put aside memories of her "Liebling" as she opened her rolodex to "producers" and then to "star-actors." Knowing that in her business nothing ever happened according to plan, she was not surprised when she found a star before she found a willing producer. She was just beginning to show Friel's script to producers when she read in *Variety* that the British stage and film actor James Mason of *The Desert Fox: The Story* of *Rommel* and *North by Northwest* was in New York where it was reported that he wanted to appear in a play. Audrey grasped at what she considered a brilliant piece of casting if the British actor could be persuaded to play the faith healer. Unknown to Audrey at the time, Mason was married to actress Clarissa Kaye, who had worked extensively on stage in her native Australia.

She called the actor at his hotel and asked if he would have time to read a script by Brian Friel. Once the Masons read the script, they offered to play the faith healer and his wife. Having solved two problems, Audrey was left with one more hurdle—the producer. She turned to Morton Gottlieb whose recent productions were *Sleuth*, *Same Time Next Year*, and *Tribute*. He was known for his interest in offbeat plays, such as *We Bombed in New*

Haven and *The Killing of Sister George* by Audrey's client Frank Marcus. Moreover, Audrey had enlisted Gottlieb to produce Friel's *Lovers* with Art Carney at the Vivian Beaumont Theatre, Lincoln Center, *Crystal and Fox* at the Mark Taper Forum Theatre in Los Angeles, and the unsuccessful *The Mundy Scheme* for Broadway. Audrey now mulled over the many questions, ranging from would Gottlieb take on another unconventional play, and, would he be interested in raising money for a show with questionable appeal as popular entertainment?[15]

Audrey presented Gottlieb with a package deal (Friel's play and the Masons). He agreed to produce and proceeded to hire José Quintero. Although the director had walked away from *The Square Root of Wonderful*, he had a long history of success with plays by another writer of Irish heritage, Eugene O'Neill. Ed Flanders was contracted for the part of the faith healer's manager. As always, the theater business proved unpredictable. Audrey went to the out-of-town opening in Boston and found audiences and reviewers responding favorably to the play and its performers. When she returned to her office, Gottlieb telephoned and calmly told her that Ed Flanders had decided to withdraw from the cast. As she listened, she thought of the quarter of a million dollars invested in the production and wondered why Gottlieb was so calm. The producer assured her that he would solve the problem—and he did. The talented Irish actor, Donal Donnelly, who had appeared as the second Gareth O'Donnell character in *Philadelphia, Here I Come!*, had just closed in a touring company production of *The Last of Mrs. Cheyney* with Deborah Kerr. Gottlieb enlisted the actor to fly to Boston and take the manager's role.

It was left to Audrey to tell the playwright of the cast change, but he was at the Abbey Theatre in Dublin attending rehearsals of a new play and a postal strike had spread to telephone workers and disrupted communications for anything other than emergency calls. Although Audrey and Friel agreed that their conversation qualified as an emergency, the telephone operator interrupted Audrey's report about the cast change with, "This is not an emergency!"[16] Audrey consoled herself with the thought that Friel would approve of his countryman in the manager's role and she would finish her explanation when he arrived to see the Broadway opening at the Longacre Theatre in early April.

Friel's play and the performances of the three actors received respectful reviews but failed to generate the excitement required to bring audiences into the theater for more than twenty performances. The *Times* reviewer called *Faith Healer* "an intriguing and sometimes powerful piece of writing," but found the monologues at times "stagnant and tedious." Praising James Mason's "remarkable eloquence," other critics were put off by the strange and unengaging play.[17] Although seemingly consigned to the ash-heap of rejected plays, Walter Kerr selected *Faith Healer* as one of the "Ten Best Plays of the Year," praising the play as a shared risk with a playwright "entirely willing to go for broke."[18]

Audrey did not dwell on the play's failure. She knew that James Mason, called by one critic "a necromancer of his craft," would continue to earn a substantial living in films.[19] Moreover, Brian Friel was already at work in Dublin on a production of his new play, *Aristocrats*, and was writing *Translations*. Only Audrey seemed melancholy over the failure of *The Faith Healer,* but faced with three more plays that required her immediate attention, she had little time to dwell on the "what ifs" of the failed production.

Audrey's attachment to *Faith Healer* was puzzling until the parallels became apparent between the healer's hit-or-miss profession, thinly disguised as a writer's doubts about the meaning and validity of his creative efforts, and her own nagging questions about her insights into what worked and what did not work in the commerce of Broadway. Audrey's intuitive responses to scripts (her flashing green lights) were as mysterious as the faith healer's sporadic powers and his ability to know in advance the success or failure of his laying on of hands. Audrey also sensed when a play, fraught with problems like Inge's *A Loss of Roses*, should be withheld from the public—if only temporarily. Nevertheless, she had no reservations about Friel's intention to craft a parable of an artist's repeated efforts, time and time again, to create remarkable outcomes with failures often outweighing the successes. It is likely that Audrey identified with the healer and his manager, both *enablers* like herself of miracles on the one hand and disappointments on the other.

When she spent years enabling the careers of playwrights and they turned against her, as had occurred with Tennessee Williams and William Inge, her disappointment was profound. Nevertheless, the morning following her dismissal by the writers, she resumed her responsibilities with renewed conviction (even "faith") in the powers of the present and future generations of playwrights. As Friel's faith healer attested about his chosen profession and the people who witnessed to it: "Yes; we were always balanced somewhere between the absurd and the momentous."[20] As an author's representative, Audrey had likewise teetered between the absurd efforts that closed on opening night and the momentous ones that went down in the history books.

Over a period of four months in the 1978–1979 season, Audrey marshaled six plays in various stages of readiness for Broadway openings. *Wings* arrived at the Lyceum in January of 1979, and settled in as a modest success. Isherwood and Bachardy's *A Meeting by the River* had a long development phase in California that did not include oversight by Audrey. She first saw a special performance of the play under the auspices of T. Edward Hambleton at the Edison Theatre on West Forty-seventh Street and was intrigued by the well-written drama, filled with provocative ideas and characters, which defied the popular musicals and romantic comedies that filled seats in Broadway's theaters. Audrey pronounced *A Meeting by the River* not an "easy play."[21]

Isherwood and Bachardy's play was the story of a young Englishman who chose to leave the material world behind and join a group of ascetic monks in India. His brother seeks him out to discover what precipitated the abrupt change in his sibling's life. Eventually, New York producers, Harry Rigby and Terry Allen Kramer, became interested in the piece following its California tryout. When the producers asked to option the play, International Creative Management's (formerly, The Ashley-Steiner-Famous Agency) West Coast office called their New York office and Audrey was requested to take over the negotiations on behalf of the authors.

As authors' agent for *A Meeting by the River*, Audrey attended the tryout production at the Clarence Brown Theatre in Knoxville, Tennessee, where the late film director Clarence Brown had endowed a new, fully equipped theater run by Ralph G. Allen—a professor in the theater department who shortly became an associate in Harry Rigby's New York office and author of *Sugar Babies*, a show based on the art of burlesque with popular entertainers Mickey Rooney and Ann Miller. The modern burlesque show became the hit of the 1979–1980 season while *A Meeting by the River* languished for lack of enhancement money, a theatrical term to explain money provided by a commercial producer to a nonprofit theater to underwrite costs for cast changes, added scenery, longer rehearsal period, and so on, in return for the rights to move the production.

When the production at the Clarence Brown Theatre with Siobhan McKenna and Simon Ward exceeded its budget, the producers faced several choices: close the play, or, cancel the Boston tryout and bring the show directly into New York's Palace Theatre for a "cold opening." (Broadway jargon for opening a show without an out-of-town tryout and ticket sales prior to opening.)

Audrey was aware that *A Meeting by the River* was not the kind of entertainment that usually filled the then $30 orchestra seats. Even though it was a well-written drama with a splendid cast, spectacular costumes and scenery, and a director, Albert Marre, who had traveled to India to witness ceremonies by neophyte monks received into their brotherhood, Audrey's experience told her that to arrive "cold" at the 1800-seat Palace Theatre, with no advance sales and without word-of-mouth, placed the show's future in the hands of a small group of critics "at a meeting not by the river but by Times Square."[22]

One week before *Faith Healer, A Meeting by the River* opened opposite Alan Ayckbourn's *Bedroom Farce* and closed after its opening performance to unenthusiastic reviews and indifferent audiences. Despite impeccable acting by Siobhan McKenna, Simon Ward, and Keith Baxter, critics found the work "static" and filled with "discursive nonsense."[23] Cowriter Don Bachardy acknowledged that the play with its monastic setting and Eastern religious rites did not fit into the Broadway theater of the day. Nevertheless, he admired Audrey Wood's "truthfulness and loyalty" in her dealings with the writers and their unusual material. Bachardy complimented the independence of their agent who was interested in the "substance and class" of the work more so than in its popularity for Broadway's marketplace. When asked about his impressions of the agent, Bachardy, a well-known visual artist, said that he wished he had painted the "distinctive-looking" woman in order to spend more time in conversation with her than rehearsals permitted.[24]

Faith Healer was still playing when David Berry's *G. R. Point* opened with Michael Moriarty as a soldier fighting in Vietnam during the 1969 build up of troop-levels. Set in a graves registration depot (the "G. R." of the title), Moriarty played a young man coming to terms with life in an ugly moment in American political history. Although Berry won Off Broadway's Obie award for Distinguished Playwriting and a Drama Desk Nomination for Best New American Play in 1977, *G. R. Point* had only a modest run.

With the clarity of hindsight, Audrey surmised that audiences were not interested in faith healers, monkish ways, or dramas reminding them of the far-off war in Vietnam. The next month, Louis LaRusso's *Knockout* with Danny Aiello proved that comedies about the boxing world had 154 times more stamina and punch with audiences than antiwar plays and Eastern mystics.

Audrey mused on her box-score for the 1978–1979 season: six productions, five closings, and a great deal of work that had come to naught other than the making of unhappy producers, out-of-work actors, discarded scenery, and reviews consigned to the ashcan of Broadway history.

"So what then does an agent do when she's had five plays by her clients close in one season?" Audrey asked herself. She found solace in the words of another pragmatic woman of the theater, the late Dorothy Fields, in the song "Pick Yourself Up."[25]

Audrey's new beginnings on the cusp of another decade involved Friel's *Translations*, reflections on her long career for her memoir, and a headlong plunge into new works by Ed Graczyk, A. E. Hotchner, David Berry, Joseph Pintauro, Sybille Pearson, and Ruth Wolff. An Irishman, a Texan, and a Chicago raconteur rounded out her client list.

At age 75, Audrey arrived at her office on the sixth floor at ICM every morning but her client list now was made up of a smaller number of new clients since she willingly handed over most newcomers to other ICM agents. Even though there were fewer and fewer plays produced on Broadway, there never seemed to be a shortage of hopeful playwrights whose names appeared in Audrey's appointment books.

A year earlier, Brian Friel sent Audrey a script of *Translations* that had premiered in Derry and subsequently toured the Irish countryside. Still smarting from her earlier mistakes as a result of not sufficiently using regional and Off Broadway theaters to prepare audiences for Friel's serious and complex plays, she looked to the Manhattan Theatre Club, an Off Broadway company under the artistic leadership of Lynne Meadow, who had earlier announced that the theater's goal was "to present well-crafted, bold challenging plays by major writers from America and around the world."[26]

Translations met the Manhattan Theatre Club's criteria. Set in 1833, as British authorities were in the process of mapping and renaming Ireland's old Gaelic towns, Friel's play engaged with the ending of traditions and cultural identity in the creation of a modern, divided Ireland. The storyline, played out an inexorable parallel with that of Romeo and Juliet, as English Lieutenant Yolland, engaged in the mapping of County Donegal, falls in love with the countryside and with a young woman named Maire, who speaks only Gaelic. Reviewers called the work "glorious," and wrote that Friel found the theme, the period of history, the language, and the passion to create a work that "resonates with poetic metaphor" and universal meaning. Clive Barnes praised the portrait of Ireland's loss of national identity and Friel's "Hibernian gift of transforming a foreign reality into native poetry."[27]

Friel's *Translations* opened on April 7, 1981, three weeks before Audrey Wood collapsed in front of the Royalton Hotel. It can be said that the agent made her exit from Broadway's obstacle course having, among her manifold accomplishments, introduced three enduring plays by Brian Friel to American audiences: *Philadelphia, Here I Come!*, *Faith Healer*, and *Translations*.

Nor was Audrey's unswerving loyalty and unusual probity forgotten by the playwright. Twenty-five years after her death, Brian Friel wrote of his American agent:

> She and I came together while she was still smarting from her loss of Tennessee Williams. And not long after she and I teamed up her beloved Bill became ill. But with characteristic fortitude she overcame those set-backs and never for a second did she allow them to interfere with her duty to her clients. I still miss her and her imperturbability (so unlikely in the emotion-charged atmosphere of theatre) and her quiet wisdom—and all those breakfasts we enjoyed together in the Algonquin where we met every morning when I'd be in New York.[28]

Part III Entrances and Exits 1971–1986

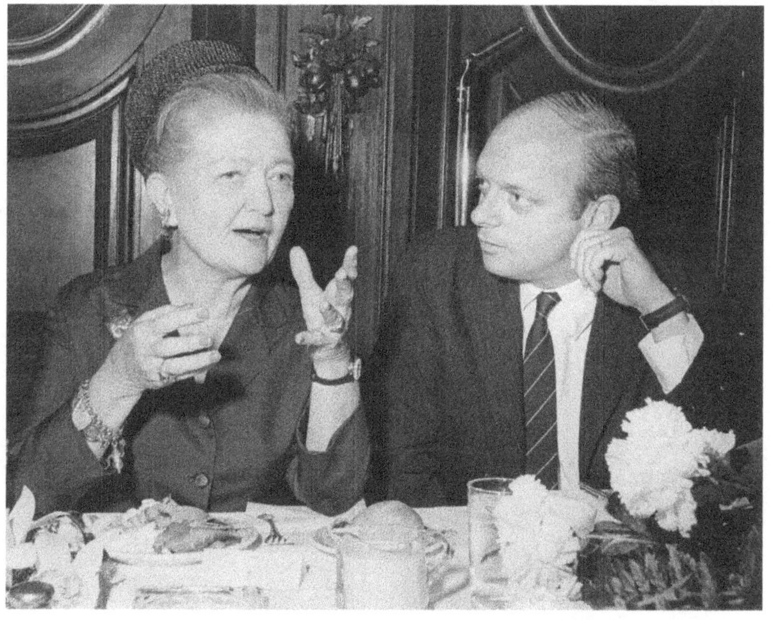

Audrey Wood with producer-director Harold Prince. (Photograph by Friedman-Abeles.) Billy Rose Theatre Division, The New York Public Library for the Performing Arts, Astor, Lenox, and Tilden Foundations.

11. Out-of-the-Ordinary

When I fall in love with a talent, I fall headlong.[1]

During Audrey Wood's last years at ICM, she was no longer actively engaged in ferreting out new clients. She continued to represent her longtime clients and nurtured several writers from the National Playwrights Conference in Waterford, Connecticut. As a senior executive at ICM, she advised the less experienced agents and took on special projects and a few unsolicited clients. Brian Friel and David Storey had arrived in her office by means of telephone calls from their respective London agents. By happenstance, she acquired a new client when her friend and ICM associate Kay Brown wanted a traveling companion to accompany her to the Dallas Theater Center. The trip resulted in an unlikely client by the name of Preston Jones.

OF TRILOGIES AND THINGS

A trilogy of plays was a new experience for the seasoned agent. Her first encounter with Preston Jones's plays was not the usual case of discovering a shining needle in the middle of a haystack of new submissions neatly stacked by her bedside for nightly reading. She fell headlong in love with *A Texas Trilogy* when she saw the first two parts onstage: *The Last Meeting of the Knights of the White Magnolia* and *Lu Ann Hampton Laverty Oberlander*. (*The Oldest Living Graduate* was unfinished at the time.)

Three years before Audrey arrived in Dallas, Paul Baker, nationally known educator and producing director of the regional theater, appointed actor Preston Jones as managing director of a small workshop space dedicated to new works. When Audrey asked the actor what inspired him to write plays, his answer was unadorned by philosophy or ideology or literary fervor. Baker had assigned him to read scripts by would-be playwrights and find one suitable for staging. "I didn't think any of 'em were any good," he told the New York agent in his distinct Western drawl, "so I decided to write a few myself." Later, when he played the stage manager in Thornton Wilder's *Our Town*, he was further inspired. "If I could write a play as beautiful as that," he said of Wilder's masterpiece, "I'd quit acting."[2]

When the curtain rose that evening on *The Last Meeting of the Knights of the White Magnolia*, Audrey's intuitive radar signaled "green." Anticipating that she had found a new client, Audrey mused on the potential problems inherent in finding a producer for a three-part evening of contemporary American plays set in a small West Texas town. The only trilogies that she knew had been written by Aeschylus and recently by Alan Ayckbourn, whose newly produced comedic trilogy, *The Norman Conquests*, was set in different areas of a house over one weekend.

As she contemplated the potential problems that she faced if she agreed to represent Preston Jones and his three plays, Audrey admitted to herself that she was captivated by the playwright's "authentic American voice."[3] During that first evening in Dallas, she went so far as to tell the amiable writer that, if he wished to have her represent him, she would send him a contract. Later, in private, she expressed astonishment that at her age she had taken on a trilogy![4]

Audrey was mindful that the emerging professional theaters across the country were replacing established tryout venues and contributing as "feeders" to the resurgence of serious plays on New York stages. Moreover, the resident theaters, located in cities with major newspapers and respected theater reviewers, also had thriving professional companies. In that season, Audrey had five clients whose plays had been first produced at the Guthrie Theater, Minneapolis; the Long Wharf Theatre, New Haven; Hartford Stage Company, Connecticut; the Mark Taper Forum Theatre, Los Angeles; and the New York Shakespeare Festival / Public Theater in lower Manhattan.

Even though tryout stages had changed, very little had altered for Broadway's leading play-agent. As always, new plays represented long months of preparation and planning, including finding the "right" producer and director, advising on the casting of leading players, and infinite hours of negotiations and contractual work.

When Audrey reflected upon the untested playwright with his multiple plays, she acknowledged that she had witnessed an original piece of playwriting on a regional canvas with the townspeople of Bradleyville, an alias for a West Texas town where Preston Jones had worked for the highway department while waiting to enroll in Baylor University. The playwright said of the real "Bradleyville" that the new highway had bypassed it—and the world was trying to do the same.[5]

Nevertheless, Audrey was realistic about Broadway's marketplace for a trilogy and for a group of plays that was not star driven. The townspeople introduced in one play reappeared in one or more of the successive plays. *The Last Meeting of the Knights of the White Magnolia* introduced the brethren of a moribund fraternal group on the evening their tired organization wholly disintegrates. *Lu Ann Hampton Laverty Oberlander* depicts the boredom and depressing life of a former high school cheerleader residing in her hometown. Lu Ann Hampton is a battered survivor of losses, involving two ex-husbands and an aging mother in a vegetative state. Finally, *The Oldest Living Graduate* takes up the twilight days of Colonel J. C. Kinkaid, a First World War veteran and the oldest living graduate of Mirabeau B. Lamar Military Academy. Confined to a wheelchair and dying, he is soon to be honored by his alma mater for an unremarkable life.

A year later Audrey learned that Paul Baker had decided to stage Jones's trilogy in a single evening. She made the trip to Dallas to attend the marathon that began at seven in the evening and ended at two the next morning. During her return flight to New York the next day, Audrey resolved to find a producer to stage the trilogy in a Broadway theater on three successive evenings.

At the outset, Audrey faced two challenges. She had not one but three plays to promote; moreover, the theater business had changed over the 40 years of her ascendant career. As she made a mental checklist of the obstacles she (and the playwright) faced, she started with the fact that in the mid-1970s, there were few knowledgeable producers still working in the commercial theater with the exception of the Shubert organization. She mourned the loss of the year-round entrepreneurs with proven track records who had retired, passed away, or who were no longer forces on Broadway. Uppermost in her mind were the absence of George Abbott, Max Gordon, Brock Pemberton, Antoinette Perry, Lawrence Langner, Theresa Helburn, Russel Crouse, Leland Hayward, Cheryl Crawford, and Kermit Bloomgarden.

As she sipped her martini on the return flight, she mused, "These days, one can count such full-time producers in New York on the fingers of both hands and have several fingers left."[6]

Many of the new producers, in Audrey's estimation, invested in Broadway shows with little or no theatrical background and were often in the business for reasons unrelated to creative considerations. Impromptu groups of moneyed investors operated on a show-by-show basis, seeking the dream "hit," and without a sustaining continuity or permanent interest in theater as a valuable art form. In Audrey's equation, the costs of producing a Broadway show and the weekly operating expenses were so enormous that ticket sales by any means had become paramount. Moreover, there was a lot of second-guessing by investors of what the *New York Times* reviewer was going to write and what audiences were going to like well-enough to buy tickets. Audrey's estimation of the new-breed of part-time producers was not flattering: "It's like they're playing the horses!"[7]

Audrey's dwindling list of full-time producers along with accelerating start-up costs accounted for her preference to begin a production in a regional or Off Broadway theater. Absent the tensions of cost-induced stresses, creative people found the freedom to function in a lesser make-or-break situation, and even gained the space to fail without too much sturm und drang.

Noted for successfully matching the three "P's" (playwright, play, and producer), Audrey remained in a quandary: "I had an author hitherto inexperienced. Pure, kind, and gentle. I wanted to find him a producer of the same ilk."[8] Her task became harder when she offended two producers.

ERODING TIME

Before she could examine her rolodex, word leaked out about the Texas trilogy and Alexander H. Cohen and Joseph Papp knocked on Audrey's office door at different times.

Even though Alexander Cohen had produced *Home* by Audrey's client, David Storey, she did not sense that he was the right producer for Jones's three plays about a small West Texas town, its characters and their foibles. She justified her rejection of Cohen based on the fact that Preston Jones, at the age of 40, was a "beginning" playwright. "He is untainted. He is kind. He is gentle," she explained to Lewis Funke. Moreover, she wanted a producer that would fit into his world and assist him.[9]

She addressed her concerns in forthright terms to Cohen and told him that, in her opinion, he was not the right producer for Jones's plays. Having made up his mind to produce the trilogy, he responded with an angry letter to the head of ICM in which he accused Audrey of being unethical in her efforts to keep him from optioning the rights to *A Texas Trilogy*.

Audrey found herself explaining her position to Marvin Josephson, her boss at ICM, who supported her decision. Meanwhile, as she tried to mollify one producer, she received a presigned contract from another. Joseph Papp, producing-director of the Public Theater in lower Manhattan, drew up a contract giving himself the right to produce *A Texas Trilogy*. Audrey was stunned by Papp's audacity not only to create a contract, but sign it and assume the deal was a fait accompli as well.

Audrey had had enough bullying. She returned the contracts to the Public Theater's impresario with a stern reminder that she acted for her client and no one else. As tempers cooled, Papp invited "Miss Wood" to a reading at the Public of *G. R. Point*, written by her client David Berry, but neglected to invite her to the post-performance conference in his office. Audrey ignored Papp's discourtesy and turned to her rolodex to continue her search for a producer.

As she reached the "W's," Robert Whitehead's name called out to her. He had taken on Carson McCullers' delicate play, *The Member of the Wedding*, and guided the inexperienced playwright through the pressure cooker of a Broadway production to a triumphant opening night. From her experience with the fragile novelist and her delicate play, Audrey knew that Whitehead had the patience and temperament to provide the meticulous care that she wanted for Preston Jones's first commercial production.

She called the producer who had heard about the plays through the Broadway rumor-mill. Betraying her desperation, Audrey pressured Whitehead to read the plays over the weekend and give her an answer on Monday. When Whitehead called Monday morning, Audrey heard the magic words: "I would like to produce the plays."[10]

As Audrey anticipated, Whitehead also brought Roger Stevens to the project. A tryout period was arranged at the Kennedy Center and A *Texas Trilogy* was officially launched with director Alan Schneider who had also staged plays by Audrey's clients Tennessee Williams, Maurice Valency, and Robert Anderson.

As auditions began, Audrey insisted that Preston Jones come to New York to keep "an eye on the casting." Probably because of its proximity to Audrey's residence across the street at the Royalton, he chose to stay at the "Algon-queen," as he pronounced the name of the hotel on Forty-fourth Street. When she met with the playwright, dressed in his usual Western garb (cowboy boots, Stetson hat, and zippered jacket), in the famous Algonquin foyer, he expressed disappointment that the notorious literary and theatrical luminaries were not engrossed in conversation at the Round Table.[11]

Although he did not find Dorothy Parker, Robert Benchley, Alexander Woollcott, George S. Kaufman, and Edna Ferber clustered around the Arthurian table, Jones went in search of other luminaries. Wandering his first night down Forty-fourth Street toward Broadway, he came to a neon sign with arrow pointing up a stairway to "Topless Girls." The next day over lunch, Audrey encouraged him to describe his nocturnal adventures. He was still incredulous that the women were not topless, but "plum naked!"[12]

Audrey got her first glimpse of the broad-shouldered Texan's stage fright the afternoon of the first rehearsal. To celebrate the true beginning of their theatrical journey, she invited her client to lunch where he proceeded to order one Bloody Mary after another and weave long tales about more nocturnal ramblings. At one point, he whispered, "You know, Miss Wood, I'm *scared*!"[13]

Audrey knew just how frightening a plunge into the Broadway theater could be for any playwright, especially for one with three plays and the New York critics looming like a modern sword of Damocles over his future. Nevertheless, Audrey was confident that he had been given the strengths of seasoned producers, a proven director, and an amazing cast with Diane Ladd as Lu Ann Hampton, and Fred Gwynne as Colonel J. C. Kinkaid.

For a short time at the Kennedy Center, it seemed that Preston Jones had a hit. The Washington newspapers and magazine critics raved about the newly discovered playwright from Texas, Alan Schneider's direction, and the remarkable cast. As she absorbed the rave reviews, the gossip columns, and the magazine articles with color photographs and bold captions ("Has Texas Spawned a New O'Neill?"), it was Audrey's turn to experience fear and dread.

Attempting to inject a note of caution into the playwright's celebratory mood, she warned that the enthusiastic reception in Washington did not mean that the same would occur in New York. Audrey knew that it was hard for outsiders to appreciate the life-and-death power of the *New York Times* critic over the success or failure of a production. In 1976, that critic was the same Clive Barnes who had dismissed William Inge as "a writer of soap operas." Audrey sensed the handwriting on the wall. "If a critic from England could not understand Kansas," she mused, "how could one expect him to relate to West Texas?"[14]

The *Texas Trilogy* company did not have long to wait for a verdict. In September of 1976, the trilogy opened at the Broadhurst Theatre on three consecutive nights. Presented in rotating repertory, the trilogy of gentle, realistic tales of small-town life in the mythical Bradleyville was an artistic success, but not a commercial one. In three consecutive reviews, the *Times* critic battered the plays with muted praise, labeling Jones's dramatic method as "all texture and little substance."[15]

Despite the volume of newsprint, the playwright had the last word on the failure of his trilogy that held on for 63 performances. When asked by a reporter about his disappointment, he countered with, "Hell, we were the longest-running Texas Trilogy in history!"[16]

Audrey admired how the playwright dealt with his hurt and disappointment. He returned to the Dallas Theater Center and began writing another play. She always thought of the writer's experience of critical rejection and failure in terms of a rider thrown from his horse, who gets up, brushes himself off, and remounts to ride again. She believed that after a bruising experienced to the creative soul, when failure takes over a beloved project, the writer had to go back to work. Tennessee Williams had taught her as much after the failure of *Camino Real.* In her view, *work* was the best medicinal salve, not some of the anodynes used by others in the face of failure.

When Audrey received Preston Jones's *A Place on the Magdalena Flats* and *Santa Fe Sunshine,* she liked the warmth and humor of the plays, found them interesting for regional audiences, but she did not encourage commercial productions. Jones accepted her decisions and followed her suggestion to sell the amateur rights to Dramatists Play Service.

Based on her experience with William Inge, who had rejected her advice to close *A Loss of Roses* before it reached Broadway, she was grateful that, despite his disappointment, Preston Jones listened to his agent who had learned from experience that often to plod stubbornly ahead was merely to postpone the inevitable.

Audrey continued to represent Preston Jones in other assignments: the development of a screenplay based on *A Texas Trilogy,* an article by the playwright depicting memories of Thanksgiving in Texas for the OP-ED page of the *New York Times,* and *Remember,* a new play based on the Irving Berlin ballad. Audrey remained hopeful that *Remember*—the story of an actor, a member of a second-rate touring company, who returns to the small town where he grew up and encounters the woman with whom he was once in love—would prove commercial. She pledged that once she found the right leading man and made a marriage between the play and a producer, she would reintroduce Preston Jones to Broadway.

Audrey was monitoring five productions when she received word of another closing that shook her world. On a warm September day in 1979, she learned that Preston Jones, rehearsing the part of the Duke of Norfolk in A *Man for All Seasons,* had been found unconscious and rushed to a Dallas hospital where he was diagnosed with bleeding ulcers and had immediate surgery. By the middle of the week he seemed to be recovering.

Audrey telephoned over the weekend, and, from his hospital bed, he told her that he was "fine" and seemed his normal, upbeat self. Two days later, he was dead of massive complications following surgery.

Audrey traveled to Dallas where she attended the memorial service during which company members of the Dallas Theater Center read from Jones's favorite authors, ending with the final lines from Sir Philip Sidney's encomium to the fallen Brutus in *Julius Caesar*, "Get Hence, Foul Grief":

> His life was gentle, and the elements
> So mix'd in him that Nature might stand up
> And say to all the world, "This was a man!"

Despite the playwright's death, NBC television proceeded with a two-hour live broadcast of the third part of Jones's trilogy from the stage of Southern Methodist University's main theater with a cast of notables, including Henry Fonda, Cloris Leachman, George Grizzard, and John Lithgow. Director Jack Hofsiss, who had earlier staged *The Elephant Man* on Broadway, now turned his hand to the television version of the trilogy. Audrey was invited, as NBC's guest, to witness the telecast of *The Oldest Living Graduate* on April 7, 1980. She arrived at the theater some 48 hours before the taping and was greeted by the cast of friends whom she had known either as Liebling's clients, waiting patiently in the outer office at 551 Fifth Avenue, or, as her own clients from her MCA days.

NBC launched the live telecast as a major programming event with full-page advertisements in national newspapers. By nine the theater was full; the glowing red lights on the TV cameras turned to green; and the house lights dimmed. Actress Jane Fonda's voice was heard introducing the play from the control booth. That evening, *The Oldest Living Graduate* appeared in millions of American homes.

A last-minute decision was made to honor Preston Jones with an afterpiece of segments taken from an earlier documentary produced by a local public television station. When the play ended, the documentary appeared on a vast television screen positioned above the proscenium. Audrey's heart ached as she looked at the large image of her late friend, smiling, puffing on his pipe, and bursting with enthusiasm as he responded to the interviewer's questions.

Earlier during that weekend in April, Audrey visited Jones's grave at the invitation of his widow. Observing the beautiful surroundings of the small cemetery, Audrey remarked upon an unusual birdhouse hanging above the headstone of a nearby grave. It contained cigarettes and other tokens left there by a gypsy family for their ancestral ghosts. Audrey was cheered by the thought that Preston Jones would have been amused by the ancient custom and by the unstated affinity between actors and gypsies.[17]

"IT'S AN ART"

While *A Texas Trilogy* was a rare undertaking for Audrey Wood, Studs Terkel, with microphone and tape recorder as his creative tools, was a most unusual client. A raconteur, radio interviewer, and published author of interviews with the ordinary and the celebrated, Terkel had written scripts for WGN radio in Chicago, and by 1950, he had become the star and host of the NBC television show "Studs' Place." Terkel and actors improvised the popular half-hour weekly show. Two years later, with McCarthyism in full flower, NBC canceled the nationally syndicated show because its creator and chief showman had a habit of signing petitions in support of left-wing causes. Like many artists caught up in the Red scare, Terkel turned to the theater and worked as an actor. He was soon hired by Chicago-based WFMT radio where he broadcast a daily hour of music, commentary, and interviews for the next 45 years with a diverse roster of guests that included Oliver Sacks, Aaron Copland, Bob Dylan, Toni Morrison, Gloria Steinem, and John Kenneth Galbraith.

Terkel was thrust into a literary career when the publisher and editor of Pantheon Books, who was looking for a writer to create the American equivalent of Jan Myrdal's *Report from a Chinese Village*, a collection of interviews that shed light on the lives of ordinary Chinese citizens living under Mao Zedong's regime, enlisted Terkel to create a uniquely American "report." With the assistance of a tape recorder, he encouraged ordinary Americans to talk about their hopes and dreams, their daily working lives, and their troubles in the hard times of the Depression years. Terkel effectively transformed his searching interviews into a serious genre and recorded on cassettes and reels the oral histories of ordinary Americans. Later, he published these interviews under such titles as *Hard Times: An Oral History of the Great Depression* and *Working: People Talk About What They Do All Day—And How they Feel About What They Do.*

When she first met Studs Terkel, Audrey was intrigued by his Chicago accent and tough-guy demeanor enhanced by his red-and-white checkered shirt and well-chewed cigar. He was a study in contrast to the sartorially impeccable Bill Liebling with high-collar white shirts and fashionable pinstriped ties. Terkel's tape recorder was also a phenomenon on Audrey's script-laden desk as well as his excited exhortations, "Just listen to this, Audrey!"

Audrey had appeared to the elfin creator of oral histories during the tryout of *The Glass Menagerie* in Chicago. Terkel remembered seeing the small woman in the pillbox hat in the audience and thought she looked like Louise Closser Hale, playwright and actress who played dowager mothers and high-toned society types. He later discovered that the "brisk lady, precise, and gentle" was the famous literary agent to whom he would send his first play, *Amazing Grace*, thereby establishing a friendship with both Audrey and Bill Liebling.[18]

While in residence at the MacDowell Colony, Terkel wrote his play with its theme of revelation attributed to the hymn. *Amazing Grace* was about an earthy woman (a variation of his mother) who ran a hotel for blue-collar workers. Actress and wife of the late Kurt Weill, Lotte Lenya, whom Terkel had interviewed, told Audrey about his play and the agent invited him to send the script to her. Audrey liked the play, but advised in her brusque way: "It needs work, dear, but the main thing is to get it on a stage."[19]

Terkel soon learned that the no-nonsense agent had an abrupt, but not unkind, telephone demeanor that rarely departed from business. He recalled the style and substance of one conversation with Audrey, saying, "'How are you, dear? Yes, dear, and we're meeting at two sharp, you be there, right?' Boom. That's it. No good-byes."[20]

Audrey attended to the business of finding a stage for *Amazing Grace* and arranged a production at the University of Michigan, Ann Arbor, which in 1967 sponsored a professional theater company. Nevertheless, the earthy woman in *Amazing Grace*, based on Terkel's volatile and impetuous mother, who had emigrated from Bialystok and managed a hotel for workers on the North Side of Chicago, was seriously miscast. The elegant actress, Cathleen Nesbitt, appeared in the leading role intended for Maureen Stapleton. *Variety* blistered the show and Terkel acknowledged that his play had not been good enough. Audrey stepped forward with her well-used prescription for disappointed playwrights: "Well, dear, we'll try again."[21]

Ten years passed before composer Stephen Schwartz approached Terkel with a proposal to adapt *Working* for the musical stage. Schwartz had written music and lyrics for *Godspell* with Michael Tebelak and for *Pippin* with Roger O. Hirson, both Broadway hits, and wanted to create a show over which he had complete creative control. Terkel understood at the start of the project that *Working* would be Schwartz's show and had no quarrel with the arrangement until later.

The composer had a plan for adapting Terkel's "conversations" for the stage, but, as director, proved unable to simplify the staging for a musical book about ordinary, everyday people, going about their jobs, and talking to the audience in dialogue and song about their lives as waitresses, truck drivers, steelworkers, and so on. Moreover, the show's producers were the new breed who had come into show business from investment backgrounds on Wall Street where they had made a great deal of money and financed shows with little understanding of the craft and perils of the commercial theater.

Terkel admitted that it was not an easy job to make the workers' conversations into a Broadway show even with an outstanding cast and a talented group of young songwriters and lyricists that included not only Schwartz but Mary Rodgers, James Taylor, Susan Birkenhead, Micki Grant, and Craig Carnelia as well. The workers' stories offered none of the usual musical-comedy glitter, no romance (boy meets girl), and no chorus lines. They were straight-forward narratives taken from the workers' mundane lives (the switchboard operator, the supermarket checker, the gas meter reader, the interstate trucker, and the bus driver's wife) with emphasis on their struggles to find meaning in their working lives.

On stage in musical numbers, Terkel's anonymous workers who keep "our country going," became clichés (what one critic called "dramatic fictions"), rather than *real* people straining to define the part of their lives that frustrated or disappointed them. One reviewer faulted the show's "inflated and banal" words and lyrics that stood in sharp contrast to Terkel's "devastating" record of working lives.[22]

A few years after the show closed, Studs Terkel remarked from the vantage point of hindsight that "perhaps the original mistake was that *Working* shouldn't have been a musical at all."[23] At the time of the Chicago tryout at the Goodman Theatre, Terkel felt that the show was overproduced. As he and Audrey watched the tryout performances, they both felt that something was basically wrong, but audiences seemed to like the show and they withheld their reservations. As the show moved into Broadway's Forty-Sixth Street Theatre, they had a revelatory experience that occurred too late to affect the success of the show.

For one matinee only, Schwartz staged an abbreviated version of *Working* for a theater-party. These parties have become an important Broadway ritual. If the groups (usually women) like the show, they buy whole performances for their charities, church groups, sisterhoods, and other organizations that use theatrical benefits to raise money. The abbreviated version of *Working* was presented with Steven Schwartz talking and performing the score with three singers from the cast. Terkel observed that "the theater-party ladies loved it, just that way, simple, and on a bare stage." Nevertheless, it was too late to discard the scenery, the dance numbers, the technology—everything that made the show glitzy and overproduced. Terkel concluded that Schwartz was in love with Broadway and its technology.[24]

Audrey was likewise astounded by the unsuitable approach to Terkel's material. Schwartz had failed to find a workable form for the fantasies, boredoms, and pleasures of "real" working-class people who were not prone to gypsy numbers with trays or musical skits that diffused true emotion into stage clichés. Faced with a losing battle and acknowledging that Audrey had done everything she could on behalf of her author, Terkel advised her to go to her house in Westport for the weekend.

On opening night, Terkel found that *Working* was subjected to the Broadway cliché: "audiences loved it, critics hated it." For 25 performances, audiences gave standing ovations, but the critical reception was too hostile to overcome.

Throughout the posting of closing notices, Audrey remained by her author's side. Observing her professionalism, Terkel developed an increasing appreciation for the toughness of the small woman in the pillbox hat. He called Audrey "a little piece of leather," not easily scuffed or scarred.[25]

When Terkel learned that Audrey was writing her memoir, he was jubilant. "Great idea! Long overdue!" he announced with enthusiasm and insisted, "But you mustn't write about *me*. You've got to let *me* talk about you."[26] Three years after *Working* closed, the Pulitzer Prize winning author of "*The Good War": An Oral History of World War II* created one of the last portraits of Audrey Wood.

In a reversal of his process perfected over 20 years of interviewing and listening to others talk, Terkel spoke into a microphone to tape, unedited, an interview with himself on the subject of Audrey Wood. He began with his first sighting of the diminutive agent in the pillbox hat during the opening-night of *The Glass Menagerie* in Chicago, remarked upon the hermetic world of the theater where she and Bill Liebling resided for over four decades (he called theirs a "Thoreauvian" world), and provided examples of Audrey's indomitable personality that persisted through the hard and the rough of the theater business.[27]

Terkel closed his self-interview with a glimpse into his agent's endearing (and enduring) toughness on behalf of her clients for the 42 years of her unparalleled career. In moments of stress, the remarkable Audrey Wood would reach out and take her client's arm to assure him of their mutual survival. "It's okay, dear boy," she would say, "we'll survive this. Don't worry."[28]

12. Guardian Angel

I've always tried to work with writers whose quality of work I admire.[1]

For the last decade of Audrey Wood's professional life, she experienced the usual highs and lows of the business. However, her deep distress over the loss of Liebling and her rejection by longtime clients William Inge and Tennessee Williams created emotional and physical stresses that finally contributed to the end of her career in a way unanticipated by all who knew her.

Inge's dismissal of his agent was a low-key affair in contrast to the murderous rage directed at her by Tennessee Williams in a backstage dressing room at Chicago's Ivanhoe Theatre.

A COMPLEX LADY

Throughout the period of failed plays in the late 1960s, Audrey persevered in her representation of Inge and Williams, even though they rejected her counsel to withhold from critical scrutiny *Where's Daddy?* and *The Two-Character Play* for further revisions on the texts. With the first failure of *The Milk Train Doesn't Stop Here Anymore*, Audrey could no longer ignore Williams's hostility, distrust of her management, and resentment of her strong-willed representation. She hastened to persuade the playwright of her good intentions as his representative and friend. Nevertheless, she reiterated her rights as his agent:

> I have the right to advise you when in my opinion I think you may be making a wrong decision about your work. You, of course, have the right to make any final decision and whatever it is, I must follow your instructions. During these last years you have made most of the major decisions and even when I have not agreed with you, I have followed your lead. Surely, you must acknowledge this to be the truth.

Reassuring him of her loyalty, Audrey ended with, "My job has been to carry your work like a banner throughout the world and this I have done and continue to do with gusto and enthusiasm."[2] A truce was not to be.

In the early 1960s, two Broadway productions of *The Milk Train Doesn't Stop Here Anymore* set off seismic quakes in Audrey's relationship the playwright. The earlier version was produced on Broadway with Hermione Baddeley as the cancer-stricken Flora Goforth. A newspaper strike prevented the tepid reviews ("one of Tennessee Williams' lesser plays") from reaching the theatergoing public and the show lasted 69 performances.[3]

Williams reshaped the script for a second production, giving it a kabuki framework, with two actors as stagehands commenting on the play's action. At the time, David Merrick, determined to produce a play by Tennessee Williams, viewed *The Milk Train Doesn't Stop Here Anymore* as an opportunity to corner the market on the playwright's work. When the revised script, staged in the out-of-the-way Barter Theatre in Abingdon, Virginia, became endangered for lack of funds to hire New York actors, Audrey asked Merrick to give the theater a subsidy and the producer gave her a signed check with no amount filled in—a first for the agent.

At the Barter, Claire Luce proved an admirable Flora Goforth, but the playwright was determined that Tallulah Bankhead, creator of Regina in *The Little Foxes* and Sabina in *The Skin of Our Teeth*, would star in the New York production of *The Milk Train Doesn't Stop Here Anymore*, directed by Tony Richardson, the notable British stage and film director, who had staged Brecht's *The Resistible Rise of Arturo Ui* for David Merrick.

Audrey recalled the first time Tallulah telephoned to invite her to her apartment to discuss the role. She heard the familiar rasping voice, "It's on Fifty-seventh Street, darling. It's a two-way street. The story of my life."[4]

The first reading of *The Milk Train Doesn't Stop Here Anymore* took place in Tallulah's apartment, overstuffed with self-portraits and mementoes. Audrey observed Tallulah sitting on the sofa beneath her famous portrait, painted years earlier by Augustus John, and recalled the contrasting images: "On the wall, a radiant young woman of the twenties, and, seated beneath it, the fragile, aging beauty, four decades—and many experiences—older."[5]

As they prepared to read a play about the imminence of death, Audrey was moved by the irony of the tableau. Seated before them was the actress, herself in fragile health, with two fingers of her right hand holding the ubiquitous cigarette permanently scarred by burns below the scarlet-lacquered nails.[6]

Within 12 months of the first production, *The Milk Train Doesn't Stop Here Anymore* began its second journey to Broadway with a star in fragile health, inadequate to the task with neither energy nor luster, and a playwright unnerved by an absent director. (Returning from a Christmas visit with his family in London, Tony Richardson was delayed eight hours on a runway at Heathrow.) All the elements—inadequate star, director temporarily grounded on another continent, and an uncertain script—came together to acerbate the playwright's paranoia. More and more, Audrey found that she had become a convenient scapegoat for the playwright's anger and frustration.

During a run-through in mid-December, Tennessee Williams was seen pacing back and forth in front of the stage when Audrey quietly entered the theater and took a seat in the rear. Somehow aware of her presence, he continued to pace and was overheard mumbling, "There's a murderer in the house! There's a murderer in the house!"[7]

Based upon what occurred later, those witnessing the incident conjectured that Audrey either did not hear the writer's imputations, or, upon hearing them, she chose to ignore his mutterings as a reaction to a stressful situation.

The Milk Train Doesn't Stop Here Any More opened at the Brooks Atkinson Theatre on the first day of 1964. Tallulah Bankhead stepped forth on opening night in a wrinkled mask of makeup to face a coterie of fans. As Audrey described them, they were "a galaxy of boys of all ages, who'd come to have themselves a hoot of a good time." She admired Tallulah's bravery, but, when the actress came to her big scenes, she simply could not rise to them with bravura and eloquence.[8]

The "milk train" stopped three nights later—and so did Tallulah Bankhead's Broadway career.

Nevertheless, it was not the failures of *The Milk Train Doesn't Stop Here Any More* that captured Audrey's attention as much as her client's bizarre behavior in public places whenever she was present, and the fact that he was not writing with his usual discipline and fervor.

Audrey was most troubled by the loss of a free exchange of opinions between them. Within a year, she sent an urgent wire: "All artists have to lay their life on the line and you above all other playwrights have been faithful in your work and true to yourself. Don't be downcast there are other mountains to climb and I am ready to come along whenever you put out your hand."[9]

Nevertheless, no heartfelt pleas on Audrey's part could offset the hostile receptions of his short plays (*The Two-Character Play*, *Slapstick Tragedy*,

The Seven Descents of Myrtle, and *In the Bar of a Tokyo Hotel*) and her perceived role in their failures.

FALLEN ANGEL

Audrey remained on the defensive for the rest of the decade. In 1967, Williams probed her reasons for the temporary relocation to Sarasota and her participation in the Wesleyan University-Eugene O'Neill Memorial Theatre Foundation program for playwrights. George C. White founded the O'Neill Memorial Theater Center on 90 acres leased for $1 a year from the town of Waterford, Connecticut, to create a laboratory for a new generation of American playwrights. As part of a core program situated on acreage near O'Neill's boyhood home in New London, White inaugurated the National Playwrights Conference and the Eugene O'Neill Theatre to develop and stage plays by unproduced playwrights. Activities began at nearby Wesleyan University in Middletown, Connecticut, and White enlisted Audrey Wood as the first artist-in-residence to hold a seminar there and mentor four promising writers of her choosing. In the initial foursome were Ron Cowan, John Guare, Tom Oliver, and Ruth Wolff.[10]

Tennessee Williams read about the new program in the *New York Times* and challenged Audrey to explain her betrayal of her clients. In an effort to make clear that she had no intention of giving up her representation of her authors at the renamed Ashley-Steiner-Famous Agency (AFA), she assured him that the position will be part-time and will not interfere with her representation of her writers, "chiefly one named T. Williams."[11]

On a deeply personal note, Audrey also explained that her relocation to Sarasota ("not an easy move for me") was motivated by dire medical reports of Liebling's heart condition coupled with emphysema that made it impossible for him to walk a block free of pain. The couple had leased the Sarasota apartment in 1966 on Sands Point Road with an unlisted telephone number in Liebling's name. She assured the playwright that Liebling had already improved in the Florida sunshine and wished her to continue the present arrangement with the agency that allowed her to travel to New York or London or Rome—whenever Williams's work called for traveling.

> Out of long habit, Audrey ended with words of reassurance: My belief in your strength as a writer and my admiration for your writing remain as pure as when you and I found each other by grace of Molly Thacher Kazan in the now far-away thirties. The other side of the moon indeed![12]

Despite her efforts to reassure the playwright that the New York–Florida arrangement did not interfere with her representation of her clients, she grew increasingly concerned that Liebling's failing health would shortly require her full-time attention. She began quietly searching for a University appointment in a warm climate where she could house Liebling, establish a playwriting institute, and transition into retirement. Preparing for a change in 1965, she quietly negotiated the sale of her "Tennessee Williams-Audrey Wood" correspondence to the Humanities Research Center at the University of Texas, Austin, to be paid in five equal installments over five years.

While casting about for a compatible institution that would meet both her needs and Liebling's, she approached Stanford University's Speech and Drama Department with an outline of a proposal to develop a small group of gifted, unrecognized playwrights in a program exclusive to playwriting.[13] Stanford's response was not encouraging and the couple proceeded to rent the Sarasota apartment and relocate Liebling to the warmer Florida climate. Audrey continued to approach other institutions, namely, New College in Sarasota and the University of Arizona, Tucson, but negotiations faltered in each case on matters of start-up costs, teaching requirements, and faculty rank. Audrey disentangled herself from an offer from the University of Arizona's Department of Drama "to teach four courses as a Lecturer." She pointed out in a few terse words that there had been a misunderstanding. Moreover, she stressed that she could not practically sever her relationship with Ashley-Steiner-Famous within three months because she had contracts for ten productions in the next season, including a musical of *Breakfast at Tiffany's* based on Truman Capote's novella, *The Killing of Sister George, The Two-Character Play*, and *The Loves of Cass McGuire.*[14] Despite the failure of her negotiations, Audrey was awarded the honorary degree of Doctor of Humane Letters for her contributions to the American theater by Florida State University, Tallahassee, in April of 1970. She stood proudly in academic cap and gown to be recognized as Dr. Audrey Wood Liebling.

In the 1967–1968 season, George White's O'Neill Memorial Foundation-Wesleyan University playwriting program answered Audrey's interests but not Liebling's situation. The Lieblings continued their dual residencies in New York and Sarasota until the close of the decade.

Back in Manhattan at AFA, little had changed in Audrey's troubled relationship with Tennessee Williams. Against Audrey's advice, he revised *The Two-Character Play* for production in an Off Broadway theater and announced to the world that Audrey Wood never approved of his "masterpiece."[15] Moreover, she continued to be pummeled by Williams's angry outbursts and paranoiac moods expressed verbally and in writing. In one expression of her imagined offenses, he wrote: "please cogitate on this: you say that you hate me but I doubt that you want to see me destroyed. You're a complex little lady, quite easily offended and I don't doubt that I have often offended you. But this has occurred through my own confusions and complexities, never through any impulse to hurt or embarrass you."[16]

In London in 1967, *The Two-Character Play* was rejected by critics as "enigmas that litter the stage like pieces of an elaborate jigsaw."[17] Audrey was in attendance at the Hampstead Theatre Club where the playwright dissolved into a spell of self-pity and Audrey surprised herself by demanding that he pull himself together and get on with his life. She later recalled that the most ironic aspect of that dreadful evening was how it was later reversed in his mind and used against her.[18]

In July of 1971, Audrey was in Chicago for the last preview of *Out Cry*, the revised *Two-Character Play*, when the fatal collision occurred. George Keathley, by then manager of the Ivanhoe Theatre, suggested a summer revival with Eileen Herlie and Donald Madden. Even though the playwright's behavior had grown increasingly erratic, Audrey appeared unaware that her client had resumed a round-the-clock dependence on drugs and she was, therefore, unprepared for the vicious encounter that followed the final preview of *Out Cry*.

When she arrived at the theater, Audrey found a cross section of Chicago theatergoers who had come to witness a preview performance of a new play by a major playwright. Mingling with the audience, Audrey observed that, although familiar with *The Glass Menagerie*, *A Streetcar Named Desire*, and *The Rose Tattoo*, they had no idea that the playwright was reentering the theatrical arena with highly subjective material drawn from elements of his childhood in which a brother and sister, trapped in a play-within-a-play, act out their confused devotion.[19] In his dismissal of the piece, one Chicago critic cited the play's reference to "a ponderously symbolic un-drama."[20]

Two years earlier, Audrey had come to the playwright's defense when she found a full-page advertisement in the *New York Times*, originally written by Stefan Kanfer for *Life* magazine, announcing the "early demise" of Tennessee Williams.[21] To ensure that her protest would be read by theater professionals, she wrote a letter to *Variety* wherein she quoted Lillian Hellman's appraisal, two months earlier, of Williams's legacy to the American theater when he was awarded the National Academy of Arts and Letters highest honor—the Gold Medal for Drama. Audrey closed her defense with, "Remembering his consistent contribution to the contemporary theatre, it is appalling to find a newspaper of the stature of the *New York Times* accepting an advertisement of the sort it did."[22]

In the backstage maelstrom in Chicago, Audrey's efforts to defend and shield the playwright from unjust criticism were ignored.

During the intermission for *Out Cry*, Audrey overheard accolades for the performers and serious discussion of the play's content. With confidence in the reception of Williams's memory play, she went backstage afterward and found the playwright in Eileen Herlie's dressing room talking with his longtime British friend, Lady Maria St. Just and Keathley. Audrey had been warned by friends about Maria St. Just's negative influence on the writer, but, thus far, had ignored the warnings.[23]

When he noticed his agent in the doorway, Williams spoke with quiet ferocity, saying, "And as for you, you have wished I was dead for the last ten years!" Audrey's first instinct was to strike him, but, the realization that he would replay the scene in a future play, stopped her. Instead, she made a quick exit, but heard Tennessee call after her, "That bitch! I'm glad I'm through with her."[24]

Eyewitnesses to the encounter later recorded their memories of the scene. George Keathley accepted responsibility for starting the fireworks by suggesting that a line of dialogue needed to be altered. The playwright's reaction was volcanic. "How dare you make such a suggestion to me," he said to the director who had initiated *Sweet Bird of Youth* in Miami. In Keathley's account, Audrey tried to calm the situation by saying in an unhurried, low-keyed voice, "Tenn, it may be a good idea—just listen to George for a moment."[25] Turning on his agent of 32 years, Williams shouted the fateful words and later blamed his outburst on Audrey's decade-long neglect of his career and their friendship.[26]

Audrey left the Ivanhoe Theatre with the harsh strains of the playwright's outcry ringing in her ears. As she had done in the past, she tried to block from her mind his incendiary words. When she awoke the next morning, she called a car and driver to take her to Milwaukee where the Wood family lived. Before visiting her relatives, she asked the driver to stop at the cemetery where her mother and father were buried. She was certain that her parents would want to congratulate their daughter for having, at last, *dared to be free*.[27]

When asked about the breakup in later years, her reply was nuanced: "I think he was not well. I think his recent plays had not gone well. You know the famous story Neil Simon is supposed to have said: 'If a play is a success, he doesn't need an agent and if the play fails, it's all the agent's fault.' "

Audrey added, "I honestly had no idea how deeply this would hurt me and I don't want to see him primarily because I'm still too deeply moved."[28]

The breakup between agent and playwright reverberated throughout Times Square. Audrey's longtime friend, James Laughlin, heard about the playwright's "defection" and offered condolences. "Surely, he knows all you have done for him," Laughlin wrote his friend, "and his wanting to hurt you in this way must be some complicated reaction in his very complicated mind, the result, perhaps, of some new stresses which have made him think he is getting even with those who write adversely about him these days by hurting the person who has been his best friend ... I just pray this will solve itself soon."[29]

The publisher had not known that Williams, once he returned to New York after the close of *Out Cry*, wrote to Audrey on Plaza Hotel stationery alluding to the final period placed on their relationship, and closed with, "I hope you will be as willing as I am to remember only the many good things about our working relationship and forget what is unpleasant and could only hurt us both."[30]

Williams changed his legal representation to Floria Laskey, then with Fitelson and Meyers, but Audrey took care to see that he remained a client of ICM. She arranged a meeting between Williams and agent Bill Barnes who represented his new client for the next seven years until he, too, was replaced.

Ten years after *Out Cry*, Tennessee Williams had the last word. At the publisher's invitation, he wrote a tribute to his agent of 32 years for inclusion in her memoir. In a lengthy note of praise, he wrote that, from the beginning, he had been a difficult client and referred to their parting as "the wearing out of a deep relationship in which, years later, no bitterness remained." He closed with,

> Audrey Wood's profession is one that has never been properly appreciated. Theatrical clients are often impossible people. No one understood them better than Audrey or knew so well that understanding was so essential to their existence.[31]

For a decade after their parting in Chicago, the revolving door of Audrey's office continued to turnout projects by David Storey, Brian Friel, Preston Jones, David Berry, Studs Terkel, Ruth Wolff, and James Costigan. *Love Among the Ruins*, Costigan's script, arrived on her desk for a second time in 1975, thus confirming her belief that "a great deal of theater history is made by *being there at the right moment, with the right people*."[32]

The early 1960s had not been the right moment for *Love Among the Ruins*, written for the Lunts. Alfred Lunt and Lynn Fontanne made their television debut in *The Magnificent Yankee* for the "Hallmark Hall of Fame," directed by George Schaefer. He discussed a new project for them with James Costigan, who came up with a period comedy for television about a grand Dame, a former Shakespearean actress involved in a breach-of-promise suit in the British courts, who seeks out a distinguished barrister to represent her.

The Lunts expressed interest and Costigan completed two drafts of *Love Among the Ruins*. Then, without explanation, the Lunts declined the project. Audrey thought it had something to do with the word *ruins,* which perhaps was unappealing to two celebrated people of advanced age.[33]

Costigan's script languished in Audrey's files for almost a decade. She tried various ways to secure a production for television but the pieces never came together to her satisfaction. One day in 1974, she was having lunch with a television producer and the conversation turned to *Love Among the Ruins* whereupon Audrey hastened to suggest Katharine Hepburn to play the leading lady.

Encouraged by her conversation, Audrey called the "formidable lady," saying, "Miss Hepburn, I have a script I'd like you to read for TV." She heard an abrupt response; "Miss Wood, I don't do TV."[34] Audrey gently reminded the actress that she had just appeared in the television versions of *The Glass Menagerie* and *A Delicate Balance.* Hepburn conceded the point and asked Audrey to send the script to her Eastside apartment.

After reading Costigan's script, Hepburn invited Audrey to tea and informed her that she liked the script but that "they" needed a *male* star. Audrey was amused that the actress had assumed the agent was oblivious to the script's casting needs. Hepburn proposed showing the script to her good friend, director George Cukor, who, in turn, proposed taking it to London to show to Sir Laurence Olivier.

Audrey thought they had lost the British knight when his London agent called to tell her that the actor was not interested. Then, Olivier's agent called a second time to say that the actor had been under the impression that he was declining a film, but if *Love Among the Ruins* was planned for television, he would reconsider. Even though the two stars were locked into the project, Audrey's work was still not done. *Billing* (whose name comes first in playbills, posters, etc.) became a possible deal breaker. Hepburn broke the impasse by proposing that she take top billing in the United States and Olivier in Great Britain. Thereafter, in Audrey's ironic view, "they would both divide up the rest of the world equally!"[35]

Ten years after Costigan wrote the script for the Lunts, the television production was spoken of as a "polished" production with a pair of "superb performances."[36] Hepburn and Olivier, incandescent in the ABC special, won Emmy Awards for Best Actress and Best Actor.

Audrey was resigned to the decades-long delay before Costigan's script appeared on American and British television. "Who knows how many plays have died, unproduced, because it was simply too difficult to put the right pieces together," she remarked.[37] Once again, Audrey's belief in the writer and the lasting value of his script prevailed.

Also, in the decade, Audrey discerned that actress Eva Le Gallienne—known for her acclaimed performances in plays by Ibsen, Chekhov, and Shakespeare, and for her roles as founding producing-director of the Civic Repertory Theatre and as cofounder of the American Repertory Theatre—was turning more and more to her for career advice. The actress's longtime agent, Jane Broder, was advanced in years and in ill-health. When novelist Barbara Wersba approached Le Gallienne to collaborate on an adaptation of *The Dream Watcher* for the stage, the actress asked Audrey Wood to represent her and the writer on *The Dream Watcher* project, Le Gallienne characterized Audrey as "wise, witty, tough, and kind."[38] Not having represented actors for many years, Audrey made an exception for Le Gallienne who was also a Connecticut neighbor.

Audrey had her ups and downs in her efforts to interest producers in bringing the flawed adaptation to the stage. Originally a best-selling juvenile novel, *The Dream Watcher* was the story of the 14-year-old Albert Scully, described as a lonely misfit who is befriended by a once-famous actress who assures him that all great people have been misunderstood by their peers. Le Gallienne was interested in finding a role that might serve, as her biographer put it, as a coda to her career.[39]

In 1973, when Audrey took on *The Dream Watcher*, she was at work representing plays by Robert Anderson, Arthur Kopit, David Storey, and Ruth Wolff. Producers and directors came and went on the *Dream Watcher* project, largely because of structural problems within Wersba's script. In August of 1975, the show was given a tryout at the White Barn in Westport, Connecticut, for three performances. Audrey attended each of the three nights. *Variety* called Le Gallienne's performance "flawless" while raising questions about the readiness of the script.

As it so happened, Audrey Wood was a far more active literary agent than Le Gallienne was accustomed to. With the future of *The Dream Watcher* caught between the playwright's reluctance to rewrite the play and the actress's decline of a salary offer from a potential producer, the theater gods continued to smile on both the agent and Le Gallienne. With *The Dream Watcher* on hold, Audrey proceeded to represent Le Gallienne as a triumphant Fanny Cavendish in George S. Kaufman's *The Royal Family*, under the direction of Ellis Rabb, first at the McCarter Theatre in Princeton, and then at the Kennedy Center, the Brooklyn Academy of Music, and on Broadway. Critical acclaim accompanied the show and Le Gallienne's performance along the way.

The Royal Family returned from its national tour in March of 1977. By September, Audrey was negotiating contracts for a New York production of *The Dream Watcher* to be produced by Burry Fredrick, who had produced the Kaufman play and now purchased the Wersba adaptation with plans to present the play at the Seattle Repertory Theatre and the Kennedy Center before its Broadway opening. Nevertheless, the theater gods failed to smile on the Seattle production. With the exception of Le Gallienne's "luminous" performance, critics panned the inferior play and the producers decided to end the run there.

Despite Le Gallienne's reputation for being difficult and demanding, Audrey represented the actress for various opportunities during 1978. Audrey developed the contract for Le Gallienne to tour with Ingrid Bergman in *Waters of the Moon*, but Bergman became ill and the tour was cancelled. Audrey also sent Le Gallienne a film script, called *Resurrection*, to star Ellen Burstyn who wanted Le Gallienne for the part of the grandmother. Without much ado, Audrey negotiated a contract for four weeks' work, costar billing, a substantial salary, and VIP accommodations at the Chateau Marmont in Los Angeles.

Although offers followed for roles in revivals at regional theaters along with television offers, Le Gallienne declined the offers until Audrey presented her with a role in Joanna Glass's new play, *To Grandmother's House We Go*. The play opened in 1980 at the Alley Theatre in Houston with raves for Le Gallienne's performance and proceeded to Broadway with the octogenarian actress praised by Walter Kerr: "So what else is new? Eva Le Gallienne is new."[40]

To Grandmother's House We Go closed on March 8, 1981. Thereafter, Le Gallienne explained to Audrey that she was tired, required dental work, and did not want to act for some time. Little did she know that her assertive agent would suffer a debilitating stroke in April and bring to an end the highly successful collaboration between the actress and the agent.[41]

In early 1981, Audrey was searching for the "right" director for Robert Anderson's *Free and Clear* under option to Roger L. Stevens for the Kennedy Center. Having become a believer in Off Broadway for untested playwrights, she was shepherding former O'Neill Center writers Sybille Pearson (*Sally and Marsha*) and Joseph Pintauro (*Snow Orchid*) into those venues. In the regional theaters, Ruth Wolff's *Sarah in America* was moving from Stratford, Connecticut, to the Kennedy Center; David Berry's *The Whales of August* was playing at Trinity Square Repertory in Providence; A. E. Hotchner's *Sweet Prince* had settled in at the Repertory Theatre of St. Louis; and Brian Friel had plays running in New York, Philadelphia, and Portland, Maine. In New York, auditions were beginning for *Nine* with Arthur Kopit's musical book, and, in mid-April, Audrey received the copyedited manuscript of her memoir for her corrections and approval. She made a note in her appointment book to return the manuscript to Doubleday on April 30.

Frequent visits to her optometrist and changes in her handwriting in her appointment book during March and April were the only indications to an outsider that Audrey was experiencing somatic difficulties. By mid-March, her cursive handwriting frequently becomes indecipherable. Names are unreadable, and, uncharacteristically, she makes frequent corrections, marking through entries. Her assistant prints in large block letters the street addresses where she has appointments away from the office. Moreover, Ruth Wolff remarked upon Audrey's frailty when her agent came to the Kennedy Center in February for the opening of *Sarah in America*. Helping Audrey across the street, the playwright remarked that Audrey seemed older than her 76 years.[42]

On Thursday, April 30, Audrey's day settled into a familiar routine. Impeccably dressed for business in suit and hat, she hailed a taxi to take her from her residence at the Royalton Hotel to the ICM building on West Fifty-seventh Street where she entered her office on the sixth floor around eleven. In the spacious corner suite, befitting a senior executive, posters of the plays she represented hung on the walls alongside framed awards won over the years by those same works. Bookshelves crowded with books and scripts took up another wall, a large desk with chair and footstool, a long sofa was covered with stacks of more scripts, and framed photographs of friends and clients appeared everywhere.

As she proceeded with the day's routines, she checked the dozens of telephone messages, putting aside those that needed her immediate attention, reviewed her appointment book, noting the day's and evening's appointments, and sorted through the business affairs that required her personal attention.

The previous Tuesday had been set aside for sessions with Max Wilk, author of books on show business, plays, and screenplays, who had become her "Boswell," as Audrey called him, to read through the 300-plus pages of copyedited manuscript of *Represented by Audrey Wood* delivered to her office by the publisher. She was determined to dot every "i" and cross every "t," as she did from long practice before affixing her name to legal documents and contracts. During the afternoon, Wilk escorted her to Doubleday's offices where, seated in a conference room, she responded to all of the red-ink queries and conferred with the editor about the schedule for the galley proofs to be returned to her in early June.

Wednesday was another typical day. It began with her usual morning office routines followed by lunch at La Côte Basque with producers interested in a revival of *Room Service*, an early dinner in the theater district, and a show to see for a second time. Friel's *Translations* had opened earlier in April, but Barnard Hughes, who had the key role of the rustic school master, had almost immediately left the cast to fulfill a film commitment and had returned to the show on April 25. After revisiting Friel's play, Audrey continued the evening at Sardi's with a business meeting that lasted until midnight. Producer and theater owner Lester Osterman, who won Tony Awards for *A Moon for the Misbegotten*, *The Shadow Box*, and *Da*, was at the table and recalled Audrey focusing the rambling discussion so that by the time the showmen left the table, they "were all operating on the same wavelength."[43]

Thursday began with a late morning appointment with Seymour Morgenstern, who controlled certain intellectual property rights for theater, film, and television. Lunch followed with friend and ICM legal executive, Morris Schrier, at the Harmonie Club on East Sixtieth Street. One of her last appointments for the day was with director-producer Joshua Logan who was interested in producing a revival of *Picnic*.

Audrey returned to the Royalton around nine that evening. Carrying a briefcase full of scripts, she stepped out of the taxi and collapsed onto the sidewalk. Hotel personnel and concerned passersby rushed to help her. She was carried to her suite, a doctor was called, and several hours later she was taken to Mount Sinai Hospital. The terrible incident and impossible verdict echoed throughout the theater district the next day and for weeks thereafter: Audrey Wood had suffered a massive cerebral hemorrhage and had lapsed into a coma.

POSTSCRIPT

During the four years Audrey lay comatose in the Carrolton Nursing Home in Fairfield, Connecticut, close friends dropped by to relay theater gossip and their views on the state of playwriting in her absence—all the while knowing the hopelessness of her condition. There was no flicker of understanding from the silent figure encased in a sarcophagus of sheets and blankets.

As the years passed, friends eventually gave up in despair and fewer made the trip to her bedside. Her death in late 1985 left friends, colleagues, and former clients with feelings of relief coupled with rage. Audrey Wood had been an impassioned supporter of the right-to-die issue and belonged to the Euthanasia Society. As Samuel G. Freedman said, "Her long demise in a Fairfield, Conn., nursing home was, for them, the bitterest of ironies."[44]

Four years before her death, she was the recipient in absentia of the Richard L. Coe Award in October 1981 at the Kennedy Center in recognition of her contributions to the theater. In 1983, with contributions from Audrey's friends, the Yale School of Drama established a scholarship for playwriting students in her name, and, the next year, an intimate stage in the Off Broadway Jack Lawrence Theatre at 359 West Forty-eighth Street was named the Audrey Wood Theatre.[45]

Audrey Violet Wood was 80 years old when she died on December 27, 1985. The obituaries that followed celebrated her as the preeminent playwright's agent and commented on "her air of quiet dignity and confidence" along with her legendary style and mode of speech sprinkled with "dears" and "darlings."

A memorial service was organized at the Shubert Theatre in the heart of the theater district on January 15, 1986. Not only was Audrey, the person and the quietly ferocious agent, remembered, but also the Broadway theater of her heyday. At the time when playwrights could make their careers and livelihoods on Broadway, Audrey was a force, shaping and delivering many of America's finest writers—Robert Anderson, Tennessee Williams, William Inge, Arthur Kopit, Carson McCullers, Murray Schisgal, and many others. Anderson, her client of 35 years, referred to her as "a condition of our life for so many years."[46]

Among the speakers were playwrights, actors, literary agents, and producers. She was called a "guardian agent" and a "divining rod for talent," spoken of as "an editor, sounding board, and surrogate mother," and fondly remembered for her disconcerting habit of hanging up the telephone without saying "Goodbye."[47]

There were memories that touched upon the painful rejections of longtime clients, most notably William Inge and Tennessee Williams. One speaker said that Williams's rejection of his agent was "a sad conclusion to one of the most fruitful relations in the modern American theater."[48]

Audrey's miniscule stature was mentioned by several in comments suggesting that this doyenne of agents should have been of Amazon-like size to match her contributions to the Broadway theater. Murray Schisgal of *Luv* fame, admitted that when he first met his agent, he was terrified. "Later, she would call every few weeks and ask me what I was doing. Imagine—an agent calling you!"[49]

Over the intervening years, others added to the legend of Audrey Wood. Screenwriter and novelist Daphne Athas described Audrey and Bill Liebling guiding her like bookends, one on each side of her as they crossed Fifth Avenue. The couple seemed like "two Lilliputian pilots, an absurdity against my abashed respect for them as reigning powers of the theater." A half century later, Athas still remembered how the power couple "grooved on the absurdity of the sight of themselves among the honks and rushing breezes of taxis."[50]

Few remember Audrey Wood today. Isobel Robins Konecky shared her memories of Audrey's "fierce but rare integrity"; George C. White spoke of her as "the pillar" of the O'Neill Center; David Berry—an undergraduate in that first class at Wesleyan University and later writer of *The Whales of August*—recalled that Audrey's clients were "set adrift, even bereft," by the loss of their "powerful, charismatic" agent. And, Ruth Wolff recalled Audrey's favorite gambit as she delivered good news to her client: "'Are you sitting down, darling?' The opposite of that was her expectation that her playwrights should take bad news standing up!" David Storey called her a "forceful and likeable nature," and Brian Friel praised her "quiet wisdom."[51]

The absence of memories is not just that too many years have passed since clients were "represented by" the agent, but the work by the author's agent, as she called herself, is largely *invisible* to actors who give life to the play, to critics who review the plays, and to audiences who buy tickets and share in the fruits of her labors. The agent is the unheralded handmaiden who facilitates the writer's career and sees to the affairs of business with a mixture of compassion, wisdom, and efficiency.

On one occasion Audrey commented that "hope" was the cornerstone of the agent's business: hope for the right producer, hope to negotiate favorable terms for the playwright, hope for the capitalization of the show, hope for booking a suitable theater, hope for the ideal director and leading actors, hope that all parties survive the pressure cooker of a Broadway opening, hope for favorable reviews, hope for the writer's next unborn script, and so on.

It is fitting to close with Audrey Wood's reflections on her chosen profession. From time to time, she summarized those qualities required of a literary agent: diplomacy, contractual skills, humor, tact, and endless amounts of patience. For over forty years, "Miss Wood," as she was called in public by clients, actors, directors, producers, and her husband William Liebling, brought these qualities both day and night to illumine *the hidden glade* of the commercial theater where, beginning with the adept and forceful agent, the playwright's work moves onto a stage, and, in the most fortunate of circumstances, into the pages of theatrical history.

Appendix: The Liebling-Wood Agency's Client List of Playwrights, 1938–1958

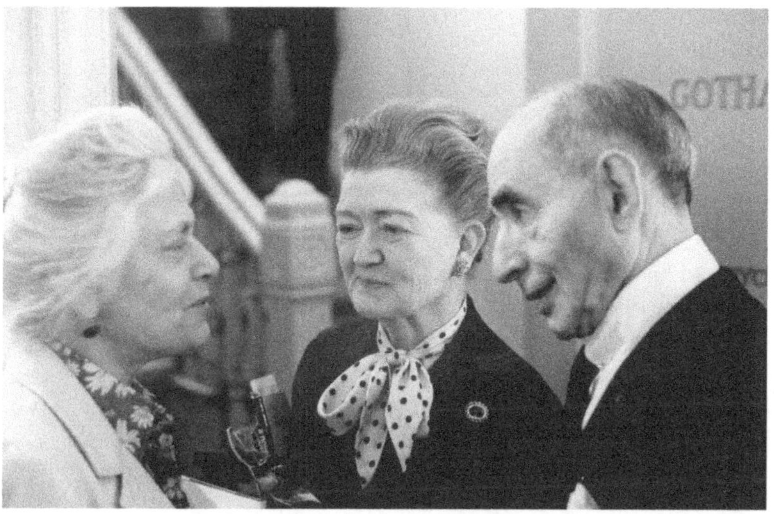

Audrey Wood and William Liebling with Frances Stoloff, founder of the Gotham Book Mart, New York City (Photograph by William Yoscary) Courtesy of Cheryl Raymond for the Estate of William Yoscary.

Audrey Wood's client list at Liebling-Wood was extended for another 23 years beyond the sale of the Liebling-Wood Agency and her relocation, first, to Music Corporation of America, and, second, to the Ashley-Steiner-Famous Agency (later, International Creative Management).

Katharine Albert
Robert Anderson
Jean Anouilh
Don Appell
Harold Arlen
Robert Ayres
Marie Baumer
Bertram Bloch
Allen Boretz
Bertolt Brecht
Jane Bowles
Marc Connelly
Luther Davis
Mel Dinelli
Friedrich Düerrenmatt
Vernon Duke
Jack Dunphy
Jacques Duval
Mignon Eberhart
Dale Eunson
John Finch
Doris Frankel
Claiborne Foster
Ketti Frings
Charlcie Garrett
Oliver Garrett
Michael Gazzo
E. B. Ginty
Jean Giraudoux
C. Givens
Jay Gorney
E. Y. ("Yip") Harburg
Roy Hargrave
Sig Herzig
Dorothy Heyward
DuBose Heyward
William Inge

Orrin Jannings
Fay Kanin
Michael Kanin
Jean Kerr
Walter Kerr
H. S. Kraft
Searle Kramer
Herbert Kubly
Clare Kummer
John LaTouche
Charles Laughton
Isabel Leighton
Carl Leo
Vera Matthews
Carson McCullers
John Murray
Liam O'Brien
Edward Paramore
Ernest Pascal
John Pen
Leo Rifkin
Howard Rigsby
Cecil Robson
Lynn Root
Fred Saidy
George Seaton
David Shaw
Elsa Shelly
Arnold Sundgaard
Frank Tarloff
Julian Thompson
Dan Totheroh
Maurice Valency
F. Wakeman
Robert Wallston
Hagar Wilde
Tennessee Williams
Calder Willingham
Donald Windham
Eva Wolas

Notes

INTRODUCTION

Epigraph: From a one-page hand-out of quotes by Audrey Wood prepared for the dedication of the Audrey Wood Theatre, New York City, on September 24, 1984, Audrey Wood Papers, HRC.

1. Audrey Wood, with Max Wilk, *Represented by Audrey Wood* (New York: Doubleday and Company, Inc., 1981), 7. Reprinted with the approval of the Audrey Wood Estate.
2. Wood, *Represented by Audrey Wood,* 130.
3. Wood, *Represented by Audrey Wood,* 13.

1 STAGESTRUCK

1. From Audrey Wood with Max Wilk, *Represented by Audrey Wood*, 22, by permission of the Audrey Wood estate and by David Wilk for the estate of Max Wilk.
2. Wood, *Represented by Audrey Wood,* 14.
3. Wood, *Represented by Audrey Wood,* 15.
4. Wood, *Represented by Audrey Wood,* 20–21.
5. Press photograph of William H. Wood, dated March 18, 1916, and inscribed to his daughter, Audrey, Audrey Wood Papers, HRC.
6. Wood, *Represented by Audrey Wood,* 28.
7. Wood, *Represented by Audrey Wood,* 29.
8. Wood, *Represented by Audrey Wood,* 31.

2 STARTING OUT

1. From Audrey Wood with Max Wilk, *Represented By Audrey Wood*, 48.
2. Wood, *Represented By Audrey Wood*, 56.
3. Wood, *Represented By Audrey Wood*, 60.
4. Wood, *Represented By Audrey Wood*, 60–61.

5. Wood, *Represented By Audrey Wood*, 61.
6. Quoted in Wood, *Represented By Audrey Wood*, 62.
7. Quoted in Wood, *Represented By Audrey Wood*, 62.
8. Jesse Zunser, "Nursemaid to Genius," *Cue* October 18, 1958, 14; in Audrey Wood Clippings File, Billy Rose Theatre Collection, NYPL.
9. Quoted in Wilfred Sheed, *The House that George Built* (New York: Random House, 2007), 67.
10. Brooks Atkinson, "Mamba's Waters," *New York Times*, January 4, 1939, 28.
11. Quoted in Wood, *Represented By Audrey Wood*, 64.
12. Wood, *Represented By Audrey Wood*, 64.
13. "William Liebling Obituary," *Variety*, December 31, 1969.
14. Quoted in Wood, *Represented By Audrey Wood*, 65.
15. Quoted in Wood, *Represented By Audrey Wood*, 65.

3 A ROOM OF THEIR OWN

1. From Audrey Wood, with Max Wilk, *Represented by Audrey Wood*, 11.
2. Wood, *Represented by Audrey Wood*, 3.
3. Quoted in Wood, *Represented by Audrey Wood*, 4.
4. Brooks Atkinson, "The Play: 'Room Service,'" *New York Times*, May 20, 1937, 16.
5. Author's telephone conversation with Gilbert Parker, January 31, 2011. Gilbert Parker, former agent for playwrights and directors at the William Morris Agency, now retired, started out as a switchboard operator at Liebling-Wood and became Audrey Wood's assistant for a time in the late 1940s.
6. Wood, *Represented by Audrey Wood*, 78.
7. In a letter to Elia Kazan, Audrey Wood recalled Liebling's account of his sing-along with Marlon Brando on the walk to Henry Miller's Theatre. Conflicting claims about the amount of money advanced to Marlon Brando to make the trip to Provincetown differ by $5—or, perhaps the actor collected a total of $45.00 from the two parties. Audrey Wood recalled that Liebling gave the actor "the magnificent sum of $25.00" to take the bus to Provincetown. From Letter from Audrey Wood to Elia Kazan, August 14, 1978, Audrey Wood Papers, HRC. Kazan also claimed that he advanced Brando $20 to make the trip. See Elia Kazan, *A Life* (New York: Alfred A. Knopf, 1988), 341.
8. Quoted in Tennessee Williams, *Memoir*s (New York: Doubleday and Company, 1975), 131. Also, Tennessee Williams, *A Streetcar Named Desire*, in *Tennessee Williams Plays 1937–1955* (New York: Library Classics of the United States, Inc., 2000), 564. Reprinted by permission of The University of the South, © 1947, renewed © 1975, by The University of the South, Sewanee, TN.
9. Quoted in Wood, *Represented by Audrey Wood*, 64.

10. Wood, *Represented by Audrey Wood*, 7. Also, from a single-sheet list of Audrey Wood quotes, prepared as a handout for the dedication of the Audrey Wood Theatre, New York, on September 24, 1984, Audrey Wood Papers, HRC.
11. Wood, *Represented by Audrey Wood*, 95.
12. Quoted in Wood, *Represented by Audrey Wood*, 96.
13. Quoted in Wood, *Represented by Audrey Wood*, 99.
14. "Obituaries," *New York Times*, October 23, 1958.
15. Richard Seff, *Supporting Player: My Life Upon The Wicked Stage* (New York: Xlibris Corporation, 2006), 100. Reprinted by permission of Richard Seff.
16. Max Wilk, *Mr. Williams and Miss Wood: A Two-Character Play* (New York: Dramatists Play Service, Inc., 1990), 7. Reprinted by permission of David Wilk.
17. Letter from Audrey Wood to Tennessee Williams, April 1, 1939, Audrey Wood Papers, HRC. Also, Lyle Leverich, *Tom: The Unknown Tennessee Williams* (New York: Crown Publishers, 1995), 300.
18. Leverich, *Tom: The Unknown Tennessee Williams,* 300–404.
19. Letter from Audrey Wood to Tennessee Williams, April 13, 1939, Audrey Wood Papers, HRC.
20. Letter from Audrey Wood to Tennessee Williams, April 28, 1939, Audrey Wood Papers, HRC.
21. Letter from Audrey Wood to Tennessee Williams, April 28, 1939, Audrey Wood Papers, HRC. Also, Leverich, *Tom: The Unknown Tennessee Williams,* 303.
22. Letter from Tennessee Williams to Audrey Wood, May 5, 1939, Audrey Wood Papers, HRC.
23. Wood, *Represented by Audrey Wood*, 130. The storied introduction between playwright and agent is repeated in Williams, *Memoirs*, 10; and also in, Leverich, *Tom: The Unknown Tennessee Williams,* 326.
24. Leverich, *Tom: The Unknown Tennessee Williams,* 326.
25. Williams, *Memoirs*, 10.
26. Letter from Tennessee Williams to Molly Day Thacher, circa late October 1939, Audrey Wood Papers, HRC.
27. Letter from Tennessee Williams to Audrey Wood, circa early November 1939, Audrey Wood Papers, HRC; also see, *Notebooks: Tennessee Williams*, ed. Margaret Bradham Thornton (New Haven, CT: Yale University Press, 2006), 166.
28. Letter from Audrey Wood to Tennessee Williams, November 8, 1939, Audrey Wood Papers, HRC.
29. Letter from Tennessee Williams to Audrey Wood, November 30, 1939, Audrey Wood Papers, HRC. See also, Leverich, 332.
30. Telegram from Audrey Wood to Tennessee Williams, December 22, 1939, Audrey Wood Papers, HRC. The Rockefeller fellowship was awarded on December 18, 1939.
31. Wood, *Represented by Audrey Wood*, 7.

4 THE BITCH GODDESS

1. From Letter from Audrey Wood to Irene Mayer Selznick, August 18, 1940, Audrey Wood Papers, HRC. Audrey Wood was communicating with the *Streetcar* principals about a future deal on a film; Irene Selznick was in London, Tennessee Williams was in Capri, and the agent was at her desk in New York.
2. *Notebooks: Tennessee Williams,* ed. Margaret Bradham Thornton (New Haven, CT: Yale University Press, 2006), 226.
3. *Selected Letters of Tennessee Williams 1920–1945*, eds. Albert J. Devlin and Nancy M. Tischler, vol. 1 (New York: New Directions Publishers, 2000), xv.
4. Audrey Wood, with Max Wilk, *Represented by Audrey Wood*, 133–34.
5. Hume Cronyn, *A Terrible Liar: A Memoir* (New York: William Morrow and Company, 1991), 188–89.
6. Lawrence Langner, *The Magic Curtain: The Story of Life in Two Fields, Theatre and Invention* (New York: E. P. Dutton, 1951), 331–32.
7. Wood, *Represented by Audrey Wood*, 135.
8. Cecil Brown, "Interview with Tennessee Williams," *Partisan Review* 45 (1978): 279.
9. Wood, *Represented by Audrey Wood*, 135–36.
10. Tennessee Williams, "*Battle of Angels*: The History of the Play (with Parentheses)," *Pharos* 1–2 (Spring 1945): 110.
11. Margaret Webster, *Don't Put Your Daughter on the Stage* (New York: Alfred A. Knopf, 1972), 72.
12. Alexander Williams, "'Battle of Angels'," *Boston Herald*, December 31, 1940.
13. Elliot Norton, "'Battle of Angels,' A Defeat But No Disaster," *Boston Post*, January 12, 1941.
14. Almost all the participants have given firsthand accounts of the aftermath of the catastrophic opening of *Battle of Angels:* Audrey Wood (*Represented By Audrey Wood*, 135–38), Tennessee Williams (*Memoirs*, 62–63), Margaret Webster (*Don't Put Your Daughter on the Stage*, 72–74), and Lawrence Langner (*The Magic Curtain*, 333.).
15. Wood, *Represented by Audrey Wood*, 136.
16. Wood, *Represented by Audrey Wood*, 137. Also, Lyle Leverich, *Tom: The Unknown Tennessee Williams* (New York: Crown Publishers, 1995), 274–75.
17. Letter from the Theatre Guild to Boston subscribers, January 20, 1941, in the Theatre Guild Collection, Beinecke Rare Book and Manuscript Library, Yale University, New Haven, CT.
18. Letter from Tennessee Williams to Audrey Wood, September 1, 1942, Audrey Wood Papers, HRC. Also, Letter from Tennessee Williams to the Williams Family, May 11, 1943, in *Letters I*, 448–50.
19. Tennessee Williams and David Newman, "The Agent as Catalyst," *Esquire* 58 (December 1962): 216, 260.

20. Letter from Audrey Wood to Tennessee Williams, June 2, 1943, Audrey Wood Papers, HRC.
21. Wood, *Represented by Audrey Wood*, 141.
22. Letter from Tennessee Williams to Audrey Wood, March 23, 1945, Tennessee Williams Papers, HRC. Also see, *Letters 1*, 556–59. 1944–1945 was a busy season for the agent and her playwright. *The Glass Menagerie* opened in Chicago on December 26, 1944 and in New York on March 31, 1945 and played for nearly 600 performances. *You Touched Me!* opened six months later on September 25, 1945.
23. Lewis B. Funke Interview with Audrey Wood, tape recording and typescript, December 4, 1976, 34, Audrey Wood Papers, HRC. Reprinted by permission of Michael J. Funke. See also Wood, *Represented by Audrey Wood*, 151–52.
24. Wood, *Represented by Audrey Wood*, 141.
25. Quoted in Wood, *Represented by Audrey Wood*, 145.
26. Wood, *Represented by Audrey Wood*, 152.
27. Quoted in Wood, *Represented by Audrey Wood*, 153. Also, Funke Interview, 36–37, Audrey Wood Papers, HRC.
28. Elia Kazan, *A Life* (New York: Alfred A. Knopf, 1988), 327–28.
29. Kazan, *A Life*, 327.
30. Cheryl Crawford, *One Naked Individual: My Fifty Years in the Theatre* (Indianapolis, IN: The Bobbs-Merrill Company, Inc., 1977), 185.
31. Quoted in Wood, *Represented by Audrey Wood*, 155.
32. Wood, *Represented by Audrey Wood*, 156.
33. Liebling-Wood Office Files, dated 1948–1952, Audrey Wood Papers, HRC.
34. Letter from Audrey Wood to Tennessee Williams, January 7, 1947, Tennessee Williams Papers, CU.
35. Wood, *Represented by Audrey Wood*, 157.
36. Brooks Atkinson, "At the Theatre: 'Summer and Smoke,'" *New York Times*, October 7, 1948, 205–06.
37. Richard Watts, Jr., "An Enigma by Tennessee Williams," *New York Post*, March 20, 1953; John Chapman, "Symbols Clash in 'Camino Real'" *New York Daily News*, March 20, 1953; Brooks Atkinson, "Tennessee Williams Writes a Cosmic Fantasy Entitled 'Camino Real,'" *New York Times*, March 20, 1953; Walter Kerr, "Casino Real," *New York Herald Tribune*, March 20, 1953; reprint, *New York Theatre Critics' Reviews 1953*, vol. 14 (New York: New York Theatre Critics Reviews, Inc., 1954), 330–31.
38. Wood, *Represented by Audrey Wood*, 162–63.
39. Funke Interview, 41, Audrey Wood Papers, HRC
40. Brooks Atkinson, *New York Times*, March 25, 1955.
41. Wood, *Represented by Audrey Wood*, 171. *Cat on a Hot Tin Roof* was the only play that Tennessee Williams dedicated to his long-serving agent and friend.
42. Funke Interview, 45–46, Audrey Wood Papers, HRC.
43. Wood, *Represented by Audrey Wood*, 169.

44. Quoted in Wood, *Represented by Audrey Wood*, 175.
45. Wood, *Represented by Audrey Wood*, 175.
46. Wood, *Represented by Audrey Wood*, 177. When the film was made in 1963, Geraldine Page played the leading role, along with Paul Newman as Chance Wayne.
47. Brooks Atkinson, "The Theatre: Portrait of Corruption," *New York Times*, March 11, 1959; Walter Kerr, "First Night Report: 'Sweet Bird of Youth,'" *New York Herald Tribune*, March 11, 1959; Robert Coleman, "'Sweet Bird' Sure-Fire Hit," *Daily Mirror*, March 11, 1959; John McClain, "Williams' Best And Maybe Best of Year," *New York Journal-American*, March 11, 1959. Reprint *New York Theatre Critics' Reviews 1959*, vol. 20 (New York: Theatre Critics Reviews, Inc., 1960), 349–350.
48. Robert Brustein, "Sweet Bird of Success," *Encounter* 12 (June 12, 1959): 59–60; Kenneth Tynan, *New Yorker* 35 (March 21, 1959): 98–100.
49. Cheryl Crawford interview with Donald Spoto, January 18, 1984. See Spoto, 243.
50. Wood, *Represented by Audrey Wood*, 198.
51. Richard Seff, *Supporting Player: My Life Upon the Wicked Stage* (New York: XLibris Corporation, 2006), 101–102.
52. Wood, *Represented by Audrey Wood*, 204.
53. Wood, *Represented by Audrey Wood*, 205.
54. *Tennessee Williams: Plays 1937–1955*, edited by Mel Gussow and Kenneth Holditch (New York: The Library of America, 2000), 1021.
55. Wood, *Represented by Audrey Wood*, 181.
56. Wood, *Represented by Audrey Wood*, 185.
57. Wood, *Represented by Audrey Wood*, 219.
58. Letter from Tennessee Williams to Audrey Wood, February 24, 1963, Audrey Wood Papers, HRC.
59. Western Union Telegram from Audrey Wood to Tennessee Williams, March 1, 1963; also, Letter from Audrey Wood to Tennessee Williams, February 23, 1963, Audrey Wood Papers, HRC.
60. Quoted in Wood, *Represented by Audrey Wood*, 198. William Liebling died in a New York hospital on December 29, 1969. The failed plays by Tennessee Williams between 1957 and 1969 were: *Orpheus Descending*, *Period of Adjustment*, *Slapstick Tragedy*, two productions of *The Milk Train Doesn't Stop Here Anymore*, and *In the Bar of a Tokyo Hotel.*

5 DANCING ON EGGS

1. From Audrey Wood, with Max Wilk, *Represented By Audrey Wood*, 118.
2. Wilfred Sheed, *The House that George Built: With a Little Help from Irving, Cole, and a Crew of About Fifty* (New York: Random House, 2007), 288.

3. Brooks Atkinson, "The New Play," *New York Times*, January 11, 1947, 23.
4. Brooks Atkinson, "Finian's Rainbow," *New York Times*, January 11, 1947, 23.
5. Wood, *Represented By Audrey Wood*, 123.
6. Quoted in Wood, *Represented By Audrey Wood*, 124.
7. Wood, *Represented By Audrey Wood*, 125.
8. Lawrence Langner, *The Play's The Thing* (New York: G. P. Putnam's Sons, 1960), 39.
9. Wood, *Represented By Audrey Wood*, 126.
10. Wood, *Represented By Audrey Wood*, 127.
11. Wood, *Represented By Audrey Wood*, 127.
12. See James K. Lyon, *Bertolt Brecht in America* (Princeton, NJ: Princeton University Press, 1980), 196–97.
13. "Galileo," *Variety*, August 6, 1947.
14. Brooks Atkinson, "Galileo," *New York Times*, August 1, 1947.
15. *Galileo* closed in Los Angeles on August 17, 1947, and Brecht was served with a subpoena to appear before HUAC on September 19.
16. Brecht's play was derived in 1943 from Jaroslav Hašek's novel *The Adventures of the Good Soldier Švejk in the World War.*
17. Letter from Bertolt Brecht to Audrey Wood, February 5, 1949, Audrey Wood Papers, HRC. Also, Lyon, *Bertolt Brecht in America*, 321.
18. James K. Lyon, writing in *Bertolt Brecht in America*, called the playwright's testimony "a polite exercise in cunning and duplicity," 329.
19. Quoted in Ronald Hayman, *Brecht A Biography* (New York: Oxford University Press, 1983), 309–10. Also see Lyon, *Bertolt Brecht in America*, 330.
20. Quoted in Lyon, *Bertolt Brecht in America*, 332.
21. See *Bertolt Brecht Journals 1934–1955*, trans. Hugh Rorrison and ed. John Willett (New York: Routledge, Chapman and Hall, Inc. 1993), 372.
22. Quoted in Wood, *Represented By Audrey Wood*, 128.
23. Brooks Atkinson, "At the Theatre," *New York Times*, December 8, 1947, 34.
24. Bertolt Brecht, *Galileo*, in *The Modern Repertoire*, Series Two, trans. by Charles Laughton and ed Eric Bentley, (Bloomington: Indiana University Press, © 1952), 474. Also, Wood, *Represented By Audrey Wood*, 129.
25. *Red Channels: The Report of Communist Influence in Radio and Television* (New York: American Business Consultants, Inc., 1950): 72–74.
26. See Milly S. Barranger, *Unfriendly Witnesses: Gender, Theater, and Film in the McCarthy Era* (Carbondale: Southern Illinois University Press, 2008), 90.
27. Quoted in Victor S. Navasky, *Naming Names*, Third Ed. (New York: Farrar, Straus and Giroux Publishers, 2003), 94–95.
28. *Touch and Go* opened on October 13, 1949 at the Broadhurst Theatre and played 176 performances.
29. See Eric Bentley, ed., *Thirty Years of Treason: Excerpts from Hearings before the House Un-American Activities Committee 1938 1968* (New York: Viking, 1971), 542–44.

30. Brooks Atkinson, "At the Theatre," *New York Times*, October 14, 1949; John Chapman, "'Touch and Go,'" New York *Daily News*, October 14, 1949; reprint *New York Theatre Critics' Reviews* 1949, vol. 10 (New York: Critics' Theatre Reviews, 1950): 250–51.
31. See Sondra K. Gorney, *Brother, Can You Spare A Dime? The Life of Composer Jay Gorney* (Lanham, MD: The Scarecrow Press, Inc., 2005), 60. Reprinted by permission of Sondra K. Gorney.
32. Sondra K. Gorney, 65. See also "*Testimony of Jay Gorney*, May 6, 1953," US Congress. House Committee on Un-American Activities. 83rd Congress, Part 3, First Session. *Hearings Regarding Investigation of Communist Activities, New York Area* (Washington, DC: US Government Printing Office, 1953), 1370–76.
33. Author conversation with Sondra K. Gorney, December 12, 2011. Reprinted with permission.
34. Author telephone conversations with Richard Seff, September 20 and 21, 2009. Reprinted with permission.
35. A commemorative US Postal Stamp, recognizing Harburg's accomplishments, was issued in 2005. He died in 1981 at 88 in an automobile accident on Sunset Boulevard in Los Angeles. Jay Gorney, afflicted in his late years with Parkinson's disease, died at the age of 94 on June 14, 1990.

6 PERSONAL MONSTERS

1. From Ronald Bergan, "Obituary: Robert Anderson," *The Guardian*, February 19, 2009.
2. David H. Ayers, "The Apprenticeship of Robert Anderson" (Ph.D. diss., Ohio State University, 1969), 17.
3. Thomas E. Adler, *Robert Anderson* (Boston: G. K. Hall and Company, 1978), 72.
4. James F. Wharton, *Life Among the Playwrights: Being Mostly the Story of the Playwrights' Producing Company* (New York: Quadrangle / New York Times Book Company, 1974), 237–51. *Tea and Sympathy* opened on September 30, 1953 (for 712 performances); *Cat on a Hot Tin Roof* opened on March 24, 1955 (for 694 performances).
5. Elia Kazan, *A Life* (New York: Alfred A. Knopf, 1988), 504.
6. Robert Anderson, *Tea and Sympathy* (New York: Random House, 1953), 88. With permission of Samuel French, Inc.
7. Quoted in Audrey Wood, with Max Wilk, *Represented by Audrey Wood*, 268. Also, in Kazan, *A Life*, 502.
8. Barranger, *Unfriendly Witnesses*, 77, 124.
9. Brooks Atkinson, "First Night at the Theatre," *New York Times*, October 1, 1953, 35.
10. Wharton, *Life Among the Playwrights*, 241.

11. Phyllis Stohl Anderson died on November 28, 1956. See "Mrs. Robert Anderson Dies Here at 49; Dramatist's Wife Aided Theatre Guild," *New York Times*, November 29, 1956, 35.
12. Wharton, *Life Among the Playwrights*, 242–44.
13. Letter from Robert Anderson to Audrey Wood, undated, in Audrey Wood Papers, HRC.
14. Brooks Atkinson, "Theatre: 'Silent Night, Lonely Night,'" *New York Times*, December 4, 1959, 36.
15. Quoted in Wood, *Represented by Audrey Wood*, 273.
16. Wood, *Represented by Audrey Wood*, 273–74.
17. Wood, *Represented by Audrey Wood*, 274.
18. Adler, *Robert Anderson*, 124–125.
19. Bruce Weber, "Robert Anderson, 91, Playwright, Dies: Made Name with 'Tea and Sympathy,'" *New York Times*, February 10, 2009.
20. Robert Anderson, *I Never Sang for my Father* (New York: Random House, 1968), 3. With Permission of Samuel French, Inc.
21. The Lieblings leased the apartment at 100 Sands Point Road in Sarasota, Florida, from May 1966 to 1970; thereafter, Audrey sublet the apartment until April 1971. The inventory of contents and their appraisal are located in the Audrey Wood Papers, HRC.
22. Clive Barnes, "Theater: 'I Never Sang for My Father,'" *New York Times*, January 26, 1968, 30.
23. Wood, *Represented by Audrey Wood*, 276
24. C. W. E. Bigsby, *Modern American Drama, 1945–1990* (New York: Cambridge University Press, 1992), 75.
25. Quoted in Wood, *Represented by Audrey Wood*, 277.
26. Maurice Valency, "Introduction," *Four Plays by Jean Giraudoux* (New York: Hill and Wang, Inc., 1958), xxi. With permission of Macmillan Publishing Company.
27. Jared Brown, *The Fabulous Lunts: A Biography of Alfred Lunt and Lynn Fontanne* (New York: Atheneum, 1986), 387–88.
28. Quoted in Wharton, *Life Among the Playwrights*, 225.
29. Brooks Atkinson, "Theatre: 'Ondine,'" *New York Times*, February 19, 1954 and February 28, 1954; Richard Watts, Jr., "Audrey Hepburn and Her Triumph," *New York Post*, February 19, 1954; reprint, *New York Critics' Theatre Reviews 1954*, vol. 15 (New York: Critics' Theatre Reviews, 1955): 362–63.
30. Wood, *Represented by Audrey Wood*, 308.
31. *Bus Stop* opened March 2, 1955 (for 478 performances); *Cat on a Hot Tin Roof* opened March 24, 1955 (for 694 performances).
32. Brown, *The Fabulous Lunts*, 399.
33. See Kenneth Tynan, "The Visit," *The Observer*, March 23, 1958.
34. Brown, *The Fabulous Lunts*, 408. Also, Margot Peters, *Design for Living: Alfred Lunt and Lynn Fontanne A Biography* (New York: Alfred A. Knopf, 2003), 203.

35. Brooks Atkinson, "Theatre: "An Unforgettable 'Visit,'" *New York Times*, May 6, 1958 and May 18, 1958; Richard Watts, Jr., "The Lunts in Striking New Play," *New York Post*, May 6, 1958; John McClain, "A Most Disturbing Play," *New York Journal-American*, May 6, 1958; reprint, *New York Critics' Theatre Reviews 1958*, vol. 19 (New York: Critics' Theatre Reviews, 1959): 294–97.

7 DARKNESS IN THE HEARTLAND

1. From Audrey Wood, with Max Wilk, *Represented by Audrey Wood*, 233.
2. William Inge, "St. Louis Personalities: 'Tennessee' Williams, Playwright, Author," *St. Louis Star-times*, November 11, 1944, 11. Reprinted in *Conversations with Tennessee Williams*, ed. Albert J. Devlin (Jackson: University Press of Mississippi, 1986), 6–8. Spoto referenced the affair between Williams and Inge, 112.
3. "Inge, William (Motter)," *Current Biography* (New York: H. W. Wilson Company, 1954), 293.
4. Telegram from Audrey Wood to William Inge, November 5, 1945, Audrey Wood Papers, HRC.
5. Letter from Audrey Wood to William Inge, November 8, 1945, Audrey Wood Papers, HRC.
6. Wood, *Represented by Audrey Wood*, 225.
7. Wood, *Represented by Audrey Wood*, 225.
8. See Ralph F. Voss, *A Life of William Inge: The Strains of Triumph* (Lawrence, Kansas: University Press of Kansas, 1989), 113–14.
9. Wood, *Represented by Audrey Wood*, 226–27.
10. Brooks Atkinson, "At the Theatre: '*Come Back, Little Sheba*,'" *New York Times*, February 16, 1950, 28; Richard Watts, Jr., "The Man, the Dog, and the Bottle," *New York Post*, February 16, 1950; reprint, *New York Theatre Critics' Reviews 1951*, vol. 11(New York: Critics' Theatre Reviews, 1951), 350.
11. Wood, *Represented by Audrey Wood*, 228.
12. Quoted in Donald Spoto, *The Kindness of Strangers: The Life of Tennessee Williams* (Boston: Little, Brown and Company, 1985), 225–26. Quoted with the permission of Donald Spoto.
13. Brooks Atkinson, *Broadway*, rev. ed (New York: Macmillan Publishing Company, Inc., 1974), 443.
14. Joshua Logan, *Josh: The Up and Down, In and Out Life* (New York: Delacorte Press, 1976), 277–285. Also, Voss, *A Life of William Inge*, 113–14.
15. Brooks Atkinson, "At the Theatre: '*Picnic*,'" *New York Times*, February 20, 1953, 14; John McClain, "A Fine Blend of Many Talents," *New York Journal-American*, February 20, 1953; reprint, *New York Theatre Critics' Reviews 1953*, vol. 14 (New York: Critics' Theatre Reviews, 1954), 348.
16. Wood, *Represented by Audrey Wood*, 230.

17. Brooks Atkinson, *Broadway*, 443. Also see, *New York Theatre Critics' Reviews 1956*, vol. 16, 347.
18. Wood, *Represented by Audrey Wood*, 13.
19. Seven pages of type-written notes, entitled "Dark at the top of the Stairs," by William Inge," from Audrey Wood to William Inge, August 5, 1957, Audrey Wood Papers, HRC.
20. Kazan, *A Life*, 572–73.
21. Brooks Atkinson, "The Theatre: Illuminations by Inge," *New York Times*, December 6, 1957, 38. Walter Kerr, "First Night Report/Walter Kerr's Review: 'The Dark at the Top of the Stairs,'" *New York Herald-Tribune*, December 6, 1957; John McClain, "Inge's Best Play—With Kazan's Aid," *New York Journal-American*, December 6, 1957; reprint, *New York Theatre Critics' Reviews 1957*, vol. 18 (New York: Critics' Theatre Reviews, Inc., 1958), 160.
22. Quoted in Spoto, *The Kindness of Strangers*, 224–25. Quoted with permission.
23. Introduction by Tennessee Williams, in *The Dark at the Top of the Stairs* (New York: Random House, 1958), vii–ix. Tennessee Williams completed the introduction in Key West on January 15, 1958, Tennessee Williams Papers, HRC.
24. Robert Brustein, "The Men-Taming Women of William Inge," *Harper's* (November 1958), 52–57.
25. William Gibson, "For Bill Inge," *New York Times*, July 24, 1973, 35.
26. Wood, *Represented by Audrey Wood*, 232.
27. Wood, *Represented by Audrey Wood*, 232–33.
28. Wood, *Represented by Audrey Wood*, 233.
29. Brooks Atkinson, "Theatre: 'Loss of Roses,'" *New York Times*, November 30, 1959; John McClain, "Inge Wilts in His Latest," *New York Journal-American*, November 30, 1959; Richard Watts, Jr., "Two on the Aisle: Everything Didn't Come Up Roses," *New York Post*, November 30, 1959; reprint, *New York Theatre Critics Reviews 1959*, vol. 20 (New York: Theatre Critics' Reviews, Inc., 1960), 211, 213.
30. Jack Balch, "Anatomy of a Failure," *Theatre Arts* (February 1960): 10.
31. Wood, *Represented by Audrey Wood*, 234.
32. Lewis B. Funke, Interview with Audrey Wood dated December 4, 1976, in Audrey Wood Papers, HRC, University of Texas, Austin, 42–43.
33. Wood, *Represented by Audrey Wood*, 234–35.
34. Wood, *Represented by Audrey Wood*, 235.
35. Wood, *Represented by Audrey Wood*, 235–36.
36. Letter from William Inge to Audrey Wood, March 29, 1962, Audrey Wood Papers, HRC.
37. Howard Taubman, "The Theater: 'Natural Affection,'" *New York Times*, February 2, 1963, 4. Richard Watts, Jr. and Norman Nadel, Reviews of "*Natural Affection,*" February 2, 1963; reprint, *New York Theatre Critics'*

Reviews 1963, vol. 24 (NewYork: Critics' Theatre Reviews, Inc., 1964), 383–84.

38. Spoto, *The Kindness of Strangers,* 77. Also, producer Margery Klain shared this instance of a client asking if Audrey Wood had any children, and her reply. Email to Author from Margery Klain, dated July 27, 2011.
39. Wood, *Represented by Audrey Wood,* 54.
40. D. Newman, "The Agent as Catalyst," *Esquire* (December 1962): 264.
41. Voss, *A Life of William Inge,* 198.
42. Stanley Kauffmann, "The Theatre: Inge's 'Where's Daddy?'" *New York Times* March 3, 1966, 27. Norman Nadel, "It's Hard to Care about Inge and His 'Daddy,'" *New York World-Telegram,* March 3, 1966; Walter Kerr, "Where's Daddy?" *New York Herald-Tribune,* March 3, 1966; reprint, *New York Theatre Critics' Reviews 1966,* vol. 27 (New York: Critics' Theatre Reviews, Inc., 1967), 348–49.
43. Winfred Blevins, "America's Ignored Dramatist," *Los Angeles Herald-Examiner,* November 10, 1968, William Inge Collection, Independence Community College, Independence, KS.
44. Funke, Interview with Audrey Wood, 42–43. Inge worked on the musical book for *Beau,* based on *Bus Stop,* with music and lyrics by Gerry Raad. Even though Inge's collaboration was announced in the *New York Times, Beau* never appeared on Broadway. See Sam Zolotow, "William Inge Helps Turn His Play into a Musical," *New York Times,* November 15, 1968, 39.

8 IRON BUTTERFLIES

1. From Audrey Wood, with Max Wilk, *Represented By Audrey Wood,* 13.
2. Wood, *Represented By Audrey Wood,* 54.
3. Wood, *Represented By Audrey Wood,* 104.
4. See T. W. Stanford, "Dorothy Heyward and DuBose Heyward," *The Dictionary of Literary Biography* (Detroit, MI: The Gale Group, Inc., 2004), 141.
5. Brooks Atkinson, *Broadway,* Revised ed. (New York: Macmillan, 1974; rpt., New York, Limelight, 1990), 251. *Porgy and Bess* played 217 performances.
6. Audrey Wood is quoted in "The Voice of Broadway: The Battle for 'Porgy,'" *New York Journal-American,* July 31, 1958.
7. Brooks Atkinson, "'*Jonica,*'" New *York Times,* April 8, 1930, 27.
8. Brooks Atkinson, "*Cinderelative,*" *New York Times,* September 19, 1930, 18.
9. Wilfred Sheed, *The House that George Built: With a Little Help from Irving, Cole, and a Crew of About Fifty* (New York: Random House, 2007), 67.
10. Tennessee Williams, *Memoirs* (New York: Doubleday and Company, 1975) 106.
11. Virginia Spencer Carr, *The Lonely Hunter: A Biography of Carson McCullers* (New York: Carroll and Graf Publishers, Inc., 1975), 274–75.
12. Carr, *The Lonely Hunter,* 278–79, 291.

13. Carr, *The Lonely Hunter*, 311.
14. Wood, *Represented By Audrey Wood*, 112.
15. Wood, *Represented By Audrey Wood*, 112.
16. Wood, *Represented By Audrey Wood*, 112–13.
17. Wood, *Represented By Audrey Wood*, 113.
18. Wood, *Represented By Audrey Wood*, 113.
19. Quoted in Wood, *Represented By Audrey Wood*, 114.
20. Wood, *Represented By Audrey Wood*, 115.
21. Brooks Atkinson, "At the Theatre," *New York Times*, January 6, 1950, 26. Robert Coleman, "'Member of the Wedding' Is a Stirring Hit," *New York Daily News*, January 6, 1950; reprint, *New York Theatre Critics' Reviews 1950*, vol. 11, 397.
22. Carson McCullers, "The Vision Shared," *Theatre Arts* (April 1950): 30.
23. Wood, *Represented By Audrey Wood*, 115.
24. Brooks Atkinson, "At the Theatre," *New York Times*, December 30, 1953, 17. Impaired by a stroke in 1957, Jane Bowles did not write another play. She died in 1973 in a clinic in Málaga, Spain.
25. Letter from Audrey Wood to Jane Bowles, February 25, 1964, Audrey Wood Papers, HRC.
26. Letter from Audrey Wood to Jane Bowles, March 27, 1964, Audrey Wood Papers, HRC. *In the Summer House* opened Off Broadway on March 25, 1964, and closed after 15 performances on April 5, 1964.
27. Wood, *Represented By Audrey Wood*, 308.
28. Letter from Audrey Wood to Carson McCullers, July 2, 1951, in Liebling-Wood Correspondence, HRC.
29. Carr, *The Lonely Hunter*, 535.
30. Wood, *Represented By Audrey Wood*, 116.
31. Wood, *Represented By Audrey Wood*, 116.
32. Carr, *The Lonely Hunter*, 451.
33. Wood, *Represented By Audrey Wood*, 117; also, Carr, *The Lonely Hunter*, 451.
34. Brooks Atkinson, "At the Theatre: 'Square Root,'" *New York Times*, October 31, 1957, 40. *The Square Root of Wonderful* closed after forty-five performances.
35. Carr, *The Lonely Hunter*, 461.
36. Carr, *The Lonely Hunter*, 458.

9 AN ACCIDENTAL CAREER

1. From Audrey Wood, with Max Wilk, *Represented by Audrey Wood*, 13.
2. Quoted in Wood, *Represented by Audrey Wood*, 280.
3. Arthur Kopit, *End of the World with Symposium to Follow* (New York: Samuel French Inc. 1984, 187), 16–17.
4. Wood, *Represented by Audrey Wood*, 280.
5. Quoted in Wood, *Represented by Audrey Wood*, 281.

6. Wood, *Represented by Audrey Wood*, 282.
7. Wood, *Represented by Audrey Wood*, 213.
8. Deborah Jowitt, *Jerome Robbins: His Life, His Theater, His Dance* (New York: Simon and Schuster, Inc., 2004), 328–29.
9. Arthur Kopit, *Oh Dad, Poor Dad, Mama's Hung You in the Closet and I'm Feelin' So Sad* in *Three Plays* (New York: Farrar, Straus, and Giroux, 1997), 79.
10. Paul Gardner, "Theater: 'Dad' Returns," *New York Times*, August 28, 1963, 31.
11. Wood, *Represented by Audrey Wood*, 215.
12. Wood, *Represented by Audrey Wood*, 286.
13. Don Shewey, "Arthur Kopit: A Life on Broadway," *New York Times*, April 29, 1984, 91. Reprinted with permission of Don Shewey.
14. Wood, *Represented by Audrey Wood*, 286.
15. Wood, *Represented by Audrey Wood*, 287.
16. Wood, *Represented by Audrey Wood*, 287.
17. Quoted in Wood, *Represented by Audrey Wood*, 280.
18. Lewis B. Funke, Interview with Audrey Wood, dated December 4, 1976, in Audrey Wood Papers, HRC, University of Texas, Austin, 79–80. *Indians* closed after 96 performances on Broadway.
19. Quoted in Wood, *Represented by Audrey Wood*, 288.
20. Wood, *Represented by Audrey Wood*, 47.
21. Shewey, "Arthur Kopit," 88–91, 105.
22. Arthur Kopit, "Preface," *Wings* (New York: Hill and Wang, 1978), xi–xii. Reprinted with permission.
23. Wood, *Represented by Audrey Wood*, 292.
24. Shewey, Arthur Kopit," 105. Reprinted with permission.
25. Shewey, Arthur Kopit," 105. Reprinted with permission.
26. Shewey, Arthur Kopit," 104. Reprinted with permission.
27. Frank Rich, "Stage: New Kopit Play," *New York Times*, May 7, 1984, C15.
28. Quoted in Wood, *Represented by Audrey Wood*, 323. Also, reprinted by permission of Arthur Kopit.

10 IRISH FICTIONS

1. From Audrey Wood, with Max Wilk, *Represented by Audrey Wood*, 42.
2. Thomas Kilroy, "The Early Plays," *The Cambridge Companion to Brian Friel*, ed. Anthony Roche (New York: Cambridge University Press, 2006), 6–17.
3. Wood, *Represented by Audrey Wood*, 291. See also Howard Kissel, *David Merrick: The Abominable Showman: The Unauthorized Biography* (New York: Applause Books, 1993).
4. "Interview with Victoria Radin (1981)," *Brian Friel Essays, Diaries, Interviews: 1964–1999*, ed. Christopher Murray (London: Faber and Faber, 1999), 93.
5. *Brian Friel Essays, Diaries, Interviews: 1964–1999*, xix.

6. Walter Kerr, "'Philadelphia, Here I Come!'" *New York Herald Tribune*, February 17, 1966.
7. Clive Barnes, "The Theater: Friel's 'Mundy Scheme,'" *New York Times,* December 12, 1969, 75; Clive Barnes, "The Theater: 'Freedom of the City,' About the Irish,"*New York Times*, February 18, 1974, 32.
8. Wood, *Represented by Audrey Wood*, 314.
9. Martin Gottfried, "The Theatre: 'Home,'" *New York Times*, November 18, 1970; Walter Kerr, "Home, The Play," *New York Herald-Tribune*, November 29, 1970; John J. O'Connor, "The Theatre: English Presence," *Wall Street Journal*, November 18, 1970; reprint, *New York Theatre Critics' Reviews 1970*, vol. 31 (New York: Theatre Critics' Reviews, Inc., 1971), 146–48.
10. T. E. Kalem, "The Theater," *New York Times*, December 18, 1972; reprint, *New York Theatre Critics' Reviews* 1972, vol. 33 (New York: Theatre Critics' Reviews, Inc., 1973), 338.
11. Lewis B. Funke, Interview with Audrey Wood, dated December 4, 1976, in Audrey Wood Papers, HRC, University of Texas, Austin, 31.
12. Wood, *Represented by Audrey Wood*, 314. Also, Martin Gottfried, "The Theater: 'The Changing Room,'" *Women's Wear Daily*, March 8, 1975; reprint, *New York Theatre Critics' Reviews 1975*, vol. 36 (New York: Theatre Critics' Reviews, Inc., 1976), 337.
13. Letter from David Storey to Author, dated May 2, 2010. Quoted with approval.
14. Letter from Brian Friel to Author, dated March 5, 2010. Quoted with approval.
15. Wood, *Represented by Audrey Wood*, 40.
16. Quoted in Wood, *Represented by Audrey Wood*, 42.
17. Richard Eder, "Drama: Friel's 'Faith Healer,'" *New York Times,* April 6, 1979; Douglas Watts, "Friel's 'Faith Healer,'" *New York Daily News*, April 6, 1979; Clive Barnes, "Friel's 'Faith' Beyond Healing," *New York Post*, April 6, 1979; reprint, *New York Theatre Critics' Reviews 1979*, vol. 40 (New York: Theatre Critics' Reviews, Inc, 1980), 297–300.
18. Walter Kerr, "Best Plays of the Year," *New York Times*, December 30, 1979.
19. T. E. Kalem, "The Theatre," *Time* (April 16, 1979); reprint, *New York Theatre Critics' Reviews 1979*, 298.
20. Brian Friel, *Faith Healer* (New York: Samuel French, Inc., 1980), 12.
21. Wood, *Represented by Audrey Wood*, 35.
22. Wood, *Represented by Audrey Wood*, 35.
23. Clive Barnes, "'River' Doesn't Have Depth of Book," *New York Post*, March 29, 1979; Douglas Watt, "Stagnant 'River,'" *New York Daily News*, March 29, 1979; reprint, *New York Theatre Critics' Reviews 1980*, 309, 310–11.
24. Author telephone conversation with Don Bachardy, July 22, 2010. Quoted with approval.
25. Wood, *Represented by Audrey Wood*, 52. See the lyrics by Dorothy Fields in "Pick Yourself Up" from the film of *Swing Time* (1936).

26. Quoted in *Cambridge Guide to American Theatre*, eds. Don B. Wilmeth and Tice L. Miller (New York: Cambridge University Press, 1996), 248.
27. Clive Barnes, "A Play's Worth of 'Translations,'" *New York Post*, April 15, 1981; Frank Rich, "Stage: 'Translations' from Brian Friel," *New York Times*, April 15, 1981; reprint, *New York Theatre Critics' Reviews 1981*, vol. 42 (New York: Theatre Critics'Reviews, Inc., 1982), 264–66.
28. Letter from Brian Friel to Author, dated March 5, 2010. Quoted with permission.

11 OUT-OF-THE-ORDINARY

1. From Audrey Wood, with Max Wilk, *Represented by Audrey Wood*, 240.
2. Quoted in Wood, *Represented by Audrey Wood*, 241.
3. Wood, *Represented by Audrey Wood*, 242.
4. Wood, *Represented by Audrey Wood*, 242.
5. See Preston Jones, *A Texas Trilogy* (New York: Hill and Wang Publishers, 1976), vii–viii.
6. Wood, *Represented by Audrey Wood*, 244.
7. Lewis B. Funke, Interview with Audrey Wood, dated December 4, 1976, in Audrey Wood Papers, HRC, University of Texas, Austin, 56.
8. Wood, *Represented by Audrey Wood*, 244.
9. Funke, Interview with Audrey Wood, 55.
10. Quoted in Wood, *Represented by Audrey Wood*, 247.
11. Wood, *Represented by Audrey Wood*, 248.
12. Quoted in Wood, *Represented by Audrey Wood*, 248.
13. Quoted in Wood, *Represented by Audrey Wood*, 249.
14. Wood, *Represented by Audrey Wood*, 252.
15. Clive Barnes, "Preston Jones's 'Texas Trilogy' Opens with Portrait of a Loser," *New York Times*, September 22, 1976, 30; Clive Barnes, "A Sentimental Texas Journey," *New York Times*, September 23, 1976, 50; Clive Barnes, "Stage: The Last of 'Texas Trilogy,'" *New York Times*, September 24, 1976, 55.
16. Quoted in Mel Gussow, "Preston Jones Playwright, Dead: Author of 'Texas Trilogy,' Was 43," *New York Times*, September 20, 1979, D23.
17. Wood, *Represented by Audrey Wood*, 257–58.
18. Wood, *Represented by Audrey Wood*, 295–96.
19. Wood, *Represented by Audrey Wood*, 296.
20. Wood, *Represented by Audrey Wood*, 295.
21. Quoted in Wood, *Represented by Audrey Wood*, 296.
22. Richard Eder, "Theater: 'Working' Opens on 46th Street," *New York Times*, May 15, 1978, C15. Douglas Watt, "'Working,'" *Daily News*, Mary 15, 1978; Howard Kissel, "'Working,'" *Women's Wear Daily*, May 15, 1978; reprint, *New York Theatre Critics' Reviews 1978* (New York: Critics' Theatre Reviews, Inc., 1979), 274–75.

23. Quoted in Wood, *Represented by Audrey Wood*, 297.
24. Quoted in Wood, *Represented by Audrey Wood*, 298.
25. Quoted in Wood, *Represented by Audrey Wood*, 300.
26. Quoted in Wood, *Represented by Audrey Wood*, 295.
27. Wood, *Represented by Audrey Wood*, 295–96.
28. Wood, *Represented by Audrey Wood*, 300.

12 GUARDIAN ANGEL

1. From Audrey Wood, with Max Wilk, *Represented By Audrey Wood*, 307.
2. Letter from Audrey Wood to Tennessee Williams, February 23, 1963, Audrey Wood Papers, HRC.
3. Richard Watts, Jr., "Milk Train," *New York Post*, January 21, 1963, reprint, vol. 24, *New York Theatre Critics' Reviews 1963,* vol. 24 (New York: Critics' Theatre Reviews, Inc., 1964), 391. The magazine critics were less kind. Richard Williams, "Mistuh Williams, He Dead," *Commonweal* 7 (February 8, 1963), 515–17, referred to the play as "creative suicide."
4. Wood, *Represented by Audrey Wood*, 187.
5. Wood, *Represented by Audrey Wood*, 187.
6. Liz Woodman, assistant to Tony Richardson, in conversation with the Author, June 10, 2008. Cited with permission of Liz Woodman. Also, Tony Richardson, *Long Distance Runner: A Memoir* (London: Faber and Faber, Ltd., 1993), 145.
7. Liz Woodman in conversation with the Author, June 10, 2008. Quoted with permission.
8. Wood, *Represented by Audrey Wood*, 188–89.
9. Telegram from Audrey Wood to Tennessee Williams, May 12, 1969, Audrey Wood Papers, HRC.
10. Letter from Audrey Wood to George C. White, November 20, 1968, Audrey Wood Papers, HRC.
11. Letter from Audrey Wood to Tennessee Williams, February 24, 1967, Audrey Wood Papers, HRC.
12. Letter from Audrey Wood to Tennessee Williams, February 24, 1967, Audrey Wood Papers, HRC.
13. Letter from Audrey Wood to the Chairman of the Department of Speech and Drama, Stanford University, October 29, 1965, Audrey Wood Papers, HRC.
14. Letter from Audrey Wood to Peter R. Marroney, May 22, 1966, Audrey Wood Papers, HRC.
15. Donald Spoto, *The Kindness of Strangers: The Life of Tennessee Williams* (Boston, MA: Little, Brown and Company, 1985), 273.
16. Letter from Tennessee Williams to Audrey Wood, November 22, 1970, Audrey Wood Papers, HRC.
17. "'The Two-Character Play,'" *Daily (London) Express*, December 13, 1967.

18. Wood, *Represented by Audrey Wood*, 192.
19. Wood, *Represented by Audrey Wood*, 199.
20. William Leonard, "'Out Cry,'" *Chicago Tribune*, July 9, 1971, 1.
21. Stefan Kanfer, "White Dwarf's Tragic Fadeout," *Life* 66 (June 13, 1969): 10.
22. Wood, *Represented by Audrey Wood*, 197–98.
23. The publisher of New Directions, James Laughlin, attributed, in part, the erosion of Audrey's relationship with Tennessee Williams to the caustic language and dismissive attitudes of the Lady Maria St. Just. See Letter from James Laughlin to Audrey Wood, August 21, 1972, Audrey Wood Papers, HRC.
24. Quoted in Wood, *Represented by Audrey Wood*, 200. Donald Spoto argued in his biography that Williams's suspiciousness, caused earlier by toxic drugs, had become ingrained. See Spoto, *The Kindness of Strangers*, 208.
25. Quoted in Spoto, *The Kindness of Strangers*, 297.
26. Tennessee Williams, *Memoirs* (New York: Doubleday and Company, 1975), 229.
27. Wood, *Represented by Audrey Wood*, 201.
28. Lewis B Funke, Interview with Audrey Wood, dated December 4, 1976, 59, 61, Audrey Wood Papers, HRC.
29. Letter from James Laughlin to Audrey Wood, August 21, 1971, Audrey Wood Papers, HRC.
30. Letter from Tennessee Williams to Audrey Wood, July 15, 1971, Audrey Wood Papers, HRC.
31. Wood, *Represented by Audrey Wood*, 325.
32. Wood, *Represented by Audrey Wood*, 308.
33. Wood, *Represented by Audrey Wood*, 308. See also Jared Brown, *The Fabulous Lunts: A Biography of Alfred Lunt and Lynn Fontanne* (New York: Atheneum, 1986), 443.
34. Quoted in Wood, *Represented by Audrey Wood*, 308. See also Anne Edwards, *A Remarkable Woman: A Biography of Katharine Hepburn* (New York: William Morrow and Company, Inc., 1985), 282–83.
35. Wood, *Represented by Audrey Wood*, 309.
36. "'Love Among' the Ruins," *Variety*, March 12, 1975.
37. Wood, *Represented by Audrey Wood*, 309.
38. Helen Sheehy, *Eva Le Gallienne: A Biography* (New York: Alfred A. Knopf, 1996), 407.
39. Sheehy, *Eva Le Gallienne*, 408.
40. Walter Kerr, "To Grandmother's House," *New York Times*, January 25, 1981. See also, *New York Theatre Critics' Reviews 1981*, vol. 42 (New York: Critics' Theatre Reviews, Inc., 1982), 385.
41. Mitch Douglas of International Creative Management took over Eva Le Gallienne's representation as both her literary agent and theater agent. Le Gallienne lived until June 3, 1991, and died at age 92.

42. Typed notes from Ruth Wolff shared with the Author, July 28, 2011. Cited with permission.
43. Quoted in Wood, *Represented by Audrey Wood*, 318.
44. Samuel G. Freedman, "The Life and Death of an Agent," *New York Times*, December 31, 1985, C9.
45. The Audrey Wood Theatre was dedicated on September 24, 1984.
46. Freedman, "The Life and Death of an Agent," C9.
47. Freedman, "The Life and Death of an Agent," C9. Also, Herbert Mitgang, "Theater Community Honors Audrey Wood," *New York Times*, January 16, 1986, B11; Author conversation with Walter Willison, July 7, 2010; and Ruth Wolff, untitled one-page typescript, dated 1981, and shared with the Author, July 28, 2011. Cited with the permission of Ruth Wolff.
48. "Top Agent Audrey Wood Dies at 80; Served Many Playwrights," *Variety*, January 1, 1986, 136.
49. Mitgang, "Theater Community Honors Audrey Wood," B11.
50. Letter from Daphne Athas to Author, dated April 3, 2011. Quoted with permission.
51. Email from Isobel Robins Konecky to Author, dated May 12, 2011; Author telephone conversation with George C. White, September 7, 2011; Ruth Wolff, untitled one-page typescript, dated 1981, shared with the Author, July 28, 2011; Author conversation with David Berry, November 10, 2011; Letter from David Storey to Author, dated May 2, 2010; and Letter from Brian Friel to Author, dated March 5, 2010. Cited with the approval of these friends, coworkers, and clients of Audrey Wood.

Bibliography

RESEARCH CENTERS AND ARCHIVAL COLLECTIONS

Key research centers and archives have preserved invaluable materials on theater in America. The following collections are applicable to research on the life and clients of Audrey Wood:

Arthur Kopit Papers, Fales Library, New York University, New York.
Robert Woodruff Anderson Papers, Houghton Library, Harvard University College Library, Cambridge, MA.
Audrey Wood Papers, Harry Ransom Humanities Research Center, University of Texas, Austin.
Audrey Wood Papers, Manuscript Division, New York Public Library for the Performing Arts, Lincoln Center.
Carson McCullers Papers, Columbus College Library, Columbus, Georgia.
Cheryl Crawford Papers, Special Collections, University of Houston Libraries, TX.
Brian Friel Papers, National Library of Ireland, Dublin.
Fred W. Todd and the Tennessee Williams Holdings, Historic New Orleans Collection, New Orleans, LA.
William Inge Collection, Independence Community College, KS.
Tennessee Williams Papers, (Rare Books, Butler Library, Columbia University in the City of New York.)
Tennessee Williams Collection, University of Delaware Library, Newark.
Tennessee Williams Papers, Harry Ransom Humanities Research Center, University of Texas, Austin.
Tennessee Williams Papers, Rare Books, Butler Library, Columbia University in the City of New York.

OTHER SOURCES

Adler, Thomas. *Robert Anderson*. Boston, MA: Twayne Publishers, 1978.
Alpert, Hollis. *The Life and Times of Porgy & Bess: The Story of an American Classic.* New York: Alfred A. Knopf, 1990.

Atkinson, Brooks. *Broadway*. Revised ed. New York: Macmillan, 1974; rpt., New York: Limelight, 1990.

Barranger, Milly S. *A Gambler's Instinct: The Story of Broadway Producer Cheryl Crawford*. Carbondale: Southern Illinois University Press, 2010.

———. *Margaret Webster: A Life in the Theater*. Ann Arbor: University of Michigan Press, 2004.

———. *Unfriendly Witnesses: Gender, Theater, and Film in the McCarthy Era*. Carbondale: Southern Illinois University Press, 2008.

Basinger, Jean, John Frazer, and Joseph W. Reed, Jr. eds. *Working with Kazan*. Middleton, CT: Wesleyan University Press, 1973.

Bentley, Eric. *The Dramatic Event: An American Chronicle*. New York: Horizon Press, 1954.

Berney, K. A., ed. *Contemporary Dramatists*. London: St. James Press, 1993.

Bigsby, C. W. E. *Modern American Drama, 1945–1990*. New York: Cambridge University Press, 1992.

Bloom, Ken. *Broadway: Its History, People, and Places An Encyclopedia*. 2nd ed. New York: Routledge, 2004.

Bogle, David. *Heat Wave: The Life and Career of Ethel Waters*. New York: HarperCollins Publishers, 2011.

Brantley, Ben, ed. *The New York Times Book of Broadway: On the Aisle for the Unforgettable Plays of the Last Century*. New York: St. Martin's Press, 2001.

Brown, Jared. *The Fabulous Lunts: A Biography of Alfred Lunt and Lynn Fontanne*. New York: Atheneum, 1986.

Brustein, Robert. *Seasons of Discontents: Dramatic Opinions, 1959–1965*. New York: Simon and Schuster Publishers, 1965.

Carr, Virginia Spencer. *The Lonely Hunter: A Biography of Carson McCullers*. New York: Doubleday and Company, 1975.

Clurman, Harold. *Lies Like Truth*. New York: Macmillan and Company, 1958.

Coult, Tony. *About Friel: The Playwright and His Work*. London: Faber and Faber, 2003.

Courtney, Marguerite. *Laurette*. New York: Holt Rinehart, 1955.

Crawford, Cheryl. *One Naked Individual: My Fifty Years in the Theatre*. Indianapolis, IN: The Bobbs-Merrill Company, Inc. 1977.

Cronyn, Hume. *A Terrible Liar: A Memoir*. New York: William Morrow and Company, Inc., 1991.

Devlin, Albert J., ed. *Conversations with Tennessee Williams*. Jackson: University Press of Mississippi, 1986.

Emert, Tim. Interview with Audrey Wood. March 11, 1975. In William Inge Collection, Independence Community College, Independence, Kansas.

Freedman, Samuel G. "Devotion to the Stage Was Her Hallmark," *New York Times*, July 1, 1984, H4–5.

———. "The Life and Death of an Agent," *New York Times*, December 31, 1985, C19.

Funke, Lewis B. Interview with Audrey Wood. Dated December 4, 1976. In Audrey Wood Papers, Harry Ransom Research Center, University of Texas, Austin.

Gassner, John. *Theatre at the Crossroads: Plays and Playwrights of the Mid-Century American Stage*. New York: Holt, Rinehart and Winston Publishers, 1960.

Goldman, William. *The Season: A Candid Look at Broadway*. New Jersey: Limelight Editions, 1984.

Gorney, Sondra K. *Brother, Can You Spare A Dime? The Life of Composer Jay Gorney*. Lanham, MD: The Scarecrow Press, Inc. 2005.

Gross, Brenda. "Audrey Wood." *Notable Women in the American Theatre: A Biographical Dictionary*. Eds. Alice M. Robinson, Vera M. Roberts, and Milly S. Barranger. Westport, CT: Greenwood Publishing Group, 1989. pp. 921–925.

Hampton, Wilborn. *Horton Foote: America's Storyteller*. New York: Free Press, 2009.

Henderson, Mary C. *Theater in America: Two Hundred Years of Plays, Players, and Productions*. New York: Harry N. Abrams, 1986.

"Inge, William (Motter)," *Current Biography*, 1953. New York: H. W. Wilson Company, 1954. pp. 292–293.

Inge, William. "Foreword" to *A Loss of Roses*. New York: Random House, 1960. p. iv.

Jowitt, Deborah. *Jerome Robbins: His Life, His Theater, His Dance*. New York: Simon and Schuster Publishers, 2004.

Kazan, Elia. *A Life*. New York: Alfred A. Knopf, 1988.

Kerr, Walter. *How Not to Write a Play*. New York: Simon and Schuster Publishers, 1955.

Kissel, Howard. *David Merrick: The Abominable Showman: The Unauthorized Biography*. New York: Applause Books, 1993.

"Kopit, Arthur." *Contemporary Authors*. Detroit, MI: Gale Reference Group, 2002.

Kopit, Arthur. "Preface" to *Wings*. New York: Hill and Wang Publishers, 1978. pp. vi–xvii.

Langner, Lawrence. *The Magic Curtain: The Story of a Life in Two Fields, Theatre and Invention*. New York: E. P. Dutton, 1951.

Laurents, Arthur. *Original Story by: A Memoir of Broadway and Hollywood*. New York: Alfred A. Knopf, 2000.

Leverich, Lyle. *Tom: The Unknown Tennessee Williams*. New York: Crown Publishers, 1995.

Lobenthal, Joel. *Tallulah! The Life and Times of a Leading Lady*. New York: HarperCollins Publishers, 2004.

Logan, Joshua. *Josh: My Up and Down, In and Out Life*. New York: Delacorte Press, 1976.

Lyon, James K. *Bertolt Brecht in America*. Princeton, NJ: Princeton University Press, 1980.

May, Hal, ed. "Audrey Wood (1905–1985)." *Contemporary Authors*. Vol. 118. Detroit, MI: Gale Research Company, 1986.

McGill, Raymond D., ed. "Audrey Wood." *Notable Names in the American Theatre*. Clifton, NJ: James T. White and Company, 1976.

Murray, Christopher, ed. *Brian Friel Essays, Diaries, Interviews, 1964–1999*. New York: Faber and Faber, 1999.

Rigdon, Walter, ed. "Audrey Wood." *The Biographical Encyclopaedia and Who's Who of the American Theatre*. New York: James H. Heineman, 1966.

Robinson, Alice M., Vera M. Roberts, and Milly S. Barranger, eds. *Notable Women in the American Theatre*. Westport, CT: Greenwood Publishing Group, 1989.

Roche, Anthony, ed. *The Cambridge Companion to Brian Friel*. New York: Cambridge University Press, 2006.

Sanford, T. W. "Dorothy Heyward and DuBose Heyward." *Dictionary of Literary Biography*. Detroit, MI.: The Gale Group, Inc., 2004. pp. 134–147.

Savigneau, Josyane. *Carson McCullers: A Life*. Trans, Joan E. Howard. Boston, MA: Houghton Mifflin, 2001.

Schanke, Robert A. *Shattered Applause: The Lives of Eva Le Gallienne*. Carbondale: Southern Illinois University Press, 1992.

Schickel, Richard. *Eliz Kazan: A Biography*. New York: HarperCollins Publishers, 2005.

Schneider, Alan. *Entrances: An American Director's Journey*. New York: Viking Penguin, 1986. Rpt. New York: Limelight Editions, 1987.

Seff, Richard. *Supporting Player: My Life Upon the Wicked Stage*. New York: XLibris Corporation, 2006.

Selznick, Irene Mayer. *A Private View*. New York: Alfred A. Knopf, 1983.

Sheed, Wilfred. *The House that George Built: With a Little Help from Irving, Cole, and a Crew of About Fifty*. New York: Random House, 2007.

Sheehy, Helen. *Eva Le Gallienne: A Biography*. New York: Alfred A. Knopf, 1996.

———. *Margo Jones: The Life and Theatre of Margo Jones*. Dallas, TX: Southern Methodist University Press, 1989.

Slavick, William H. *Dubose Heyward*. Boston, MA: Twayne Publishers, 1981.

Schneider, Alan. *Entrances: An American Director's Journey*. New York: Viking Penguin, 1986.

Spoto, Donald. *The Kindness of Strangers: The Life of Tennessee Williams*. Boston, MA: Little, Brown and Company, 1985.

St. Just, Maria. ed. *Five O'Clock Angel: Letters of Tennessee Williams to Maria St. Just, 1948–1982*. New York: Alfred A. Knopf, 1990.

Thornton, Margaret B., ed. *Notebooks: Tennessee Williams*. New Haven, CT: Yale University Press, 2006.

Turan, Kenneth, and Joseph Papp. *Free for All: Joe Papp, The Public, and the Greatest Theater Story Ever Told*. New York: Doubleday, 2009.

Vinson, James, ed. "Robert Anderson." *Contemporary Dramatists*. London: St. James Press, 1973. pp. 334–336.

Voss, Ralph F. *A Life of William Inge: The Strains of a Triumph.* Lawrence: University Press of Kansas, 1989.

Wallach, Eli. *The Good, the Bad, and Me: In My Anecdotage.* New York: Harcourt, 2005.

Weales, Gerald. *American Drama Since World War II.* New York: Harcourt, Brace and World, 1962.

Webster, Margaret. *Don't Put Your Daughter on the Stage.* New York: Alfred A. Knopf, 1972.

Wertheim, Arthur Frank. *Vaudeville Wars: How the Keith-Albee and Orpheum Circuits Controlled the Big-Time and Its Performers.* New York: Palgrave Macmillan, 2006.

Wharton, John F. *Life among the Playwrights: Being Mostly the Story of The Playwrights Producing Company.* New York: Qadrangle/The New York Times Book Company, 1974.

Wilk, Max. *Mr. Williams and Miss Wood: A Two-Character Play.* New York: Dramatists Play Service, 1990.

Williams, Dakin, and Shepherd Mead. *Tennessee Williams: An Intimate Biography.* New York: Arbor House Publishing Company, 1983.

Williams, Tennessee. Introduction to *William Inge, The Dark at the Top of the Stairs.* New York: Random House, 1958. pp. viii–ix.

———. *Memoirs.* New York: Doubleday and Company, 1975.

———. *The Selected Letters of Tennessee Williams 1945–1957.* 2 vols. Eds. Albert J. Devlin and Nancy M. Tischler. New York: New Directions Publishing, 2004.

Williams, Tennessee, and David Newman. "The Agent as Catalyst," *Esquire,* 58 (December 1963): 216–217, 260.

Wilmeth, Don B., and Tice L. Miller, eds. *Cambridge Guide to American Theatre.* New York: Cambridge University Press, 1993.

Windham, Donald, ed. *Tennessee Williams' Letters to Donald Windham 1940–1965.* New York: Holt, Rinehart and Winston, 1977.

Wolff, Ruth. *Notable Women and a Few Equally Notable Men: Nine Plays by Ruth Wolff.* New York: Broadway Play Publishing, 2010.

Wood, Audrey, with Max Wilk. *Represented by Audrey Wood.* Garden City, NY: Doubleday and Company, 1981.

Author's Note

Milly S. Barranger is author of books on twentieth-century women and modern American theater: *Margaret Webster: A Life in the Theater*; *Unfriendly Witnesses: Gender, Theater, and Film in the McCarthy Era*; and *A Gambler's Instinct: The Story of Broadway Producer Cheryl Crawford* (a finalist for the 2011 George Freedley Award sponsored by the Theatre Library Association). She is coeditor of *Notable Women in the American Theatre: A Biographical Dictionary.*

Barranger holds the title of Distinguished Professor Emerita of Dramatic Art at the University of North Carolina, Chapel Hill. She is former producing director of PlayMakers Repertory Company; Past President of the National Theatre Conference and the American Theatre Association; and Dean Emerita of the College of Fellows of the American Theatre.

Index

GPSR Compliance
The European Union's (EU) General Product Safety Regulation (GPSR) is a set of rules that requires consumer products to be safe and our obligations to ensure this.

If you have any concerns about our products, you can contact us on

ProductSafety@springernature.com

In case Publisher is established outside the EU, the EU authorized representative is:

Springer Nature Customer Service Center GmbH
Europaplatz 3
69115 Heidelberg, Germany

www.ingramcontent.com/pod-product-compliance
Lightning Source LLC
Chambersburg PA
CBHW051444050726
47593CB00005B/1920

* 9 7 8 1 1 3 7 3 8 5 4 7 5 *